THE MUSIC OF LIFE

**The Omega Uniform Edition of the
Teachings of Hazrat Inayat Khan**

*The Awakening of the Human Spirit
Spiritual Dimensions of Psychology
The Music of Life
The Art of Being and Becoming
Complete Sayings
Tales
Mastery Through Accomplishment*

THE MUSIC
OF
LIFE

Hazrat Inayat Khan

OMEGA PUBLICATIONS
New Lebanon

Much of the material in this book originally appeared in Volumes II, IV, VII, X, and XI of *The Sufi Message of Hazrat Inayat Khan*. Additional sections were taken from several series of previously unpublished lectures.

Photo credits: Page 1, cymatic photograph of glycerine excited by oscillation, by Hans Jenny. © 1967 by Basilius Presse AG. Page 61, the dance of the Mevlevi dervishes, by Ira Friedlander. © 1975 by Ira Friedlander. Page 141, Hazrat Inayat Khan playing the vina. Page 261, micrograph of iridium atoms, by Dr. Erwin Mueller. Courtesy of Ms. Jutta Mueller Schwab. Page 285, tonoscopic photograph of a toccata and fugue of Bach, by Hans Jenny. © 1967 by Basilius Presse AG.

Published by:
OMEGA PUBLICATIONS INC.
256 DARROW ROAD
NEW LEBANON, NY 12125-2615
www.omegapub.com

Printed in the United States of America.
ISBN 0-930872-38-X

10 9 8 7 6 5

CONTENTS

FOREWORD
by
Pir Vilayat Inayat Khan

"Fare forth to the West as a musician of the soul and tune the hearts of men to the divine harmony." Such was the briefing that Hazrat Inayat Khan received from his dying predecessor, Khwaja Abu Hashim Madani of the Chishti Order.

Indeed, this answers the direct need of most people, which is (whether they know it or not) to resonate creatively with the universe, to express in a personalized way the present trend of the universe in its forward thrust.

Musicians and music lovers intuit that there is a dimension of the music tbey cultivate which expresses this order (dynamic rather than static) of the universe. Grasping this would give a clue as to what they are striving to achieve in perfecting their musical skills.

Somehow we know that all objects (and objects are actually beings) *are* really their signature tunes. Their structures are wave patterns frozen into relative permanence, rather as a whirlpool sustains its form although fed by an ever-changing flow of water. In light of this modern view, the Qur'anic sura, "God revealed to Adam the names of all things," falls into perspective. If we should discover the optimal frequency to which our cells respond—that is, their signature tune—we would indeed be learning their names. Speaking their language by imprinting upon them the appropriate vibrations, we would enlist their response, opening up new perspectives for the therapy of the future.

Seen in a high state of meditation, a crystal looks like a frozen yet pulsing and shimmering symphony of light. The sparkling signalings and the eloquence of the living cell convey a meaning we have difficulty in deciphering. Tbe congruent, concerted meaningfulness and purposefulness underlying the infinitely complex network of sonic oscillations at the scale of the body, ranging from the electrons to organs like the brain, heart, or pancreas and indeed to the whole organism, spell consternation to our intelligence. How this symphony diffuses, interfaces, intermeshes, and resonates with the unimaginable symphony of the whole universe is precisely Hazrat Inayat Khan's mind- (and heart-) leap, which transpires through his words as we read them.

Moreover, if the physical universe is the crystallization of an incommensurable cosmic thinking pattern, our thoughts may equally be looked upon as wave interference patterns of a type of energy that we can only describe as psychic or noetic. Thoughts are endowed with their own lifespan and reproductivity and are capable of explicating themselves out of archetypes into our vocabulary and syntax, or conversely of transfiguring themselves into updated thought Gestalts having an existence in their own right.

This would mean that strains of the neotic symphony of the universe may be expressed by the human on the planet and that, conversely, the human psalmody may stir the heavens, calling for a response and thus leading to a pulsing colloquy.

Pir-o-Murshid Inayat Khan captures the echoes of this colloquy, conveying some of its lyricism, and gives clues as to the way of establishing a connection with the cosmic symphony in order to be able to express something of its splendor creatively in our personalities.

The meditations to which this book leads are particularly recommended to musicians who are seeking a bridge linking them with their source of inspiration. Some of its themes, based upon the mysterious science of the *mantram* (in Sufi terminology, the *wazifa*), have indeed been introduced into present-day musical compositions, capturing the undertones and harmonic overtones of the symphony of the spheres and thus opening untold vistas for the music of the future.

PART I

THE MYSTERY OF SOUND

The knower of the mystery of sound knows the mystery of the whole universe.

In the beginning of a world all the matter which will eventually form a complete whole is already in existence, but in a state of chaos. It is not that any new thing or world or being is to be created, but that there shall be a rearrangement of all the parts until the whole is complete. The number and arrangement of every atom has yet to be made. Every electron and every atom of electricity must take its own appointed place in the mighty scheme. This is the great evolutionary process. The God buried in humanity must be uncovered and placed on His throne in the heart of man. The difficulty is that all, from atom to human being, are continually trying to fit into a place to which they belong. The upheaval of nature, the great unrest, the world revolutions, the shedding of bodies, and the separations and divisions among men —all these things are caused by the parts of the whole trying to stay in a place to which they do not belong. As soon as man is in his own place he has peace; until then he cannot have it.

A world in the making can be likened to a great jigsaw puzzle whose separate parts have life and are capable of independent movement. Each part has its own particular place and its relation to every other part, and no thing or being can live to itself alone. But if things are in their wrong places, the hand of God must move them before the complete picture can be revealed.

The way in which man can find his own place is to tune his instrument to the keynote of the chord to which he belongs. Sound is the force which groups all things from atoms to worlds. The chording vibration sounds in the innermost being of man and can only be heard in silence. When we go into the inner chamber and shut the door to every sound that comes from the life without, then will the voice of God speak to our soul and we will know the keynote of our life.

Chapter 1

"MY SOLE ORIGIN IS SOUND"
(VIBRATIONS)

The life absolute from which has sprung all that is felt, seen, and perceived, and into which all again merges in time, is a silent, motionless, and eternal life which among the Sufis is called *zat*. Every motion that springs forth from this silent life is a vibration and a creator of vibrations. Within one vibration are created many vibrations. As motion causes motion, so the silent life becomes active in a certain part and creates every moment more and more activity, losing thereby the peace of the original silent life. It is the grade of activity of these vibrations that accounts for the various planes of existence. These planes are imagined to differ from one another, but in reality they cannot be entirely detached and made separate from one another. The activity of vibrations makes them grosser, and thus the earth is born of the heavens.

The mineral, vegetable, animal, and human kingdoms are the gradual changes of vibrations, and the vibrations of each plane differ from one another in their weight, breadth, length, color, effect, sound, and rhythm. Man is not only formed of vibrations, but he lives and moves in them; they surround him as the fish is surrounded by water, and he contains them within him as the tank contains water. His different moods, inclinations, affairs, successes

5

and failures, and all conditions of life depend upon a certain activity of vibrations, whether these be thoughts, emotions, or feelings. It is the direction of the activity of vibrations that accounts for the variety of things and beings. This vibratory activity is the basis of sensation and the source of all pleasure and pain; its cessation is the opposite of sensation. All sensations are caused by a certain grade of activity of vibration.

There are two aspects of vibration, fine and gross, both containing varied degrees; some are perceived by the soul, some by the mind, and some by the eyes. What the soul perceives are the vibrations of the feelings; what the mind conceives are the vibrations of the thoughts; what the eyes see are the vibrations solidified from their ethereal state and turned into atoms which appear in the physical world, constituting the elements ether, air, fire, water, and earth. The finest vibrations are imperceptible even to the soul. The soul itself is formed of these vibrations; it is their activity which makes it conscious.

Creation begins with the activity of consciousness, which may be called vibration. Every vibration starting from its original source is the same, differing only in the tone and rhythm caused by a greater or lesser degree of force behind it. On the plane of sound, vibration causes diversity of tone, and in the world of atoms, diversity of color. It is by massing together that the vibrations become audible, but at each step towards the surface they multiply, and as they advance they materialize. Sound gives to the consciousness an evidence of its existence, although it is in fact the active part of consciousness itself which turns into sound. The knower so to speak becomes known to himself; in other words the consciousness bears witness to its own voice. It is thus that sound appeals to man. All things being derived from and formed of vibrations have sound hidden within them, as fire is hidden in flint, and each atom of the universe confesses by its tone, "My sole origin is sound." If any solid or hollow sonorous body is struck it will answer back, "I am sound."

All existing things that we see or hear, that we perceive, vibrate. If it were not for vibration, precious stones would not show us their color and their brilliance; it is vibration that makes trees grow, fruit ripen, and flowers bloom. Our existence is also according to the law of vibrations, not only the existence of our physical body but also that of our thoughts and feelings. If it were not for vibrations, drugs and herbs would not have any effect upon us. If any explanation of electricity can be given, it is that its mystery lies only in vibrations. Vibrations are productive and produce electricity; electricity is composed of vibrations. In other words, that aspect of vibration which produces form could not do so if it could not first produce light. The Bible hints at this when it says that first there was light and then the world was produced. Light is the first form; all other forms come afterwards.

Vibrations can be understood both as cause and as effect. Vibration causes movement, rotation, circulation, but on the other hand it is the rotation of the planets and the circulation of the blood which cause vibration. Thus the cause as well as the effect of all that exists is vibration.

Whether a thing is visible or audible, perceptible or imperceptible depends upon the speed of the vibrations. Everything that is visible is audible at the same time, and everything that is audible is visible also. If it does not appear so, this only demonstrates the limitation of our organs of perception. What our physical eyes cannot see we say is not visible, but this only means that it is not visible to us; in itself it is visible. And what we cannot hear we say is not audible, but it is only inaudible to our ears; in itself it is audible.

This means that everything has its sound and its form. Even things which we can perceive though they are not visible have a form. They could not be intelligible if they had no form. Although they have no physical form they have a form just the same, and if our physical eyes do not see that form, the eyes of our mind can see it and recognize it. This explains why there are things that are felt and things that are seen or heard. It is only a difference of vibrations and of the planes on which the vibrations take place. Vibrations cause life to take form; and it is the different degrees of vibrations which make that form visible or otherwise perceptible.

What we know about vibration is only what we perceive through manmade instruments; what is moving beyond this we do not recognize as vibration. But as there is no other word this is the only one we can use for it, for it is the same force that sets everything in motion on the physical plane, and this continues on all the other planes of existence, setting them all in motion. It also explains to us that it is a certain degree of vibration that brings to the earth the things of the inner world, the world that is perceived though not seen. And a change of vibrations takes away the things that are seen into the unseen world.

What we call life and death are both a recognized existence within a certain degree of vibrations. For instance when a person says, "This leaf is dead," what has made it dead is the change of vibrations. It has no longer the same vibrations that it had when it was on the tree. Yet it has not lost its vibrations; it still has them. Thus according to the vibrations it is not dead; it has only changed into a different rhythm of vibrations. If that leaf were dead then herbs would not have any effect upon a man when he takes them as medicine.

And so it is with the dead body of an animal or a person. We may say that life has gone out of it, but it is only the life that we recognize as life that has gone out of it. For we recognize as life only a certain pitch of vibrations; anything beyond it or below it we do not recognize as living. Yet it has not died; it is still vibrating, for nothing can exist and not vibrate, and nothing can vibrate and not be living in the real sense of the word. One might say that there is no movement in a dead body, that there is no heat in it, but do we not use fish and flesh of slaughtered animals as food? If these did not possess any life we would not be benefited by eating them, for it is only life that can help life to go on. If they were really dead, if all the property which is called life were gone from them, they would do us harm instead of good. This shows that though we call them dead there is some life left in them, and that this change is only a question of degree in the vibrations.

When a fruit has decayed, when a flower has faded, there has been a change of vibrations. It is wonderful to watch a flower when it is still a bud and to see how it grows every day, how it vibrates differently every moment of the day until it comes to such a culmination that it begins to radiate, reflecting the sun. Besides its color and form we can see something living in the flower, something sparkling. It can best be seen when the flower is still on the plant. And then, when it has reached its culmination, it begins gradually to fade, and that again is according to the law of vibrations. But even when its petals have dropped there is still a form of life left, for even in the dry leaves of the rose there is a fragrance, and from the dried rose leaves an effective medicine can be made. This medicine has a certain action on the blood, and it also nourishes the intestines; it is most purifying. In ancient Greek medicine the rose was used in many ways. It cools the blood as well as being very strengthening.

There is a great difference between the eating of fresh vegetables and of preserved vegetables, a difference of vibrations. The former are nearer to our life, and the latter, which have gone further from our life, have less influence on us. And so it is with everything. When we begin to see life from this point of view it will appear that birth and death are only our conceptions of life, that there is no such thing as death and that all is living. It only changes from one form to the other, subject to the law of vibrations. The difference in the vibrations of dead and living bodies is a difference of their speed; it is a difference of rhythm.

Chapter 2

THE LAW OF RHYTHM

A keen observation shows that the whole universe is a single mechanism working by the law of rhythm. The law of rhythm is a great law which is hidden behind nature. It is in accordance with this law that every form is made and that every condition manifests to view. The creation therefore is not merely a phenomenon of vibrations without any restrictions. If there were no rhythm, if it were not for the law of rhythm, we would not have distinct forms and intelligible conditions. There is no movement which has no sound, and there is no sound which has no rhythm. In order to show rhythm we need not take a conductor's baton and beat "*one*-two"; we only need to wave our hand. Divide one and it is two; double one and it is two. This shows that in one there is two; it proves that duality comes from unity.

Then, if we look at it from another point of view, we see that duality is in fact nothing but unity; in other words that two is one. The most interesting point in this is that as soon as we see two, each of the two at once takes a different and particular position in our view. This is clear with man and woman, but also each of our hands shows a particular power and a particular function, and each foot has its peculiar place in life; the right foot is distinctly different from the left foot. Also, the sight of the two eyes is not the same. One eye is always better and stronger than the other, or at least different from the other, and if there were no difference the eyes would not be a proper instrument for seeing. If there were no difference between the power and strength of person's left and right sides, one could not live.

It is this difference that causes duality, and it is this duality that maintains the existence of things. The finer aspect of this phenomenon can be seen in musical rhythm. When we say,"*one*–two, *one* –two," then we understand what it is that makes us emphasize the one, and what it is that makes the two like an echo, a reflection, something that responds to the one. Suppose that we only say, " *one–one–one–one–one,* " all with the same emphasis: this will not satisfy us. We will not feel any rhythm until the one is accented and the two, or whatever we say next, follows it; then it becomes perfect. We see the same happening in the action of walking, which is accomplished by both legs: if we practice walking on one leg we will find something missing in the rhythm.

This shows that rhythm is a hidden law of nature. The rising and the setting of the sun, the waxing and the waning of the moon, the regular change of the tides in the sea, and the seasons as they come and go all show rhythm. It is rhythm that makes the birds fly; it is rhythm that makes the creatures of the earth walk. If we delve deeper into the science of rhythm we find that it is rhythm that causes a certain thing to be made in a certain way. If it is made triangular or square or round or five-pointed, whatever geometrical form has been given to it, the reason behind its form is the rhythm of the power that has made it. It is that rhythm that is the cause of its formation.

Harmonious forms are manifestations of a right rhythm, and inharmonious forms are manifestations of a disorder in rhythm. Colors such as blue and green and red and yellow appear distinct and different for the reason that a particular color vibrates according to a certain rhythm, and it is this rhythm that gives to the colors the appearance that makes us distinguish them.

There is the law of rhythm behind good weather and bad weather; and the influence of good or bad weather, acting on living beings, creates a similar result in their lives. Good weather gives a desirable rhythm to living beings, and bad weather brings about an undesirable result in their health. It would therefore not be an exaggeration to say with the ancient yogis that birth and death, as well as the limited time that separates birth from death, are the fulfillment of a certain appointed rhythm. If we go a little further in exploring this idea, we shall see, as the ancient yogis saw, that by controlling this rhythm one can prolong one's life, and also that by neglecting this rhythm one can shorten it.

Why is it that music that emphasizes rhythm gives everyone the desire to dance? Even horses begin to move to the rhythm of the band playing before the cavalry; even the most downhearted and discouraged soldiers feel encouraged when they hear the emphatic rhythm of a march played by a military band. An infant is soothed when its mother is patting it on its back; the mother without knowing it instinctively gives a rhythm to its body. By waving our hand we give our departing friend a rhythm against the regret or despair with which he leaves, in order to keep him rhythmic on all planes of life.

What repulses or attracts us in a person is very often his rhythm. One person is rhythmic, and his influence is soothing; another is out of rhythm, and he upsets everybody.

Why should rhythm have such an influence upon us? Because we ourselves are rhythm. The beating of our heart, the pulse throbbing in our wrist or head, our circulation, the working of the whole mechanism of our body is rhythmic. When this rhythm is obstructed, then disorder and illness come; all discomfort, despair, and disappointment follow the breaking of the rhythm.

When we look at this question symbolically we find that our gain and our loss, our success and our failure, have much to do with the rhythm with which we pursue our motive in life. It will always prove to be true that when a person takes no heed of rhythm, whether he does right or wrong, good or evil, in either case a wrong rhythm will make him fail. For rhythm is not only a law to which nature is subjected, but it is something that maintains things as they are and gives things and beings the power to continue to live and to progress.

To know rhythm one must develop the sense of rhythm. How readily one notices it when one has a little pain! This shows that a person intuitively knows the effect of rhythm. For instance sometimes congestion causes illness; but what is congestion and what can it do? It is something that stops the rhythm. The rhythm with which the blood was circulating is stopped by congestion; that is why illness comes. By being regular one maintains rhythm in everything one does, and an irregular person will always find himself lost, because he cannot accomplish anything for want of rhythm.

Rhythm is a great mystery, and a sense which one should develop more than anything else in life. But if one were to explain what the right rhythm of work and rest is, the whole western way of life would be in question, for when we look at it from the point of view of rhythm and balance, there is far too much activity in the life of the West. It would make any person abnormal. The bad effects of this are continually felt, but since people are so absorbed in life, they are not yet able to realize to what an extent they suffer from these bad effects. However, before long there will come a time when thoughtful people will begin to realize that this problem has been neglected too long. And what has caused it? This life of competition: the whole misery is caused by competition. People do things not for their own pleasure or for the pleasure of God, but in order to compete with one another.

The law of rhythm can be considered as governing four actions: right or wrong rhythm in feeling, right or wrong rhythm in thinking, right or wrong rhythm in speaking, and right or wrong rhythm in acting. Not only hate but even love that is not maintained by rhythm will fail; not only an evil thought but even a good one will prove to be disastrous without regard for rhythm. Not only false but even true speech which has no rhythm will prove to be fatal; not only a wrong action but even a right one devoid of rhythm will prove to be out of place.

With the wrong person, even if we do right it sometimes turns into wrong; for instance when we say to someone who is in a rage and who has just been quarreling, "You have done wrong." By saying this we have not given him a good thought but have only added fuel so that he may fight with us too. One often sees that when two people are fighting and a third person approaches them with the best intentions, they both turn on him, and that will make three persons fighting at the same time.

Every plane of man's being is dependent upon the other planes. For instance if the body has lost its rhythm, something goes wrong with the mind; if the mind has lost its rhythm, the body goes wrong; if the heart has lost its rhythm, the mind is puzzled; and if the rhythm of the soul is lost, then all is wrong. To say that the virtue of a sinner is sin and the sin of the virtuous is virtue is an extreme statement, but it would not be an exaggeration.

The rhythm of the soul is influenced by the mind and by action. The soul does not have its own rhythm. As in a higher sense the soul is pure from all things that can be distinguished and divided, one may ask, "How then can it happen that the rhythm of the soul is lost?" But if we see our friend in great grief we will also feel grief. It is not because we have a grief ourselves; we feel it only because our friend's grief reflects on us. The soul is not subjected to a right rhythm or a wrong rhythm, but a right rhythm or a wrong rhythm can be reflected in the soul. For instance when a person says of something that it is ugly, what is ugly is outside him. Then why does he feel discomfort or ugliness? Because it reflects upon him. For the moment that he is looking at the ugly thing, that ugly thing is in his eyes and in his mind, just as when we are standing in front of a mirror our image is not engraved upon the mirror but is only reflected there and will remain there as long as we are standing before it. Thus the soul may experience misery or wretchedness, a wrong rhythm or a right rhythm, but when these are removed the soul is again free from them. In order to maintain a perfect condition in life one must be the master of rhythm. The mechanism of every kind of machinery that works by itself is arranged and kept going by the law of rhythm; and this is another proof of the fact that the whole mechanism of the universe is based on the law of rhythm.

Chapter 3

ATMOSPHERE

The pulse of space beats to the rhythm it is charged with, and this we call atmosphere. Space itself does not have an atmosphere. Space is negative in that it allows its pulse to beat to the rhythm it is charged with, and at the same time it is positive in that it absorbs and assimilates all, sooner or later. When a person says that the atmosphere of a place is quiet or exciting, this only means that the impression of someone who has charged the atmosphere of that place lingers there. This shows that every individual is a tone, a rhythm; a tone that draws the tone of every other person to its own pitch, a rhythm that compels every other person to follow the same rhythm.

Atmosphere can be of two kinds: the atmosphere of presence and the atmosphere of absence. The atmosphere of presence changes with the change that takes place in someone. When a person is sitting in meditation, when he is practicing silence or repose, the atmosphere is quietening; when a person is restless, uneasy, cross, or agitated, the atmosphere takes on the same rhythm. The reason for this is that the atmosphere is made of vibrations, and the life substance in it is charged with the same rate of vibrations as that of the person who happens to be there.

The atmosphere one creates and leaves in a place remains unchanged, although in time it loses its vitality. But it is difficult to believe how long an atmosphere created by someone in a certain place remains vibrating; it stays there much longer than one would think.

Not only does a person create an atmosphere, but an atmosphere is also created in a person. A peaceful person can feel uneasy where there is an atmosphere of restlessness, and a very restless person may feel quiet in an atmosphere of peace. To those who can perceive it, the atmosphere tells stories. One may ask how a person can read the atmosphere which is nothing but vibrations, but the perception of vibrations is in itself the understanding of a language, just as to a musician every note says something. In his mind it is distinct; he knows what note it is, what chord it is, what theme it is; he knows its feeling, its nature, its character, its sense, its effect. To anyone who is not a musician music may be comforting, healing, and soothing, but to him who understands music it is a living thing; it speaks to him, his soul communicates with it. In the same way the one who perceives atmosphere fully knows all about it.

There is another way of looking at this question: not only does every person have his particular atmosphere, but everything one feels, thinks, says, and does is creative of an atmosphere. The wicked will create a wicked atmosphere; the pious will create an atmosphere of piety; a singer by singing, a player by playing, a dancer by dancing, a painter by painting will create an atmosphere expressive of his action. Each feeling such as humor, grief, anger, passion, wonder, attachment, fear, or indifference shows its distinct character in the atmosphere that it has created. No matter what a person may try to hide, his atmosphere will speak of it. No one is ever able to create a false atmosphere, that is to say an atmosphere that is different from his own condition. Someone once asked my murshid what the sign of the godly is. He said, "Judge him not by what he says or by what he does. Feel his atmosphere, and his atmosphere will tell you whether he is godly or not." People do not differ much from one another in size, but the difference in the horizons that their atmosphere occupies is so great that very often there is no comparison possible, and this is the secret behind the personalities of the sages, saints, and prophets, as well as behind their work and their influence in the world.

Since there must be something to hold everything that is significant, what is it that holds the atmosphere in space? It is capacity; space offers capacity. In other words, in space a capacity is formed of an element invisible to our eyes and yet solid enough to hold the vibrations within it. This will become clearer if we study the mystery of the wireless and of mirage. Why does not the air scatter the sounds and words spoken many miles away? It is true that the airwaves carry them a certain distance, but what holds them? It is capacity; it is a fine element which surrounds them, not allowing them to break up, although our ears do not ordinarily hear them in space. It is the same with the phenomenon of mirage. One sees in the desert a picture that is nothing but a reflection on the waves of light of something really existing. But what holds this picture intact, not allowing it to be scattered, is capacity, which in Sanskrit is called *akasha*.

Is the atmosphere visible? All that is intelligible is audible and visible in the finer sense of these words. Our ears may not hear it, yet we may feel that we have heard it; our eyes may not see it, and yet we may feel that we have seen it. What is audible is visible, and what is visible is audible at the same time; it is only to our senses that it is either audible or visible. If a certain thing appeals to our sense of sight, it makes an impression upon that sense and our sense of hearing does not pay any attention to it; and if a thing appeals to our sense of hearing our sense of sight does not take any interest in it. This is because two senses cannot both experience something fully at the same time.

Even when two senses perceive a thing simultaneously, what they experience at that time will not be a full experience. Only the experiencing of everything through one sense at a time can give satisfaction. But apart from experiencing fully through two senses, do not think that it is an exaggeration to say that even two eyes cannot see as fully as one eye. When we close one eye in order to see a thing more clearly, we see it much better. We get a fuller vision of it, for fuller experience needs a single ray of penetration, which reveals the nature, the secret, and the mystery of the object one looks at. One particular sense is capable of experiencing vibra-

tions according to its own capacity, and the vibrations that appeal
to a particular sense engage that sense which experiences them; the
other senses experience the same, but indirectly, through the sense
that is actually experiencing them.

The visible atmosphere is called the aura. Those who do not feel
its vibrations sometimes see it in the form of colors or light. There
are some quite unevolved people who see auras, for the same
reason that some very unevolved people also communicate with
spirits, which is really something that only an evolved person
should venture upon. But they are made like that by nature, and
they are like someone who has never been trained in the technique
of art yet draws a beautiful picture. It is in him, it is a gift, it is
his finer soul and his nervous temperament that are susceptible to
finer vibrations.

The aura therefore may be called a visible atmosphere, or the
atmosphere an invisible aura. Just as different degrees of the vibrations of the atmosphere have a distinct influence upon the person
who percieves them, so the different colors of the aura have their
particular effect upon those who see this aura. There are many
who are not yet awakened to perceive an atmosphere, to see an
aura, although they will feel it in the depths of their being; they
cannot help it.

This shows us that there is another world besides the world that
our physical eyes can see and whose sound our physical ears can
hear, and it is not even very far away. We live in it and we feel
it and we are influenced by it, whether we know it or not. This
is the world of the atmosphere, which is finer than the physical
world, though in a sense it is physical too. It is something we feel;
it is something that will touch our body. And though the body
may not perceive it, yet it is influenced by it. The mind perceives
it more clearly. If we are asked to what plane atmosphere belongs,
we can only say that it is a bridge between the physical and the
mental planes; it is on both planes.

Chapter 4

CAPACITY

The secret of the whole of creation can be traced to the understanding of what is meant by capacity. Capacity is, so to speak, the egg of creation; all of this manifestation which is known to us, as well as that which is unknown to us, is formed in some capacity. The sky is a capacity. Capacity is that which makes a hollow in which the action of the all-pervading existence may produce a substance. All the stars and planets that we have discovered and those that are not yet discovered, what are they? They are all capacities. And what do they contain? They contain, each one according to its capacity, whatever that capacity is able to preserve within it and give birth to; that is why one planet is not like another planet, nor one star like another star.

Just as the sea is a capacity in which all the animals of the water are born and live and die, so the air is a capacity in which many creatures live and move and have their being, and the earth is a capacity which conceives within itself the plants, the trees, and all the different stones, metals, minerals, and other substances which come out of it. Again, everything, the stone, the tree, a fruit or a flower, is a capacity in which a perfume or a savor may be formed. Thus the living being is a capacity, an *akasha,* and man is a finished capacity. People generally think that *akasha* means the sky, but in reality it means everything. Everything in its turn is an *akasha,* just as all substance is a capacity; and according to that capacity it produces what it is meant to produce.

By studying anatomy one will learn that the organs of the senses are all capacities according to their construction, and when capacity is clogged, broken, or in any way troubled, then that organ of sense does not function properly. The tubes and veins of the body are capacities for the blood to circulate in, and when this capacity becomes stopped up, however strong the body may be, life cannot circulate and congestion and illness come. Again, every blood cell is a capacity. If it keeps itself open life comes into it and a person feels healthy, but when a blood cell loses this capacity life does not function anymore in it, and all kinds of diseases develop. So with the pores of the skin: each pore is a capacity; and when for some reason or other this capacity is clogged, then the life cannot circulate there; it stops and diseases become manifest. The digestive organs and the lungs are capacities which breathe life in and function according to the life that is breathed in, that is radiated through them; and when they do not function properly illness and disorder follow.

Then there are the intuitive centers in this physical body of man, each center being a capacity. Few know about them, and they become clogged because man leads such a material life and consequently the intuitive faculties become blunted. All the mystical practices which are followed by the adepts are given in order that these capacities may be opened up and activated, may be put in order so that through them man may experience that which is meant to be experienced. It is lack of air and energy and magnetism that blocks these capacities and centers, and it is this which blunts the intuitive faculties. Thus a person who never gives a thought to this question loses his intuitive faculties, and this itself shows that by thinking about something one produces a capacity, just as one does by action, by movement; and when that movement is dull, when it is not active, then the capacity remains unemployed.

It is capacity which makes the soul a soul; otherwise it would be spirit. For instance, when the sun comes into our house in the morning, the sunlight passing through the window will be square or round according to that window, or triangular if the window is shaped like that. The sun is not triangular or square; it is the window that is that shape. We say it is the sun that comes into the house, but we could call it something else. The sun may be likened to the spirit, and its entry through the window, which is a capacity and which gives it a form—triangular, square, or whatever it may be—may be called the soul. The soul becomes identified with qualities and merits because of the capacity through which it expresses itself; if not it would be spirit.

Life has two divisions, of which one is accepted but the other is not yet. The accepted division of life is what we call substance; the division of life that is not yet accepted can be called vacuum. If we speak to a person about oxygen, he understands that there is oxygen in space; but if we speak about vacuum he does not understand. He says, "What is it? It must be something. If my instrument registers something, I can say that it is something; if it does not, then it is nothing." But in reality vacuum is everything and all things. In certain periods of the world's history man has discovered a finer substance; scientists have discovered atoms and electrons and still finer particles. But then what? Then, they say, there is nothing. The fact is that one wishes to perceive that which is called vacuum by the same method with which one perceives substance, and this is not possible. Therefore, however far one may advance in the discovery of life, one can only reach the most extremely fine substance. In this way people may search for thousands of years, and they may succeed in finding a still finer substance, perhaps even a most useful substance, but it will still be a substance and not a vacuum.

Capacity is matter. It is not merely matter in the everyday sense of the word, for in reality all that is perceptible is matter. It is substance; even if it is the finest substance it is still a substance. That which is above substance is spirit. Spirit is the absence of matter even in its finest condition. Spirit is beyond that, and thus the finest capacity will still be a substance.

Now we come to the following question: if all this manifestation comes from one source, one life, one spirit, then why is there such a variety of things and beings, each different in its nature and character?

There are two principal reasons for this. One is the speed of vibrations; the other is the direction that a certain action takes. In order to make this comprehensible one may divide the speed of vibrations into three stages, slow, moderate, and quick, or as they are called in Sanskrit, *sattva, rajas,* and *tamas.* The first stage is creative in its effect, the second stage is progressive, and the third stage is destructive. This gives us the reason for death and decay and destruction: every living being and every object decays or dies when it strikes that particular speed which is destructive. Besides, as every object looks different when seen from different angles, so every creative force manifests differently when it takes different directions. This explains why a person's right hand is stronger than his left, with few exceptions; and why the right leg is always inclined to go forward first and not the left leg. There is always more strength in the right side of a person than in the left side. It is the law of direction which causes this. For a person to be left-handed is exceptional, it is not normal. It is normal for the right side to be stronger, and if a person is left-handed this shows that his right side has not the proper energy. It does not mean that the left side is stronger than the right side or that the left side takes the place of the right side; it only means that the right side has been weakened and that the left side therefore seems stronger than the right side. It does not mean that this person's positive side is the left and his negative side the right.

The three rhythms mentioned above may also be called mobile, regular, and irregular. It is because of them that manifestation has various forms, qualities, colors, and features. The rhythm that is mobile goes straight; the rhythm that is regular strikes right and left, first forming the perpendicular line and next the horizontal line; and the third is destructive; it is zigzag or irregular. This can also be seen when one examines one's breath: the breath that is flowing through the right nostril gives power; when it flows through the left nostril it takes away that power; and its flow through both nostrils at the same time causes destruction.

What was there before creation? Was there stillness or was there motion? As far as science can reach it finds that there is motion behind all. This is true, for what we call stillness is in reality an imperceptible motion. That is why mountains can exist and trees

can live and people can act and animals can move by the power
of movement, vibration. Their health, their joy, their sorrow, and
their destruction are all caused by a quicker or a slower speed or
a particular activity of these vibrations. Disease and health both
depend upon the law of vibrations.

A diamond is bright because it is vibrating; it is the vibration of
the diamond that makes it brilliant. And so is the brilliant person
whose intelligence is vibrating; according to the rhythm of its
vibration it is capable of understanding. One will always see that
it is the brilliant person who understands more quickly, more
deeply, and better; and it is the one who is not brilliant who takes
time to understand.

In conclusion we arrive at the understanding that the whole
phenomenon is a phenomenon of capacity, and according to that
capacity all that it contains is formed. As each thing or being
vibrates, it acts in accordance with the capacity, and the results are
in accordance with this capacity too. We ourselves are also *akashas,*
and in our *akasha* we get the resonance of our rhythm. This resonance is like the feelings we have when we are tired, depressed,
joyous, or strengthened. It is our *akasha* that feels all these different conditions that which we feel, and what causes this is our
rhythm.

Every word once spoken, every deed that is done, every sentiment felt is recorded somewhere; it has not gone, it is not lost. We
do not see it because it is not always recorded on the ground. If
a seed is sown in the ground, it is recorded in the ground; it comes
out in big letters, proving, "I am an apple tree," "I am a rosebush."
But when something is thrown into space, space does not lose it
either. It has received it and it holds it; and it shows it to those who
can build a capacity around the space and gets its reflection in that
capacity. There is a capacity that is the whole of life; in fact
everything is a recording capacity. But then there is a reading
capacity, and that we have to make ourselves. We must be able to
make a capacity in order to read what is written. In the Qur'an it
is said, "Their hands shall speak and their feet shall bear witness
of their deeds," which means the same thing: that everything is
recorded, written down. When a thief comes from the house
where he has stolen something, he may dig a hole in the ground

and bury his spoils and appear with nothing in his hands, yet there is something written on his face about what he has done. It is written, he cannot efface it; and those who can read will read it. Nothing of what we say, do, or think is lost; it is recorded somewhere, if we only know how to read it.

Chapter 5

"BE, AND ALL BECAME"
(THE ABSTRACT SOUND)

Abstract sound is called *saut-e sarmad* by the Sufis; all space is filled with it. The vibrations of this sound are too fine to be either audible or visible to the material ears or eyes, since it is even difficult for the eyes to see the form and color of the ethereal vibrations on the external plane. It was the *saut-e sarmad,* the sound of the abstract plane, that Muhammad heard in the cave of Ghar-e Hira when he became lost in his divine ideal. The Qur'an refers to this sound in the words, "Be! and all became." Moses heard this very sound on Mount Sinai, when in communion with God; and the same word was audible to Christ when absorbed in his heavenly Father in the wilderness. Shiva heard the same *ana-had nada* during his samadhi in a cave of the Himalayas.

The flute of Krishna is symbolic of the same sound. This sound is the source of all revelation to the masters, to whom it is revealed from within. It is because of this that they know and teach one and the same truth.

The Sufi knows of the past, present, and future, and about all things in life, by being able to know the direction of sound. Every aspect of one's being in which sound manifests has a peculiar effect upon life, for the activity of vibrations has a special effect

25

in every direction. The knower of the mystery of sound knows the mystery of the whole universe. Whoever has followed the strains of this sound has forgotten all earthly distinctions and differences, and has reached that goal of truth in which all the blessed ones of God unite. Space is within the body as well as around it; in other words the body is in space and space is in the body.

This being the case, the sound of the abstract is always going on within, around, and about man. As a rule one does not hear it because one's consciousness is entirely centered in material existence. One becomes so absorbed in one's experiences in the external world through the medium of the physical body that space, with all its wonders of light and sound, appears blank to one.

This can be easily understood by studying the nature of color. There are many colors that are quite distinct by themselves, yet when mixed with others of still brighter hue they become altogether eclipsed; even bright colors embroidered with gold, silver, diamonds, or pearls serve merely as a background to the dazzling embroidery. So it is with the abstract sound compared with the sounds of the external world. The limited volume of earthly sounds is so concrete that it dims the effect of the sound of the abstract to the sense of hearing, although in comparison to it the sounds of the earth are like that of a whistle to a drum. When the abstract sound is audible all other sounds become indistinct to the mystic.

The sound of the abstract is called *anahad* in the Vedas, meaning unlimited sound. The Sufis name it *sarmad,* which suggests the idea of intoxication. The word "intoxication" is here used to signify upliftment, the freedom of the soul from its earthly bondage. Those who are able to hear the *saut-e sarmad* and meditate on it are relieved from all worries, anxieties, sorrows, fears, and diseases; and the soul is freed from captivity in the senses and in the physical body. The soul of the listener becomes the all-pervading consciousness, and his spirit becomes the battery that keeps the whole universe in motion.

Some train themselves to hear the *saut-e sarmad* in the solitude at the seashore, on the river bank, and among the hills and dales; others attain it while sitting in the caves of the mountains or when wandering constantly through forests and deserts, keeping themselves in the wilderness apart from the haunts of men. Yogis and ascetics blow *sing* (a horn) or *shankha* (a shell), which awakens in them this inner tone. Dervishes play *nai* or *algosa* (a double flute) for the same purpose. The bells and gongs in the churches and temples are meant to suggest to the thinker the same sacred sound, and thus lead him towards the inner life.

This sound develops through ten different aspects because of its manifestation through ten different tubes of the body. It sounds like thunder, the roaring of the sea, the jingling of bells, running water, the buzzing of bees, the twittering of sparrows, the vina, the whistle, or the sound of *shankha* until it finally becomes *hu,* the most sacred of all sounds.

This sound *hu* is the beginning and end of all sounds, be they from man, bird, beast, or thing. A careful study will prove this fact, which can be realized by listening to the sound of the steam engine or of a mill, while the echo of bells or gongs gives a typical illustration of the sound *hu.*

The Supreme Being has been called by various names in different languages, but the mystics have known him as *Hu,* the natural name, not manmade, the only name of the Nameless, which all nature constantly proclaims. The sound *hu* is most sacred. The mystics called it *ism-e Azam,* the name of the Most High, for it is the origin and end of every sound as well as the background of each word. The word *hu* is the spirit of all sounds and and of all words, and is hidden within them all, as the spirit is in the body. It does not belong to any language, but no language can help belonging to it. This alone is the true name of God, a name that no people and no religion can claim as their own. This word is not only uttered by human beings, but is repeated by animals and birds. All things and beings proclaim this name of the Lord, for every activity of life expresses distinctly or indistinctly this very sound. This is the word mentioned in the Bible as existing before light came into being: "In the beginning was the word, and the word was with God, and the word was God."

The mystery of *hu* is revealed to the Sufi who journeys through the path of initiation. Truth, the knowledge of God, is called by a Sufi *haqq.* If we divide the word *haqq* into two parts, its assonant sounds become *hu ek, hu* signifying God or truth and *ek* in Hindustani meaning one. Both together express one God and one truth. *Haqiqat* in Arabic means the essential truth, *hákim* means master, and *hakím* means knower, all of which words express the essential characteristics of life.

Aluk is the sacred word that the *vairagis,* the adepts of India, use as their sacred chant. In the word *aluk* are expressed two words: *al* meaning "the," and *haqq,* "truth," both words together expressing God the Source from which all comes.

The sound *hu* becomes limited in the word *ham,* for the letter *m* closes the lips. In Hindustani this word expresses limitation because *ham* means "I" or "we," both of which words signify ego. The word *hamsa* is the sacred word of the yogis which illumines the ego with the light of reality. The word *huma* in the Persian language stands for a fabulous bird. There is a belief that if the *huma* bird sits for a moment on someone's head it is a sign that he will become a king. Its true meaning is that when a person's thoughts so evolve that they break all limitation, then he becomes as a king. It is the limitation of language that it can only describe the Most High as something like a king. It is said in the old traditions that Zoroaster was born of a *huma* tree. This explains the words in the Bible, "Except a man be born of water and the spirit, he cannot enter the kingdom of God." In the word *huma,* *hu* represents spirit, and the word *mah* in Arabic means water. In English the word "human " explains two facts which are characteristic of humanity: *hu* means God and *man* means mind, which word comes from the Sanskrit *mana,* mind being the ordinary person. The two words united represent the idea of the God-conscious person; in other words *hu,* God, is in all things and beings, but it is man by whom He is known. *"Human"* therefore may be said to mean God-conscious, God-realized, or God-man. The word *hamd* means praise, *hamid,* praiseworthy, and *Muhammad,* praiseful. The name of the Prophet of Islam was significant of his attitude to God.

Hur in Arabic means the beauties of heaven; its real meaning is the expression of heavenly beauty. *Zahur* in Arabic means manifestation, especially that of God in nature. *Ahura Mazda* is the name of God known to the Zoroastrians. The first word, *Ahura,* suggests *hu,* upon which the whole name is built.

All of these examples signify the origin of God in the word *hu* and the life of God in every thing and being.

Hayy in Arabic means everlasting, and *Hayat* means life, both of which words signify the everlasting nature of God. The word *huwal* suggests the idea of omnipresence, and *Huvva* is the origin of the name of Eve, which is symbolic of manifestation. As Adam is symbolic of life, they are named in Sanskrit *Purusha* and *Prakriti*.

Jehovah was originally Yahuva, *ya* suggesting the word *oh* and *hu* standing for God, while the *a* represents manifestation. *Hu* is the origin of sound, but when sound first takes shape on the external plane, it becomes *a*. Therefore *alif* or *alpha* is considered to be the first expression of *Hu*, the original word. The Sanskrit alphabet as well as that of most other languages begins with the letter *a*, as does the name of God in several tongues. The word *a* therefore expresses in English one or first, and the sign of *alif* expresses the meaning one as well as first. The letter *a* is pronounced without the help of the teeth or tongue, and in Sanskrit *a* always means without.

The *a* is raised to the surface when the tongue rises and touches the roof of the mouth when pronouncing the letter *l (lam)*, and the sound ends in *m (mim)*, the pronunciation of which closes the lips. These three essential letters of the alphabet are brought together as the mystery in the Qur'an. With *a* deepened by *ayn* the word *ilm* is formed, which means knowledge. *Alim* comes from the same root and means knower. *Alam* means state or condition, the existence that is known.

When *alif* the first and *lam* the central letters are brought together they make the word *al*, which means "the" in Arabic. In English *"all"* suggests the meaning of the entire or absolute nature of existence.

The word *Allah*, which in Arabic means God, if divided into three parts may be interpreted as "the One who comes from nothing." *El* or *Ellah* has the same meaning as *Allah*. The biblical words *Eloi, Elohim,* and *Hallelujah* are related to the word *Allahu*.

The words *om, omen, amen,* and *amin,* which are spoken in all houses of prayer, are of the same origin. *A* in the commencement of the word expresses the beginning, and *m* in the midst signifies the end; *n,* the final letter, is the re-echo of *m,* for *m* naturally ends in a nasal sound, the producing of which signifies life.

In the word *Ahad,* which means God, the Only Being, two meanings are involved by assonance. *A* in Sanskrit means without, and *hadd* in Arabic means limitation.

It is from the same source that the words *vahdat, vahdaniat, hadi, hudadi, huda,* and *hidayat* all come. *Vahdat* means the consciousness of self alone; *vahdaniat* is the knowledge of self; *hadi,* the guide; *huda,* to guide; *hidayat* means guidance.

The more a Sufi listens to *saut-e sarmad,* the sound of the abstract, the more his consciousness becomes free from all the limitations of life. The soul floats above the physical and mental planes without any special effort on the person's part, which shows its calm and peaceful state; a dreamy look comes into his eyes and his countenance becomes radiant. He experiences the unearthly joy and rapture of *wajad,* or ecstasy. When ecstasy overwhelms him he is neither conscious of the physical existence nor of the mental. This is the heavenly wine, to which all Sufi poets refer, that is totally unlike the momentary intoxications of this mortal plane. A heavenly bliss then springs in the heart of a Sufi, his mind is purified from sin and his body from all impurities, and a pathway is opened for him towards the world unseen. He begins to receive inspirations, intuitions, impressions, and revelations without the least effort on his part. He is no longer dependent upon a book or a teacher, for divine wisdom, the light of his soul, the holy spirit, begins to shine upon him. As Sharif says, "I by the light of soul realize that the beauty of the heavens and the grandeur of the earth are the echo of Thy magic flute."

Chapter 6

SOUND, THE CREATOR GOD
(FORM)

The light from which all life comes exists in three aspects, namely, the aspect that manifests as intelligence, the light of the abstract, and the light of the sun. The activity of this one light functions in three different aspects. The first is caused by a slow and solemn activity in the eternal consciousness which may be called consciousness or intelligence. It is intelligence when there is nothing before it to be conscious of; when there is something intelligible before it, the same intelligence becomes consciousness. A normal activity in the light of intelligence causes the light of the abstract at the time when the abstract sound turns into light. This light becomes a torch for the seer who is journeying towards the eternal goal. The same light in its intense activity appears as the sun. No person would readily believe that intelligence, abstract light, and the sun are one and the same, yet language does not contradict itself, and all three have always been called by the name of light.

These three aspects of the one light form the idea that lies behind the doctrine of the Trinity, and that of *trimurti* which existed thousands of years before Christianity among the Hindus and which denotes the three aspects of the One, the One being three. Substance develops from a ray to an atom, but before this it exists as a vibration. What a person sees he accepts as something existent, and what he cannot see does not exist for him. All that one perceives, sees, and feels is matter, and that which is the source and cause of all is spirit.

The philosophy of form may be understood by the study of the process by which tbe unseen life manifests into the seen. As the fine waves of vibrations produce sound, so the gross waves produce light. This is the manner in which the unseen, incomprehensible, and imperceptible life becomes gradually known, by becoming first audible and then visible; and this is the origin and only source of all form.

The sun therefore is the first form seen by the eyes, and it is the origin and source of all forms in the objective world. As such it has been worshipped by the ancients as God, and we can trace the origin of all religions in that mother-religion. We may trace this philosophy in the words of Shems-i Tabriz, "When the sun showed his face then appeared the faces and forms of all worlds. His beauty showed their beauty; in his brightness they shone out; so by his rays we saw and knew and named them."

All the myriad colors in the universe are but the different grades and shades of light, the creator of all elements, that has decorated the heavens so beautifully with sun, moon, planets, and stars; that has made the land and water; with all the beauties of the lower spheres, in some parts dull and in some parts bright, that people have named light and shade. The sun, moon, planets, and stars; the brilliance of electricity; the lesser light of gas, lamps, candles, coal, and wood, all show the sun reappearing in different forms. The sun is reflected in all things, be they dull pebbles or sparkling diamonds, and their radiance is according to their capability of reflection. This shows that light is the one and only source, and the cause of the whole creation. "God is the light of heaven and of the earth," the Qur'an says, and we read in Genesis, "And God said: let there be light, and there was light."

All forms, on whatever plane they exist, are molded under the law of affinity. Every atom attracts towards itself the atom of its own element; every positive atom attracts the negative atom of its own element, and the negative attracts the positive; yet each attraction is different and distinct. These atoms group together and make a form. The atoms of the abstract plane group together and make forms of light and color; these and all different forms of the finer forces of life are seen by the seer. The forms of the mental plane are composed of the atoms of that plane; these are seen by the mind's eye and are called imagination. On the physical plane this process may be seen in a more concrete form.

The mystic sees on the abstract plane one or another element predominating at a certain time, ether, air, fire, water, or earth. Every element in the finer forces of life is rendered intelligible by the direction of its activity and color, and the various forms of light show its different rates of activity. For instance the feeling of humor develops into greater humor, and sadness into a deeper sorrow. And so it is with the imagination: every pleasant thought develops pleasure and expands into a still pleasanter thought, and every disagreeable imagination grows and becomes more intense. Again, on the physical plane we see not only people dwelling together in cities and villages, but even beasts and birds living in flocks and herds. Coal is found in coalmines, and gold in gold-mines; the forest contains thousands of trees, whereas the desert holds not a single one. All this proves the power of affinity that collects and groups kindred atoms, and makes of them numerous forms, thereby creating an illusion before the eyes of humanity, which thus forgets the one source in the manifestation of variety.

The direction taken by an element to make a form depends upon the nature of its activity. For instance, an activity following a horizontal direction shows the earth element, a downward direction the water element, an upward direction the fire element. The activity that moves in a zigzag direction shows the air element, and the form taken by ether is indistinct and misty. Therefore the nature of all things is made plain to the seer by their form and shape, and from their color their element is known, yellow being the color of earth, green that of water, red that of fire, blue that of air, and grey that of ether. The mingling of these elements produces mixed colors of innumerable shades and tones, and the variety of color in nature bears evidence of the unlimited life behind it.

Every activity of vibrations produces a certain sound according to its dome of resonance and according to the capacity of the mold in which the form is shaped. This explains the idea behind the ancient Hindu phrase *nada Brahma,* which means sound, the creator God.

By the law of construction and destruction, as well as by addition and reduction, the different forms in this objective world group together and change. A close study of the constant grouping and dispersing of the clouds will reveal many different forms within a few minutes, and this is a key to the same process that can be seen all through nature. Construction and destruction, addition and reduction in forms all take place under the influence of time and space. Each form is shaped and changed subject to this law, for the substance differs according to the length, breadth, depth, height, and shape of the mold wherein the form is fashioned and the features are formed according to the impression pressed upon it. It takes time to make a young and tender leaf green, and again to change it from green to red and yellow; and it is space that makes of water either a ditch, well, pond, stream, river, or ocean.

The dissimilarity in the features of various races in different periods can be accounted for by the law of time and space, together with climatic and racial causes. The Afghans resemble the natives of the Punjab, and the Senegalese the people of Madras; Arabs are similar in feature to the Persians, and the Chinese closely resemble the Japanese. Tibetans resemble the natives of Bhutan, and the Burmese closely resemble the Siamese. All this proves that the proximity of the lands which they inhabit is largely the cause of likeness in feature. As wide as is the distance of space, so wide is the difference in feature among people. The similarity in form of germs, worms, and insects is accounted for by the same reason. Twin children as a rule resemble each other more closely than other children.

Form depends mostly upon reflection; it is the reflection of the sun in the moon that makes the moon appear round like the sun. All the lower creation evolves by the same law. Animals that begin to resemble man are those which are in his surroundings and see him daily. A man who has the care of animals begins to resemble them, and we see that the butler of a colonel has the bearing of a soldier, and a maid working in a nunnery in time becomes like a nun.

As all things are subject to change, no one thing is the same as it was a moment before, although the change may not be noticeable, for only a definite change is perceptible. In a flower there is the change from bud to blossom, and in a fruit from the unripe to the ripe state. Even stones change, and some among them have been known to become perceptibly altered even in the course of twenty-four hours.

Time has a great influence upon all things and beings, as may be seen by the change from infancy to youth, and from middle age to old age. In Sanskrit, therefore, time is called *kála,* which means destruction, as no change is possible without destruction. In other words destruction may be described as change. All things natural and artificial that we see today differ vastly in form from what they were several thousand years ago. This can be noticed not only in such things as fruit, flowers, birds, and animals, but also in the human race, for from time to time the structure of the human being has undergone various changes.

The form of man is divided into two parts, each part having its special attributes. The head is the spiritual body and the lower part the material body. Therefore, in comparison with the body, the head has far greater importance; thereby one individual is able to recognize another, as the head is the only distinctive part of man. The face is expressive of a person's nature and condition of life; also of his past, present, and future.

When asked if the face would be burned in the fire of hell, the Prophet answered, "No, the face will not be burned, for Allah hath said, 'We have modeled man in Our own image.'"

The likeness between things and beings, as well as between beasts and birds, animals and man, can tell us a great deal about the secret of their nature. The sciences of phrenology and physiology were discovered not only by examining the lives of persons of various features, but chiefly by studying the similarity that exists between them and animals. For instance a person having the features of a tiger will have a dominant nature, coupled with courage, anger, and cruelty. A person with a face resembling a horse's is by nature subservient; a person with a face like that of a dog will have a pugnacious tendency, while a mouse-like face shows timidity.

There are four sources from which the human face and form are derived, and these account for the changes that take place in them. These are: the inherent attributes of the soul; the influence of one's heritage; the impressions of one's surroundings; and lastly the impression of oneself and of one's thoughts and deeds, the clothes one wears, the food one eats, the air one breathes, and the way one lives.

In the first of these sources a person is helpless, for he has no choice, it was not the desire of the tiger to be a tiger; neither did a monkey choose to be a monkey; and it was not the choice of the infant to be born a male or a female. This proves that the first source of man's form depends upon the inherent attributes brought by his soul. Words never can express adequately the wisdom of the Creator who not only fashioned and formed the world, but has given to each being the form suited to its needs. The animals of the cold zones are provided with thick fur as a protection against the cold; to the beasts of the tropics a suitable form is given; the birds of the sea have wings fit for the sea, and those of the earth are provided with wings suitable for the earth. Birds and animals have forms that accord with their habits in life. The form of the human being proclaims his grade of evolution, his nature, and his past and present, as well as his race, nation, surroundings, character, and fate.

In the second instance one inherits beauty or its opposite from his ancestors, but in the third and fourth one's form depends upon how one builds it. The build of the form depends upon the balance and regularity of one's life, and upon the impressions one receives from the world. For in accordance with the attitude one takes towards life, one's every thought and action adds or takes away, or removes to another place, the atoms of the body, thus forming the lines and muscles of form and feature. For instance a person's face speaks his joy, sorrow, pleasure, displeasure, sincerity, insincerity, and all that is developed in him. The muscles of his head tell the phrenologist his condition in life. There is a form in the thought and feelings that produces a beautiful or ugly effect. It is the nature of evolution for all beings, from the lowest to the highest stage of manifestation, to evolve by being connected with a more perfect form. Animals approaching humanity in their evolution resemble primitive people, and animals in contact with people acquire in their form traces of the human likeness. This may be understood by a close study of people's features in the past, and of the improvement that has been made in them.

The nature of creation is that it is progressing always towards beauty. "God is beautiful, and He loves beauty," says the Qur'an. The nature of the body is to beautify itself; the nature of the mind is to have beautiful thoughts; the longing of the heart is for beautiful feelings. Therefore an infant should grow more beautiful every day; and ignorance seeks to become intelligence. When the progress is in a contrary direction, it shows that the individual has lost the track of natural progress. There are two forms, the natural and the artificial, the latter being a copy of the former.

Chapter 7

SOUND AND LIGHT:
TWO ASPECTS OF MOVEMENT
UNITED BY HARMONY

It seems that what science realizes in the end, mysticism realizes
from the beginning, according to the saying of Christ, "First seek
ye the kingdom of God, and all will be added." When one hears
of the present discoveries about sound and color from the scientific
point of view, one begins by being surprised. One says, "What!
A new discovery, something we have never heard of? It is something quite new." And yet when you open the Bible, there it says,
"First was the Word, and the Word was God." And if you open
the still older scriptures of the Vedanta, you read in their verses
that in the Creator there was the word, or the vibration. When we
come to the Qur'an we read there, "First there was the word Be
and then it became." The religions of the world, the prophets and
mystics who existed thousands of years ago, knew of these things.
Today a person comes with a photographic plate and says, "Here
I have a photograph of sound. This shows how important vibration is and its action upon the plate." One does not realize that it
is something that has always been known, only it has been spoken
of in spiritual terms. What has been spoken we do not think about;
what is being spoken we think is something new. But when we

realize, as Solomon has said, that there is nothing new under the sun, we begin to enjoy life, seeing how time after time the same wisdom is revealed to man. The one who seeks truth through science, the one who searches for it through religion, the one who finds it through philosophy, the one who finds it through mysticism—in whatever manner one seeks truth, one finds it in the end.

Once in New York I was introduced to a scientist who was also a philosopher, and the first thing he said about his accomplishments was "I have discovered the soul." It amused me very much that while all the scriptures, thinkers, mystics, and prophets have spoken about it, this man should come and say, "I have discovered the soul"! I thought, "Yes, that was the new discovery that we were expecting, something that we never knew." Such is the attitude of mind today, the childish attitude. When one looks into the past, the present, and the future, one sees that life is eternal; and what one can discover is that which has always been discovered by those who seek. Philosophy or science, mysticism or esotericism, will all agree on one point if they touch the summit of their knowledge, and that point is that behind the whole of creation, behind the whole of manifestation, if there is any subtle trace of life that can be found, it is motion, it is movement, it is vibration.

Now this motion has two aspects. And this is because we have developed two principal faculties, sight and hearing. One aspect appeals to hearing, the other to sight. The aspect of movement or vibration that appeals to our hearing is what we call audible, or sound. The aspect that appeals to our sight we call light or color, and we call it visible. In point of fact what is the origin of all that is visible, all that is audible? It is motion, it is movement, it is vibration; it is one and the same thing. Therefore, those who can see can trace color even in that which is audible and which is called sound; and to those who can hear even the sound of color is audible.

Is there anything that unites these two things? Yes, there is. And what is it? It is harmony. It is not a particular color that is in itself harmonious or that lacks harmony; it is the blending of that color, it is the frame in which it is placed, how the color is arranged. In accordance with that it has its effect upon the one who sees. And so it is with sound. There is not any sound that is harmonious or inharmonious in itself; it is the relation of one sound to another sound that creates harmony. Therefore one cannot point out that this or that certain thing is harmony. Harmony is a fact. Harmony is the result of the relation between color and color, the relation between sound and sound, and the relation between color and sound.

The most interesting aspect of this knowledge is how different colors appeal to different people, and how different people enjoy different sounds. The more one studies this, the more one finds its relation with the particular advancement of a person's evolution. For instance one will find that at a certain stage of one's evolution one loved a certain color, and then one lost contact with that color. With one's growth and evolution in life one begins to like some other color. It also depends upon a person's condition, whether he is emotional, passionate, romantic, warm, or cold, whether sympathetic or disagreeable. Whatever be his emotional condition, in accordance with that he has his likes or dislikes in colors. It is that which makes it easy for the seer, for the knower, to read the character of a person even before having seen his face, by seeing only his clothes. His preference for a certain color expresses what the person is like and what is his liking. His liking for a certain flower, his liking for a certain gem or jewel, his liking for a certain environment in his room, the color on his wall, all that shows what a person is like, what is his preference.

And as one evolves spiritually through life, so one's choice of color changes. With each step forward one changes; one's ideas about color become different. There are some to whom striking colors appeal; to others pale colors. The reason is that striking colors have intense vibrations, and pale colors have smooth and harmonious vibrations, and it is according to ones emotional condition that one enjoys different colors.

It is the same with sound. Every person, whether he knows it or not, has a predilection for a certain sound. Although most people do not study this subject and therefore usually remain ignorant of the idea, yet every person has a special liking for a certain sound. This explains the saying or belief that each person has his note. The fact is that each person has his sound, a sound that is akin to his particular evolution. Besides all the divisions

THE MYSTERY OF SOUND   41

that have been made, such as tenor, bass, or baritone, each person has his particular pitch and each person has his special note on which he speaks, and that particular note is expressive of his life's evolution, expressive of his soul, of the condition of his feelings and of his thoughts.

It not only has an effect upon people to hear certain sounds and to see certain colors, but it also has an effect upon animals. Colors have a great effect and influence upon all living creatures, animals or birds or human beings. Without their knowing it the influence of color works in their lives, turning them to this or that inclination. Once I was visiting a house which had been rented by a certain club, and one of the members told me, "It is a very great pity. Since we have taken this house there is always disagreement in our committee." I said, "No wonder. I see it." They asked, "Why?" I said, "The walls are red; they make you inclined to fight."

A striking color from all around gives you the inclination to disagree; the emotions are touched by it, and certainly those inclined to disagreement are helped by it. And it is from this psychological point of view that one finds in the East the ancient custom, especially at weddings, of a certain color being chosen for the time of wedding and certain colors for other times and festivities. It all has its meaning; it has a psychological significance at the back of it.

Since color and sound are perceived differently and we have different senses to perceive them, we have made a distinction between visible and audible things; but in reality those who meditate, who concentrate, who enter within themselves, those who trace the origin of life begin to see that behind these outer five senses there is one sense hidden. And this sense is capable of doing everything that we seem to do or to experience.

We distinguish five external senses. They are five because we know five organs of sense. But in reality there is only one sense. It is that sense which through these five different organs experiences life and distinguishes life in five different forms. So all that is audible and all that is visible is one and the same. It is this that is called in Sanskrit *purusha* and *prakriti;* and in the terms of the Sufis, *zat* and *sifat.* The manifested aspect is called *sifat,* the outer appearance. It is in the manifestation as *sifat* that one sees the distinction or the difference between what is visible and what is audible; in their real aspect of being they are one and the same. According to Sufi mystics the plane of existence where they are one and the same is called *zat*, that knowledge of the inner existence in which one sees the source and goal of all things.

Color and sound are a language that can be understood not only in the external life but also in the inner life. For the physician and the chemist color has a great significance. The deeper one goes into the science of medicine and of chemistry, the more one recognizes the value of color and realizes that each element and the development or change of each object is distinguishable by the changing of color. The physicians of old used to recognize diseases by the color of the face and the body. Even today there are physicians whose principal way of recognizing a person's complaint is from the color in his eyes, of the tongue, the nails, and the skin. In every condition it is color that is expressive of a person's condition. Also in objects the condition and the change of the object is recognized by the change of color. The psychologists have recognized the condition of objects by their sound and that of people by their voice. What kind of person someone is, whether strong or weak, what his character is, what his inclinations are, and what his attitude is towards life—all this can be known and understood through his voice.

Color and sound are not only the language by which one communicates with external life, but also the language by which one communicates with the inner life. One might ask how this is done. The answer is found in certain scientific experiments: special plates are made, and by speaking near such a plate, one makes marks upon it with sound and with vibration. Those marks make either harmonious forms or inharmonious forms. But every person from morning till night is making an invisible form in space by what he says. He is creating invisible vibrations around him and he is thereby producing an atmosphere. Somebody may come into the house and before he speaks you are tired of him, you wish to get rid of him. Before he has said or done anything you are finished with him, you would like him to go away, for he is creating in his atmosphere a sound and this sound is disagreeable. There may be another person with whom you feel sympathy, to whom you feel drawn, whose friendship you value, whose presence you long for; harmony is continually created through him. That is a sound too.

If this be true, then it is not only the external signs, but also the inner condition which is audible and visible. Though not visible to the eyes and not audible to the ears, yet it is audible and visible to the soul. We say, "I feel his vibrations; I feel this person's presence; I feel sympathy (or antipathy) towards that person." There is a feeling; and a person creates a feeling without having said anything or done anything. Therefore a person whose vibration is wrong, without doing or saying anything wrong creates the wrong atmosphere; and you find fault with him. It is most amusing to see how people may come to you with a complaint, "I have said nothing, I have done nothing, and yet people dislike me and are against me!" That person does not understand that it is not what one says or does, it is what one *is* that speaks louder than anything one says; it is being. It is life itself that has its tone, its color, its vibration; it speaks aloud.

One may wonder what it is and where it is to be found. The answer is that what little man knows about himself is only about his body. If you ask someone to say where he is, he will point at his arm, his hand, his body; he knows little beyond that. There are many who if asked, "But where do you think you are in your body?" will say, "In my brain." They limit themselves to that small physical region which is called body, thus making themselves much smaller than they really are. The truth is that man is one individual with two aspects, just like one line with two ends. If you look at the ends, it is two; if you look at the line, it is one. One end of the line is limited; the other end of the line is unlimited. One end is man; the other end is God. Man forgets that end and knows only the end of which he is conscious; and it is the consciousness of limitation that makes him more limited. Otherwise he would have far greater means of approaching the Unlimited that is within himself, which is only the other end of the same line, the line that he calls, or that he considers to be, himself. And when a mystic speaks of self-knowledge this does not mean knowing how old one is, or how good one is or how bad, or how right or how wrong; it means knowing the other part of one's being, that deeper, subtler aspect. It is upon the knowledge of that being that the fulfilment of life depends.

One might ask, "How can one get closer to it?" The way that has been found by those who searched after truth, those who sought after God, those who wished to analyze themselves, those who wished to sympathize with life is one single way, and that is the way of vibrations. It is the same way as of old: by the help of sound they have prepared themselves. They made these physical atoms which had gradually become deadened live again by the help of sound; they have worked with the power of sound. As Zeb un-nisa says, "Say continually that sacred name which will make thee sacred." The Hindus have called it *mantra yoga;* the Sufis have termed it *wazifa.* It is the power of the word that works upon each atom of the body, making it sonorous, making it a medium of communication between the external life and the inner life.

What one realizes as the first experience of one's spiritual development is that one begins to feel in communion with living beings, not only with human beings but with animals, with birds, with trees, and with plants. It is not a fairytale that the saints used to speak with the trees and the plants. You can speak with them today if you are in communication. It was not only the ancient times which were thus blessed with the old blessing; the old blessing is not old today, it is new. It is the same ancient one that was, that is, and that will be, and no privilege was ever limited to any period of the world's history. Man has the same privilege today if he will realize that he is privileged. When he himself closes his heart, when he allows himself to be covered by the life within and without, no doubt he becomes exclusive, no doubt he is cut off from the whole of manifestation, which is one whole and is not divided. It is man himself who divides himself; for life is undivided, indivisible.

And it is opening communication with external life which makes a person wider. Then one does not say of a friend, "This is my friend; I love him," but, "This is myself; I love him." When one has reached this point one can say that one has arrived at the realization of love. As long as one says, "I feel sympathy with him because he is my friend," one's sympathy has not yet been fully wakened. The real wakening of sympathy is on that day when one

sees a friend and says this is oneself. Then the sympathy is wakened; then there is the communication within oneself. People do
not close themselves only from external life, but also from the
inner part, which is still more important. That inner part is also
sound; that inner part is light. When one realizes this one knows
that language which is the language of heaven, a language that is
expressive of the past and the present and the future, a language
that reveals the secret and the character of nature, a language that
is always receiving and giving the divine message that the prophets have tried at times to reveal.

The nature of creation is the doubling of one. It is this doubling
aspect that is the cause of all duality in life: one part is positive,
the other negative; one expressive, the other responsive. Therefore
spirit and nature in this creation of duality stand face to face. The
first aspect is sound, and the next is light. In these nature aspects,
or responsive aspects, at first only the light works, but when one
goes deeper in creation there is sound. In nature, which is face-to-
face with spirit, what is first expressed is light, or what one first
responds to is light; and what one responds to next, what touches
one deeper, is sound.

The human body is a vehicle of the spirit, a completed vehicle
that experiences all the different aspects of creation. This does not
mean that all other forms and names that exist in this world (some
as objects, others as creatures) are not responsive to the expression
of the spirit. In reality every object is responsive to the spirit and
to the work of the spirit, which is active in all aspects, names, and
forms of the universe. One reads in the *Masnavi* of Rumi that the
earth, the water, the fire, and the air before humanity are objects,
but before God they are living beings. They work at His command,
as we understand living beings working under the command of a
master. If creation can be explained, it is the phases of sound or
of vibration, which manifest in different grades in all the various
forms in life.

Even what we call matter or substance, and all that does not
seem to speak or sound, is in reality all vibration. And the beauty
of the whole of creation is this, that creation has worked in two

ways: in one way it has expressed and in the other way it has made itself a responsive mold. For instance, there is substance, matter to touch, and there is a sense to feel, to touch. There is sound, and at the same time there are ears that can hear sound. There is light, there is form, there are colors, and at the same time there are eyes to see them. What we call beauty is the harmony of all one experiences. What after all is music? What we call music is the harmony of the audible notes; but in reality there is music in color, there is music in lines, there is music in the forest where there is a variety of trees and plants, and there is harmony in how they correspond with each other. The more widely one observes nature, the more it appeals to one's soul. Why? Because there is a music there. And the wider one's outlook on life becomes, the deeper one's understanding of life, the more music one can listen to , the music which answers the whole universe. But the one whose heart is open need not go as far as the forest; in the midst of the crowd he can find music. At this time human ideas are so changed, owing to materialism, that there is hardly any distinction of personality. But if one studies human nature, one sees that even a piano of a thousand octaves could not reproduce the variety of human nature. How people agree with one another, how they disagree; some become friends after a contact of a moment, some in many years cannot become friends. If one could only see to what pitch the different souls are tuned, in what octaves different people speak, what standards different people have! Sometimes there are two people who disagree, and there comes a third person and all unite together. Is that not the nature of music? The more one studies the harmony of music and then studies human nature—how people agree and how they disagree, how there is attraction and repulsion —the more one will see that it is all music.

But now there is another question to be understood, that what a person knows is generally the world he sees around him. Very few trouble to think that there is something beyond what they see around them. To many it is only a fable when they hear that there are two worlds. But if one looked deep within oneself one would see that there are not only two worlds but so many worlds that it is beyond expression. That part of one's being which is receptive is mostly closed in the average man. What he knows is expressing outwardly and receiving from the same sphere whence he can receive himself. For instance, the difference between a simple person and a thinking person with deeper understanding is that when a simple person has received a word he has heard it only in his ears; whereas the thinking person has received the same word as far as his mind. The same word has reached the ears of the one and the heart of the other. If this simple example is true, it shows that one person lives only in this external world, another person lives in two worlds, and a third person lives in many worlds at the same time. When a person says, "Where are those worlds? Are they above the sky, or down below the earth?" the answer is that all these worlds are in the same place as that person is himself.

As a poet has said, "The heart of man, if once expanded, becomes larger than all the heavens." The deep thinkers of all ages have therefore held that the only principle of awakening to life is the principle of emptying the self. In other words, making oneself a clearer and more complete accommodation in order to accommodate all experiences more clearly and more fully. The tragedy of life, all its sorrows and pains, belongs mostly to the surface of the life of the world. If one were fully awake to life, if one could respond to life, if one could perceive life, one would not need to look for wonders, one would not need to communicate with spirits, for every atom in this world is a wonder when one sees with open eyes.

In answer to the question as to what is the experience of those who dive into life and who touch the depth within, Hafiz has said, "It is not known how far is the destination, but so much I know, that music from afar is coming to my ears." The music of the spheres, according to the point of view of the mystic, is like the lighthouse in the port that a person sees from the sea, which tells him that he is coming nearer to his destination. What music may this be? If there were no harmony in the essence of life, life would not have created harmony in this world of variety. And man would not have longed for something which was not in his spirit. Everything in this world that seems to lack harmony is in reality the limitation of a person's own vision. The wider the horizon of his observation becomes, the more harmony of life he enjoys. In the very depth of man's being the harmony of the working of the whole universe is summed up in a perfect music. Therefore the music of the spheres is the music that is the source of creation, the music that is heard while traveling towards the goal of all creation. And it is heard and enjoyed by those who touch the very depth of their own lives.

Chapter 8

MUSIC:
THE MYSTICISM OF
TONE AND PITCH

When we pay attention to nature's music, we find that everything on the earth contributes to its harmony. The trees joyously wave their branches in rhythm with the wind; the sound of the sea; the murmuring of the breeze; the whistling of the wind through rocks, hills, and mountains; the flash of the lightning and the crash of the thunder; the harmony of the sun and moon; the movements of the stars and planets; the blooming of the flower and the fading of the leaf; the regular alternation of morning, evening, noon, and night: all reveal to the seer the music of nature.

The insects have their concerts and ballets, and the choirs of birds chant in unison their hymns of praise. Dogs and cats have their orgies, foxes and wolves have their *soirées musicales* in the forest, while tigers and lions hold their operas in the wilderness. Music is the only means of understanding among birds and beasts. This may be seen by the gradation of pitch and the volume of tone, the manner of tune, the number of repetitions, and the duration of their various sounds; these convey to their fellow creatures the time for joining the flock, the warning of coming danger, the declaration of war, the feeling of love, and the sense of sympathy, displeasure, passion, anger, fear, and jealousy, making a language of itself.

In man breath is a constant tone, and the beat of the heart, pulse, and head keeps the rhythm continuously. An infant responds to music before it has learned how to speak; it moves its hands and feet in time, and expresses its pleasure and pain in different tones.

In the beginning of human creation, no language such as we now have existed, but only music. Man first expressed his thoughts and feelings by low and high, short and prolonged sounds. The depth of tone showed strength and power, and the height of pitch expressed love and wisdom. Man conveyed his sincerity, insincerity, inclination, disinclination, pleasure, or displeasure by the variety of his musical expressions.

The tongue touching various points in the mouth and the opening and the closing of the lips in different ways produced the variety of sounds. The grouping of the sounds made words conveying different meanings in their various modes of expression. This gradually transformed music into a language, but language could never free itself from music.

A word spoken in a certain tone shows subservience, and the same word spoken in a different tone expresses command; a word spoken in a certain pitch shows kindness, and the same word spoken in a different pitch expresses coldness. Words spoken in a certain rhythm show willingness, and the same words express unwillingness when spoken at a different degree of speed. Up to the present day the ancient languages Sanskrit, Arabic, and Hebrew cannot be mastered by simply learning the words, pronunciation, and grammar, because a particular rhythmic and tonal expression is needed. The word in itself is frequently insufficient to express the meaning clearly. The student of language by keen study can discover this. Even modern languages are but a simplification of music. No words of any language can be spoken in one and the same way without the distinction of tone, pitch, rhythm, accent, pause, and rest. A language, however simple, cannot exist without music in it; music gives it a concrete expression. For this reason a foreign language is rarely spoken perfectly; the words are learned, but the music is not mastered.

Language may be called the simplification of music; music is hidden within it as the soul is hidden in the body. At each step toward simplification the language loses some of its music. A study of ancient traditions reveals that the first divine messages were given in song, as were the psalms of David, the Song of Solomon, the gathas of Zoroaster, and the gita of Krishna.

When language became more complex, it closed, as it were, one wing, the sense of tone, keeping the other wing, the sense of rhythm, outspread. This made poetry a subject distinct and separate from music. In ancient times religions, philosophies, sciences, and arts were expressed in poetry. Parts of the Vedas, Puranas, Ramayana, Mahabaharata, Zend Avesta, Kabbala, and Bible are to be found in verse, as well as different arts and sciences in the ancient languages. Among the scriptures only the Qur'an is entirely in prose, and even this is not devoid of poetry. In the East, even in recent times, not only were manuscripts of science, art, and literature written in poetry, but the learned even discoursed in verse. In the next stage, man freed the language from the bond of rhythm and made prose out of poetry. Although man has tried to free language from the trammels of tone and rhythm, yet in spite of this the spirit of music still exists. Man prefers to hear poetry recited and prose well read, which is in itself a proof of the soul seeking music even in the spoken word.

The crooning song of the mother soothes the infant and makes it sleep, and lively music gives it an inclination to dance. It is music that doubles the courage and strength of a soldier when he marches towards the field of battle. In the East, when the caravans travel from place to place on a pilgrimage, they sing as they go. In India the coolies sing when at work, and the rhythm of the music makes the hardest labor become easy for them.

All spiritualists who have really sounded the depths of spiritualism have realized that there is no better means of attracting the spirits from their plane of freedom to the outer plane than by music. They make use of different instruments that appeal to certain spirits, and sing songs that have a special effect upon the particular spirit with whom they wish to communicate. There is no magic like music for making an effect upon the human soul.

The taste for music is inborn in man, and it first shows in the infant. Music is known to a child from its cradle, but as it grows in this world of delusion its mind becomes absorbed in so many and various objects that it loses the aptitude for music which its soul possessed. When grown-up a person enjoys and appreciates music in accordance with his grade of evolution and with the surroundings in which he has been born and brought up. The person of the wilderness sings his wild lays, and the person of the city his popular song. The more refined a person becomes, the finer the music he enjoys. The character in each person creates a tendency for music akin to it; in other words the carefree person enjoys light music, while the serious-minded person prefers classical; the intellectual takes delight in technique, while the simpleton is satisfied with his drum.

There are five different aspects of the art of music: popular, that which induces motion of the body; technical, that which satisfies the intellect; artistic, that which has beauty and grace; appealing, that which pierces the heart; uplifting, that in which the soul hears the music of the spheres.

The effect of music depends not only on the proficiency but also upon the evolution of the performer. Its effect upon the listener is in accordance with his knowledge and evolution; for this reason the value of music differs with each individual. For a self-satisfied person there is no chance of progress, because he clings contentedly to his taste according to his state of evolution, refusing to advance a step higher than his present level. He who gradually progresses along the path of music in the end attains to the highest perfection. No other art can inspire and sweeten the personality like music; the lover of music attains sooner or later to the most sublime field of thought.

India has preserved the mysticism of tone and pitch discovered by the ancients, and its music itself signifies this. Indian music is based upon the principle of the raga, which shows it to be akin to nature. It has avoided limitations of technique by adopting a purely inspirational method.

The ragas are derived from five different sources: the mathematical law of variety, the inspiration of the mystics, the imagination of the musicians, the natural lays peculiar to the people residing in different parts of the land, and the idealization of the poets. These made a world of ragas, calling one *rag,* the male, another *ragini,* the female, and others *putra,* sons, and *bharja,* daughters-in-law.

Raga is called the male theme because of its creative and positive nature; *ragini* is called the female theme on account of its responsive and fine quality. *Putras* are such themes as are derived from the mingling of *ragas* and *raginis;* in them can be found a likeness to the *raga* and the *ragini* from which they are derived. *Bharja* is the theme which responds to the *putra.* Six ragas, thirty-six *raginis* (six belonging to each raga), forty-eight *putras,* and forty-eight *bharjas* constitute this family.

Each raga has an administration of its own, including a chief, *mukhya,* the keynote; *wadi,* a king, a principal note; *samwadi,* a minister, a subordinate note; *anuwadi,* a servant, an assonant note; *viwadi,* an enemy, a dissonant note. This gives to the student of the raga a clear conception of its use. Each raga has its image distinct from the others. This shows the highest reach of imagination.

The poets have depicted the images of ragas just as the picture of each aspect of life is clear in the imagination of the intelligent. The ancient gods and goddesses were simply images of the different aspects of life, and in order to teach the worship of the immanence of God in nature these various images were placed in the temples, so that God in His every aspect of manifestation might be worshipped. The same idea has been worked out in the images of ragas, which create with delicate imagination the type, form, figure, action, expression, and effect of the idea.

Every hour of the day and night, every day, week, month, and season has its influence upon man's physical and mental condition. In the same way each raga has power upon the atmosphere, as well as upon the health and mind of man. It has the same effect as that shown by the different times in life, subject to the cosmic law. By the knowledge of both time and raga the wise have connected them to suit each other.

There are instances in ancient tradition when birds and animals were charmed by the flute of Krishna, rocks were melted by the song of Orpheus, and the *dipak* raga sung by Tansen lighted all the torches, while he himself was burned by reason of the inner fire his song produced. Even today snakes are charmed by the *pungi,* the flute of the snake charmers in India. All this shows us how the ancients must have dived into the most mysterious ocean of music.

The secret of composition lies in sustaining the tone as solidly and as long as possible through all its different degrees; a break destroys its life, grace, power, and magnetism, just as the breath holds life and has all grace, power, and magnetism. There are some notes that need a longer life than others, acccording to their character and purpose.

In a true composition a miniature of nature's music is seen. The effects of thunder, rain, and storm and the pictures of hills and rivers make music a real art. Although art is an improvisation on nature, yet it is only genuine when it keeps close to nature. The music that expresses the nature and character of individuals, nations, or races is still higher. The highest and most ideal form of composition is that which expresses life, character, emotions, and feelings, for this is the inner world that is only seen by the eye of mind. A genius uses music as a language to express fully, without the help of words, whatever he may wish to make known; for music, a perfect and universal language, can express feeling more comprehensively than any tongue.

Music loses its freedom by being subject to the laws of technique, but mystics in their sacred music, regardless of the world's opinion, free both their composition and improvisations from the limitations of technicality.

The art of music in the East is called *kalá,* and has three aspects: vocal, instrumental, and the expression of movement.

Vocal music is considered to be the highest, for it is natural; the effect produced by an instrument which is merely a machine cannot be compared with that of the human voice. However perfect strings may be, they cannot make the same impression on the listener as the voice that comes direct from the soul as breath, and has been brought to the surface through the medium of the mind and the vocal organs of the body. When the soul desires to express itself in the voice, it first causes an activity in the mind, and the mind by means of thought projects finer vibrations in the mental plane. These in due course develop and run as breath through the regions of the abdomen, lungs, mouth, throat, and nasal organs, causing the air to vibrate all through, until they manifest on the surface as voice. The voice therefore naturally expresses the attitude of mind, whether true or false, sincere or insincere.

The voice has all the magnetism that an instrument lacks, for voice is nature's ideal instrument, upon which all other instruments of the world are modeled.

The effect produced by singing depends upon the depth of feeling of the singer. The voice of a sympathetic singer is quite different from that of one who is heartless. However artificially cultivated a voice may be, it will never produce feeling, grace, and beauty unless the heart be cultivated also. Singing has a twofold source of interest, the grace of music and the beauty of poetry. In proportion as the singer feels the words he sings, an effect is produced upon the listeners; his heart, so to speak, accompanies the song.

Although the sound produced by an instrument cannot be produced by the voice, yet the instrument is absolutely dependent upon the player. This explains clearly how the soul makes use of the mind, and how the mind rules the body. Yet it seems as though the body works, not the mind, and the soul is left out. When one hears the sound of the instrument and sees the hand of the player at work, one does not see the mind working behind, nor the phenomenon of the soul.

At each step from the inner being to the surface there is an apparent improvement, which appears to be more positive; yet every step towards the surface entails limitation and dependence.

There is nothing that is unable to serve as a medium for sound, although tone manifests more clearly through a sonorous body than through a solid one, the former being open to vibrations while the latter is closed. All things that give a clear sound show life, while solid bodies choked up with substance seem dead. Resonance is the preserving of tone; in other words it is the rebound of tone which produces an echo. On this principle all instruments are made, the difference lying in the quality and quantity of the tone, which depend upon the construction of the instrument. The instruments of percussion such as the *tabla,* or the drum, are suitable for practical music, and stringed instruments like the *sitar,* violin, or harp are meant for artistic music. The *vina* is especially constructed to concentrate the vibrations; as it gives a faint sound, sometimes audible only to the player, it is used in meditation.

The effect of instrumental music also depends upon the evolution of the player, who expresses with the tips of his fingers upon the instrument his grade of evolution; in other words his soul speaks through the instrument. A person's state of mind can be read by his touch upon any instrument, for however great an expert he may be, he cannot produce by mere skill, without a developed feeling within himself, the grace and beauty which appeal to the heart.

Wind instruments especially, like the flute and the *algosa,* express the heart quality, for they are played with the breath, which is the very life. Therefore they kindle the heart's fire.

Instruments stringed with gut have a living effect, for they come from a living creature that once had a heart. Those stringed with wire have a thrilling effect and the instruments of percussion such as the drum have a stimulating and animating effect upon people.

After vocal and instrumental music comes the music of the dance. Motion is the nature of vibration. Every motion contains within itself a thought and feeling. This art is innate in humans: an infant's first pleasure in life is to amuse itself with the movement of hands and feet; a child on hearing music begins to move. Even beasts and birds express their joy in motion. The peacock proud in the vision of his beauty displays his vanity in dance; likewise the cobra unfolds his hood and rocks his body on hearing the music of the *pungi.* All this proves that motion is the sign of life, and when accompanied by music it sets both the performer and onlooker in motion.

The mystics have always looked upon this subject as a sacred art. In the Hebrew scriptures we find David dancing before the Lord. And the gods and goddesses of the Greeks, Egyptians, Buddhists, and Brahmans are represented in different poses, all having a certain meaning and philosophy, relating to the great cosmic dance that is evolution.

Even up to the present time among Sufis in the East dancing takes place at their sacred meetings called *sama,* for dancing is the outcome of joy. The dervishes at the *sama* give an outlet to their ecstasy in *raqs,* dancing, which is regarded with great respect and reverence by those present, and is in itself a sacred ceremony.

The art of dancing has greatly degenerated owing to its misuse. People for the most part dance either for the sake of amusement or for exercise, often abusing the art in their frivolity.

Tune and rhythm tend to produce an inclination for dance. To sum up, dancing may be said to be a graceful expression of thought and feeling without uttering a word. It may be used also to impress the soul by movement, by producing an ideal picture before it. When beauty of movement is taken as the presentation of the divine ideal, then the dance becomes sacred.

The music of life shows its melody and harmony in our daily experiences. Every spoken word is either a true or a false note, according to the scale of our ideal. The tone of one personality is hard like a horn, while the tone of another is soft like the high notes of a flute.

The gradual progress of all creation from a lower to a higher evolution, its change from one aspect to another, is shown as in music where a melody is transposed from one key into another. The friendship and enmity among people and their likes and dislikes are as chords and discords. The harmony of human nature and the human tendency to attraction and repulsion are like the effect of the consonant and dissonant intervals in music.

In tenderness of heart the tone turns into a halftone, and with the breaking of the heart the tone breaks into microtones. The more tender the heart becomes, the fuller the tone becomes; the harder the heart grows, the more dead it sounds.

Each note, each scale, and each strain expires at the appointed time, and at the end of the soul's experience here the finale comes. But the impression remains, as a concert in a dream, before the radiant vision of the consciousness.

With the music of the Absolute the bass, the undertone, is going on continuously. But on the surface, beneath the various keys of all the instruments of nature's music, the undertone is hidden and subdued. Every being with life comes to the surface and again returns whence it came, as each note has its return to the ocean of sound. The undertone of this existence is the loudest and the softest, the highest and the lowest; it overwhelms all instruments of soft or loud, high or low tone, until all gradually merge in it; this undertone always is, and always will be.

The mystery of sound is mysticism; the harmony of life is religion. The knowledge of vibrations is metaphysics, the analysis of atoms is science, and their harmonious grouping is art. The rhythm of form is poetry, and the rhythm of sound is music. This shows that music is the art of arts and the science of all sciences; and it contains the fountain of all knowledge within itself.

Music is called a divine or celestial art not only because of its use in religion and devotion and because it is in itself a universal religion, but also because of its fineness in comparison with all other arts and sciences. Every sacred scripture, holy picture, or spoken word produces the impression of its identity upon the mirror of the soul. But music stands before the soul without producing any impression of this objective world, in either name or form, thus preparing the soul to realize the infinite.

Recognizing this, the Sufi names music *ghiza-e ruh,* the food of the soul, and he uses it as a source of spiritual perfection. For music fans the fire of the heart, and the flame arising from it illumines the soul. The Sufi derives much more benefit from music in his meditations than from anything else. His devotional and meditative attitude makes him responsive to music, which helps him in his spiritual unfoldment. The consciousness by the help of music first frees itself from the body and then from the mind. This once accomplished, only one step more is needed to attain spiritual perfection.

Sufis in all ages have taken a keen interest in music, in whatever land they may have dwelled; Rumi especially adopted this art by reason of his great devotion. He listened to the verses of the mystics on love and truth, sung by the *qawwals,* the musicians, to the accompaniment of the flute.

The Sufi visualizes the object of his devotion in his mind, which is reflected upon the mirror of his soul. The heart, the factor of feeling, is possessed by everyone, although with everyone it is not a living heart. This heart is made alive by the Sufi who gives an outlet to his intense feelings in tears and in sighs. By his so doing the clouds of *jelal,* the power that gathers with his psychic development, fall in tears as drops of rain, and the sky of his heart is clear, allowing the soul to shine. This condition is regarded by Sufis as the sacred ecstasy.

Since the time of Rumi music has become a part of the devotions in the Mevlevi order of the Sufis. The masses in general, owing to their narrow, orthodox views, have cast out the Sufis and opposed them for their freedom of thought, thus misinterpreting the Prophet's teaching, which prohibited the abuse of music, not music in the real sense of the word. For this reason a language of music was made by Sufis, so that only the initiated could understand the meaning of the songs. Many in the East hear and enjoy these songs not understanding what they really mean.

A branch of this order came to India in ancient times, and was known as the Chishtia school of Sufis; it was brought to great glory by Khwaja Moinuddin Chishti, one of the greatest mystics ever known to the world. It would not be an exaggeration to say that he actually lived on music. Even at the present time, although his body has been in the tomb at Ajmer for many centuries, yet at his shrine there is always music given by the best singers and musicians in the land. This shows the glory of a poverty-stricken sage compared with the poverty of a glorious king: the one during his life had all things, which ceased at his death, while the glory of the sage is ever-increasing. At the present time music is prevalent in the school of the Chishtis who hold meditative musical assemblies called *Sama* or *qawwali.* During these they meditate on the ideal of their devotion, which is in accordance with their grade of evolution, and they increase the fire of their devotion while listening to the music.

Wajad, the sacred ecstasy that the Sufis experience at *Sama,* may be said to be union with the Desired One. There are three aspects of this union that are experienced by Sufis of different stages of evolution. The first is the union with the revered ideal from that plane of earth present before the devotee, either the objective plane or the plane of thought. The heart of the devotee, filled with love, admiration, and gratitude, then becomes capable of visualizing the form of his ideal of devotion while listening to the music.

The second step in ecstasy, and the higher aspect of union, is union with the beauty of character of the ideal, irrespective of form. The song in praise of the ideal character helps the love of the devotee to gush forth and overflow.

The third stage in ecstasy is union with the divine Beloved, the highest ideal, who is beyond the limitation of name or form, virtue or merit, with whom it has constantly sought union, and whom the soul has finally found. This joy is unexplainable. When the words of those souls who have already attained union with the divine Beloved are sung before the one who is treading the path of divine love, he sees all the signs on the path described in those verses, and it is a great comfort to him. The praise of the One so idealized, so unlike the ideal of the world in general, fills him with joy beyond words.

Ecstasy manifests in various aspects. Sometimes a Sufi may be in tears, sometimes he will sigh, sometimes ecstasy expresses itself in *raqs,* motion. All this is regarded with respect and reverence by those present at the *Sama* assembly, as ecstasy is considered to be divine bliss. The sighing of the devotee clears a path for him into the world unseen, and his tears wash away the sins of ages. All revelation follows the ecstasy; all knowledge that a book can never contain, that a language can never express nor a teacher teach, comes to him of itself.

PART II

THE HARMONY OF LIFE

In the very depth of man's being the harmony of the working of
the whole universe is summed up in perfect music.

Music has a mission not only with the multitudes but with individuals, and its mission with the individual is as necessary and great as its mission with the multitude. All the trouble in the world and all the disastrous results arising out of it all come from lack of harmony. This shows that the world needs harmony today more than ever before. So if the musician understands this, his customer is the whole world. When a person learns music, he need not necessarily learn to be a musician or to become a source of pleasure and joy to his fellow man; no, but by playing, loving, and hearing music, he must develop music in his personality. The true use of music is to become musical in one's thoughts, words, and actions. We must be able to give the harmony for which the soul yearns and longs every moment. All the tragedy in the world, in the individual and in the multitude, comes from lack of harmony. And harmony is best given by producing harmony in one's own life.

During my travels throughout the world, I have heard the music of many different places, and always I have felt that intimate friendship and brotherhood existing in music. I always have had a great respect for music and for the devotee of music. One thing I believe (and when in India was convinced of it time after time in meeting those who have touched some perfection in music) that not only in their music but in their life one can feel the harmony that is the real test of perfection. If this principle of music were followed there would be no need for an external religion. And someday music will be the means of expressing universal religion. Time is wanted for this, but there will come a day when music and its philosophy will become the religion of humanity.

Chapter 9

THE WORD THAT WAS LOST

"The word that was lost" is a symbolical phrase of the mystics which has existed in the East and among the wise for ages. Many spiritual and mystical schools have been formed to try to understand this particular problem; but it is a fact that whoever has solved the problem says very little about it afterwards.

There is an ancient story in the East that tells that there was a wall of mystery. Whenever anyone tried to climb up the wall to look at the other side, he smiled and jumped over, and never came back again. So the people of that country became very curious to know what mystery was behind the wall. Once when someone was climbing up the wall to see what was on the other side they put chains on his feet, and held him so that he would not go over. When he looked at the other side, he too was delighted with what he saw and smiled; and those standing at the foot of the wall, curious to know what he had to say, pulled him back. But to their great disappointment he had lost his speech.

The mystery of life has a great charm; every soul is curious about it. But when one wants to explain the mystery of life, words are not adequate. There are many reasons for this speechlessness, for this silence. The first is that the person who has seen what is on the other side of the wall finds himself among children when he returns. To him all the things to which people attach great importance and value seem worthless. For him truth and fact are two different things; for everybody else truth and fact are the same.

The followers of various faiths and religions, those who have different opinions and different ideas, dispute and argue and differ from one another. Do they dispute and differ in the realization of truth? No. All the differences and disputes are caused by the various facts that are all different from one another. There are many facts and one truth; there are many stars and one sun. And when the sun has risen the stars become pale. To the one before whom the sun has risen, to whom the truth has manifested, facts make little difference. The light of truth falling upon the facts makes them disappear.

It is very interesting to observe that there are many people who are both deaf and dumb. This shows that deafness and dumbness are connected, and according to a certain point of view it is the same thing to be deaf as to be dumb. It is just like two ends of one line: when you look at the ends you may say "deaf" and " dumb"; when you look at the whole line it is one. In the same way perception and expression are the two ends of one line. In other words, the faculty of speaking and the sense of hearing are the same. If one is lost, the other is lost.

The difference between science and mysticism is very slight; it is only that one goes a certain distance, but the other goes further. Considering the idea of creation from a material point of view, a scientist goes as far as realizing that there are certain elements which cause creation and form various objects. When he goes on he goes as far as atoms, molecules, and electrons, and then he comes to vibrations; and here he stands still. He says that the basis of the whole of creation must be movement, and that the finest aspect of movement is what is called vibration.

According to the point of view of a mystic, what existed before creation was the Perfect Being—perfect not in the ordinary sense of the word, because in everyday conversation we call many things perfect which are limited, but in the sense of the spirit of the word. The spirit of the meaning of perfection is beyond words. By divine perfection a mystic means the perfection of beauty, wisdom, and power; the perfection of love and the perfection of peace. But at the same time where there are eyes there must be an object to look at, to admire; that is how the purpose of the eyes if fulfilled. Where there are ears there must be a sound to be heard in order to enjoy its beauty; therein lies the fulfillment of the existence of the ears. Thus it was necessary for the Perfect Being, in order to realize His own perfection, to create a limited perfection of His own Being and this is accomplished by the One being divided into three aspects. This is really the secret behind the conception of trinity: the seer, the seen, and sight.

It is the work of biology and other sciences to explain in detail the gradual development of creation. But the outline that the mystics of all ages have given is that first there took place the creation of the mineral kingdom, then that of the vegetable, then that of the animal kingdom, and lastly that of man. They taught that through this entire process of development there has been a certain purpose that has led creation on to the fulfillment of a certain object. But in studying the whole process, the mineral, the vegetable, the animal kingdom, and man, the seer finds something that was missing but that appears as development goes on further. What is it that was missing? It is expression and perception; and it is this which the mystics have pointed out in their symbolic phrase, "the word that was lost." What makes them say that the word was lost? It is that in the beginning there was the word; there was movement, vibration, and there was the consciousness of the Perfect Being. The rocks were not made even from a scientific point of view, before manifestation manifested. Vibration came first, and afterwards came the rocks. But the difference between the mystical and the scientific point of view is this, that the scientist says that from the rock intelligence developed by a gradual process, whereas the mystic says that the rock was only a grade of intelligence; intelligence was first, and the rock came afterwards.

The whole process of manifestation suggests that it is working towards one and the same object. There are two points of view from which to look at it: one is that a mountain will someday turn into a volcano, or a tree will someday bear fruits, and thus the object of its being is fulfilled. The other point of view, which is perhaps more perfect, is that the stones and trees and animals and humanity are all working towards one object, and that the whole process of creation is working towards it. And what is that purpose towards which every aspect of creation is working? What is it that the woods, the trees are waiting for? What moment? What object? What is it that all animals are seeking for besides food? What is it that is giving importance to every activity of man, and after the fulfillment of each activity draws him on to another? It is one object, but covered under many forms. It is the search after that word, the word that was lost. The further creation develops, the greater is its longing to hear this word.

As there is a gradual process of evolution from the mineral to the human kingdom, so there is also a gradual process from a certain state of human evolution to a state of perfection. What is it that makes a person want to hear a word of admiration or a word of praise that satisfies him? What is it that pleases him in hearing the voice, the word, of his friend? What is it that charms him in music or in poetry, and that gives him joy? It is the same word that was lost appearing in different forms.

It seems that in the beginning creation—I mean material creation—is deaf and dumb. And what is it that feels this pain of realizing being deaf and dumb? It is that spirit of perfection which has been perfect in perception and expression. What Jelaluddin Rumi says about the soul in the *Masnavi* explains the main tragedy of life. Although every person, every soul suffers pain to a certain degree, and every soul will describe the cause of that pain differently, yet beneath the different causes is one cause, and that cause is the captivity of the soul. In other words, that the word has been lost.

Souls at different stages of evolution try to search for this word that was lost in the way in which they are accustomed to search. Ways have been made to search for this word that have become right ways and wrong ways, sins and virtues. For this reason the wise person is tolerant towards all, for he sees that every soul has its own way of following its purpose. But in the accomplishment of all these purposes there is one purpose, and that is in the finding of the word that was lost.

No soul, however, will find satisfaction unless it touches that perfection which is spoken of in the Bible, "Be ye perfect as your Father in heaven is perfect." In other words this means that the spirit of God itself has gone through different phases in order to realize this perfection; and although it is limited in comparison with the perfection of God's own Being, yet it is intelligible. The satisfaction is in that.

What explanation can be given of this perfection? What is it? What experience is it? This perfection is what words can never explain, except by saying that the eyes of the soul become open, and that from all sides that word that was lost comes to the ears of the soul. The poets of the East have pictured it in beautiful imagery in stories like that of Rama and Sita. They have described the joy of this perfection as a lover who, having lost his beloved, has found her again. But no imagery can better explain this idea than the picture of a person who has lost his soul and has found it again.

Chapter 10

THE MUSIC OF THE SPHERES

By this title I do not mean to encourage any superstition or any idea that might attract people into fields of curiosity. My aim is to direct the attention of those who search for truth towards the law of music that is working throughout the universe, and that in other words may be called the law of life: the sense of proportion, the law of harmony, the law that brings about balance, the law that is hidden behind all aspects of life, which holds this universe intact and works out the destiny of the whole universe, fulfilling its purpose.

There are many in this world who look for wonders; if one only noticed how many wonders there are in this world, which is all phenomena! The deeper one sees into life, the wider life opens itself to one, and every moment of one's life then becomes full of wonders and full of splendor.

What we call music in our everyday language is only a miniature, which our intelligence has grasped from that music or harmony of the whole universe which is working behind everything, and which is the source and origin of nature. It is because of this that the wise of all ages have considered music to be a sacred art. For in music the seer can see the picture of the whole universe. The wise can interpret the secret and the nature of the working of the whole universe in realm of music.

This is not a new idea; yet at the same time it is always new. Nothing is as old as the truth, and nothing is as new as the truth. It is a human desire to search for something traditional, for something original, and for something new. All these tendencies can be satisfied in the knowledge of truth.

All the religions have taught that the origin of the whole of creation is sound. No doubt the way in which this word is used in our everyday language is a limitation of that sound which is suggested by the scriptures. Language deals with comparative objects, but that which cannot be compared has no name. Truth is that which can never be spoken; and what the wise of all ages have spoken is what they have tried their best to express, little as they were able to do so.

The music of the universe is the background of the small picture that we call music. Our sense of music, our attraction to music, shows that there is music in the depth of our being. Music is behind the working of the whole universe. Music is not only life's greatest object, but it is life itself. Hafiz, the great and wonderful Sufi poet of Persia, says, "Many say that life entered the human body by the help of music, but the truth is that life itself is music." What made him say this? He referred to a legend that exists in the East which tells how God made a statue of clay in His own image and asked the soul to enter into it. But the soul refused to be imprisoned, for its nature is to fly about freely and not to be limited and bound to any sort of capacity. The soul did not wish in the least to enter this prison. Then God asked the angels to play their music, and as the angels played the soul was moved to ectasy, and through that ecstasy, in order to make the music more clear to itself, it entered this body. It is told that Hafiz said, "People say that the soul, on hearing that song, entered the body; but in reality the soul itself was song!"

It is a beautiful legend, and much more so is its mystery. The interpretation of this legend explains to us two great laws. One is that freedom is the nature of the soul, and for the soul the whole tragedy of life is the absence of that freedom which belongs to its original nature. The next mystery that this legend reveals to us is that the only reason why the soul has entered the body of clay or matter is to experience the music of life and to make this music clear to itself. When we sum up these two great mysteries, the third mystery, which is the mystery of all mysteries, comes to our mind. This is that the unlimited part of ourselves becomes limited and earthbound for the purpose of making this life, which is the outward life, more intelligible.

Therefore there is a loss and a gain. The loss is the loss of freedom, and the gain is the experience of life, which is fully gained by coming into this limited life that we call the life of an individual.

What makes us feel drawn to music is that our whole being is music: our mind and our body, the nature in which we live, the nature that has made us, all that is beneath and around us, it is all music. We are close to all this music, and live and move and have our being in music.

Therefore music interests us and attracts our attention and gives us pleasure, because it corresponds with the rhythm and tone that are keeping the mechanism of our whole being intact. What pleases us in any of our arts, whether drawing, painting, carving, architecture, sculpture, or poetry, is the harmony behind it, the music. What poetry suggests to us is music, the rhythm in the poetry or the harmony of ideas and phrases. Besides this, in painting and drawing it is our sense of proportion and our sense of harmony that give us all the pleasure we gain in admiring art. What appeals to us in being near to nature is nature's music, and nature's music is more perfect than that of art. It gives us a sense of exaltation to be moving about in the woods and to be looking at the green, to be standing near the running water, which has its rhythm, its tone, and its harmony. The swinging of the branches in the forest, the rising and falling of the waves—all has its music. And once we contemplate and become one with nature our hearts open to its music.

We say that we enjoy nature. But what is it in nature that we enjoy? It is music. Something in us has been touched by the rhythmic movement, by the perfect harmony that is so seldom found in this artificial life of ours; it lifts one up and makes one feel that nature is the real temple, the true religion. One moment standing in the midst of nature with open heart is a whole lifetime, if one is in tune with nature.

When one looks at the cosmos, the movements of the stars and planets, the law of vibration and rhythm, all perfect and unchanging, it shows that the cosmic system is working by the law of music, the law of harmony. Whenever that harmony in the cosmic system is lacking in any way, then in proportion disaster comes to the world, and its influence is seen in the many destructive forces that manifest there. The whole of astrological law, and the science of magic and mysticism behind it, are based upon music.

Therefore the whole life of the most illuminated souls who have lived in this world, like the greatest prophets in India, has been music. From the miniature music that we understand, they expanded the whole universe of music, and in that way they were able to inspire. The one who receives the key to the working of life is he who becomes intuitive; it is he who has inspiration. It is he to whom revelations manifest, for then his language becomes music. Every person who comes to us, every object we see, is revealing. In what form? It tells us its character, nature, and secrets. Every person tells us his past, present, and future. In what way? Every person explains to us all that they contain. In what manner? In the form of music, if only we can hear it.

There is another language: it is rhythm and tone. We hear it, but we do not hear it with our ears. A friendly person shows harmony in his voice, in his words, in his movement and manner. An unfriendly person in his very movements, in his glance and expression, in his walk, in everything, will show disharmony if one can but see it. I had a friend in India who became cross very easily. Sometimes when he visited me I would say, "Are you cross today?" He would ask, "Now how do you know I am cross today?" I said, "Your turban tells me. The way you tie your turban wrongly shows disharmony."

One's very actions show an inharmonious or harmonious attitude. There are many things one can perceive in handwriting, but the principal thing in reading handwriting is the harmonious or inharmonious curves. It almost speaks to you and tells you the mood in which the person wrote. Handwriting tells you many things: the grade of evolution of the person who has written, his attitude towards life, his character, and his mood when writing. You do not need to read the whole letter he wrote, you only have to see his handwriting, for line and curve will show him to be either harmonious or inharmonious if only one can see it.

In every being you can see this, and if one looks with deep insight into the nature of things one will read it even in a tree. According to the fruit or flowers that the tree bears one discovers what music it expresses.

You can see from the attitude of a person whether that person will prove to be your friend or will end in being your enemy. You need not even wait until the end; you can see at the first glance whether his inclination is friendly or not, because every person is music, perpetual music, continually going on day and night, and your intuitive faculty can hear that music. That is the reason why one person is repellent and the other attracts you. It is the music he expresses; his whole atmosphere is charged with it.

There is a story of Omar, the well-known khalif of Arabia. Someone who wanted to harm Omar was looking for him, and he heard that Omar did not live in palaces, though he was a king, but that he spent most of his time with nature. This man was very glad to think that he would have every opportunity to accomplish his object. As he approached the place where Omar was sitting, the nearer he came the more his attitude changed, until in the end he dropped the dagger which was in his hand and said, "I cannot harm you. Tell me what is the power in you that keeps me from accomplishing the object that I came to accomplish?" And Omar answered, "My at-one-ment with God."

What did Omar mean by that "at-one-ment with God?" He meant being in tune with the Infinite, in harmony with the whole universe. In other words, Omar was the receptacle of the music of the whole universe.

The great charm that the personality of the holy ones has shown in all ages has been their reponsiveness to the music of the whole being. That has been the secret of how they became the friends of their worst enemies. But it is not only the power of the holy ones. It manifests in every person to a greater or lesser degree. Everyone shows harmony or disharmony according to how open he is to the music of the universe. The more one is open to all that is beautiful and harmonious, the more one's life is tuned to that universal harmony and the more one will show a friendly attitude towards everyone one meets. One's very atmosphere will create music around one.

The difference between the material and the spiritual point of view is that the material point of view sees matter as the first thing, and considers that intelligence and beauty and everything else evolved from it. From the spiritual point of view we see intelligence and beauty first, and from them comes all that exists. From the spiritual point of view we see that one considers last to be the same as first. Therefore in the essence of this whole being, as the basis of all that exists, there is music. One can see that in the essence of the seed of the rose there is the rose itself, its fragrance, form, and beauty; and although in the end it may not be manifested, at the same time it is there. The one who tunes himself not only to the external but to the inner being and to the essence of all things gets an insight into the essence of the whole being, and therefore he can to the same extent find and enjoy even in the seed the fragrance and beauty which delight him in the rose.

The greatest error of this age is that activity has increased so much that there is little margin left in one's everyday life for repose. And repose is the secret of all contemplation and meditation, the secret of getting in tune with that aspect of life which is the essence of all things. When one is not accustomed to taking repose, one does not know what is behind one's being. This condition is experienced by first preparing the body and the mind by means of purification. By making the senses fine one is able to tune one's soul with the whole Being.

It seems complex, and yet it is so simple. When one is open to one's tried friend in life, one knows so much about him. It is only a question of the opening of the heart; it is the at-one-ment with one's friend. We know his faults and his merits, but we know also how to experience and to enjoy friendship. Where there is hatred and prejudice and bitterness, there is loss of understanding. The deeper the person, the more friends he has. It is smallness, narrowness, lack of spiritual development that make a person exclusive, distant, different from others. He feels superior, greater, better than the others; the friendly attitude seems to have been lost. In this way he cuts himself off from others, and in this lies his tragedy. That person is never happy. The one who is happy is he who is ready to be friends with all. His outlook on life is friendly. He is friendly not only to persons, but also to objects and conditions.

It is by this attitude of friendship that a person expands and breaks down those walls which keep him in prison. And by breaking down the walls he experiences at-one-ment with the Absolute. This at-one-ment with the Absolute manifests as the music of the spheres, and this he experiences on all sides in the beauty of nature, in the color of flowers, in everything he sees and in everything he meets. In the hours of contemplation and solitude and in the hours when he is in the midst of the world, the music is always there; he is always enjoying its harmony.

Chapter 11

VIBRATIONS IN MAN

The silent life experiences on the surface through activity. The silent life appears as death in comparison with the life of activity on the surface. Only to the wise the life eternal seems preferable on account of the ever-changing and momentary nature of mortal life. Life on the surface seems to be the real life, because it is in this life that all joy is experienced.

In the silent life there is no joy but only peace. The soul's original being is peace and its nature is joy, both of which work against each other. This is the hidden cause of all life's tragedy. The soul originally is without any experience; it experiences all when it opens its eyes to the exterior plane and keeps them open, enjoying the life on the surface until satisfied. The soul then begins to close its eyes to the exterior plane, and constantly seeks peace, the original state of its being.

The inward and essential part of every being is composed of fine vibrations, and the external part is formed of gross ones. The finer part we call spirit and the grosser matter, the former being less subject to change and destruction and the latter more so. All that lives is spirit, and all that dies is matter; and all that dies in spirit is matter, and all that lives in matter is spirit. All that is visible and perceptible appears to be living, although subject to death and decay, and is becoming every moment resolved into its finer element. But the sight of man is so deluded by its awareness of the seeming world that the spirit that really lives is covered under the garb of matter and its true being is hidden. It is the gradually increasing activity that causes vibrations to materialize, and it is the gradual decrease of the same which transmutes them again into spirit. As has been said, vibrations pass through five distinct phases while changing from the fine to the gross. Each element—ether, air, fire, water, and earth—has a savor, color, and form peculiar to itself. Thus the elements form a wheel which brings them all in time to the surface. At each step in their activity they vary and become distinct from each other; and it is the grouping of these vibrations that causes variety in the objective world. Man calls the law that causes them to disperse destruction.

Vibrations turn to atoms, and atoms generate what we call life. Thus it happens that their grouping, by the power of nature's affinity, forms a living entity; and as the breath manifests through the form, so the body becomes conscious. In one individual there are many fine and small beings hidden: in his blood, in his brain cells, in his skin, and in all planes of his existence. As in the physical being of an individual many small germs are born and nourished which are also living beings, so in his mental plane there are many beings, termed *muwakkals,* or elementals. These are still finer entities born of man's own thoughts and as the germs live in his physical body so the elementals dwell in his mental sphere. People often imagine that thoughts are without life; he does not see that they are more alive than the physical germs and that they have a birth, childhood, youth, age, and death. They work for man's advantage or disadvantage according to their nature. The Sufi creates, fashions, and controls them. He drills them and rules them throughout his life; they form his army and carry out his desires. As the germs constitute man's physical being and the elementals his mental life, so the angels constitute his spiritual existence. These are called *farishtas.*

Vibrations as a rule have length as well as breadth. They may last the least fraction of a moment or the greater part of the age of the universe. They make different forms, figures, and colors as they shoot forth, one vibration creating another, and thus myriads arise out of one. In this way there are circles beneath circles and circles above circles, all of which form the universe. Every vibration after its manifestation becomes merged again in its original source. The reach of vibrations is according to the fineness of the plane of their starting point. To speak more plainly, the word uttered by the lips can only reach the ears of the hearer, but the thought proceeding from the mind reaches far, shooting from mind to mind. The vibrations of mind are much stronger than those of words. The earnest feelings of one heart can pierce the heart of another; they speak in silence, spreading out into the sphere, so that the very atmosphere of a person's presence proclaims his thought and emotions. The vibrations of the soul are the most powerful and far-reaching; they run like an electric current from soul to soul.

All things and beings in the universe are connected with each other, visibly or invisibly, and through vibrations a communication is established between them on all the planes of existence. As an ordinary instance, if one person coughs in an assembly, many others begin to do the same; and the same is the case with yawning. This also applies to laughter, excitement, and depression. This shows that vibrations convey the conditions of one being to another; therefore the seer knows of the past, present, and future, and perceives conditions on all planes of existence.

Vibrations work through the chord of sympathy existing between man and his surroundings and reveal past, present, and future conditions. This explains why the howling of dogs foretell death and the neighing of horses the approach of danger. Not only animals show this, but even plants in times of sorrow begin to die and flowers to fade, while during times of happiness they grow and flourish. The reason why plants and animals can perceive the vibrations and know of coming events while man is ignorant of them is that he has blinded himself with egotism. The influence of vibrations is left on the chair on which one sits, in the bed where one has slept, in the house where one lives, in the clothes one wears, in the food one eats, and even in the street where one walks.

Every emotion arises from the intensity of vibrations, which when active in different directions produce different emotions, the main cause of every emotion being simply activity. Every vibration while active raises the consciousness to the outermost surface, and the mist caused by this activity collects clouds that we call emotion. The clouds of emotion obscure the clear sight of the soul. Therefore passion is called blind. The excess of the activity of vibrations not only blinds but weakens the will, and a weak will enfeebles the mind and body.

It is the state of vibrations to which a person is tuned that accounts for his soul's note. The different degrees of these notes form a variety of pitches divided by the mystics into three distinct grades. First, the grade that produces power and intelligence, and may be pictured as a calm sea. Second, the grade of moderate activity, which keeps all things in motion and is a balance between power and weakness, which may be pictured as the sea in motion. Third, the grade of intense activity, which destroys everything and causes all weakness and blindness; it may be pictured as a stormy sea.

In the activity of all things and beings the pitch is recognized by the seer, as a musician knows the key in which any particular music is written. A person's atmosphere tells of the grade of activity of his vibrations.

If vibratory activity is properly controlled, one may experience all life's joy and at the same time not be enslaved by it. It is most difficult to control activity when it is once started and on the increase, for it is like trying to control a runaway horse. Yet in control abides the whole of what is called mastership.

The saints and sages spread their peace not only in the place where they sit, but even in the neighborhood where they dwell; the town or the country where they live is at peace in accordance with the power of the vibrations they send out from their soul. This is the reason why association with good or bad has a great influence upon the life and character of man. The vibrations of thought and feeling create, procure, and prepare of themselves all the necessary means for their manifestation on the surface. For example a person may desire to eat fish, and instead of ordering it might think strongly of it. His thought vibrations thus speaking to the mental ears of the cook transmit this desire, and perhaps his strong feeling even attract a fishmonger to the house. In this way the thoughts of sages work out their destiny, according to the strength, power, and purity of their minds. A certain degree of thought power is needed to bring about a certain result, as so much dynamite is required to blast a single rock, and an infinitely greater quantity is necessary to make a tunnel through a mountain.

The length of time that the thought is held has also much to do with its accomplishment, for the thought vibrations have to be active for a certain time to bring about a certain result. A certain length of time is required for the baking of a cake: if it is hurried the cake will be uncooked, and with too great a heat it will burn. If the operator of the mental vibrations lacks patience then the power of thought will be wasted, even if it is half way to its destiny or still nearer to a successful issue. If too great a power of thought is given to the accomplishment of a certain thing, it destroys while preparing it.

In order to reflect thought and feeling on another, one should observe the same rule as in voice and word. The louder a person speaks in an assembly the more attention he attracts, and all those present perforce give him a hearing. In the same way, if a Sufi sends forth the vibrations of his thought and feeling, they naturally strike with a great strength and power on any mind on which they happen to fall. As sweetness of voice has a winning power, so it is with tenderness of thought and feeling. Thought vibrations to which the spoken word is added are doubled in strength, and with a physical effort this strength is trebled. Reason is like fire; it gives light to the thought. But thought overheated loses its power, as heat can weaken the physical body. Reason gives birth to doubt, which destroys the thought power before it is able to fulfill its destiny.

The strength of thought power consists in confidence or faith. Reason confuses, and doubts scatter the waves of thought vibrations, which disperse and go off in different directions from lack of the strength that binds. One should never think or speak against one's desire, for it weakens the thought vibrations and often brings about contrary results. A variety of thoughts springing up at the same time naturally enfeebles the power of mind, for none of them has a chance to mature.

The disharmony between one's desire and one's ideal always causes a great confusion in life, for they constantly work against each other. When a person speaks, thinks, or feels either harshly or kindly of another, it reaches the spirit of that one, either consciously or unconsciously, by the power of vibration. If we happen to be offended with someone and do not show it in speech or action, yet it still cannot be hidden, for the vibrations of our feeling will reach directly to the person in question, and he will begin to feel our displeasure, however far away he may be. The same is the case with our love and pleasure: however we may try to conceal it in speech or action, it cannot be hidden. This explains the old adage that even walls have ears, which really means that even the wall is not impervious to vibrations of thought.

Sufis give special attention to the good and bad wishes of people. They strive continually to attract the good wishes of others, whether worthy or unworthy, by every means in their power. Intensity of activity produces strong vibrations named in Sufi terms *jelal;* gentleness of activity causes mild vibrations called *jemal.* the former activity works as stength and power, the latter as beauty and grace. The conflict of these forces is termed *kemal,* and causes nothing but destruction.

The standard of right and wrong, the conception of good and evil, and the idea of sin and virtue are understood differently by the people of different races, nations, and religions. Therefore it is difficult to discern the law governing these opposites. It becomes clear, however, by understanding the law of vibrations. Every thing and being on the surface of existence seems separate from every other, but in every plane beneath the surface they approach nearer to each other, and in the innermost plane they all become one. Therefore every disturbance caused to the peace of the smallest part of existence on the surface inwardly affects the whole. Thus any thought, speech, or action that disturbs peace is wrong, evil, and a sin; if it brings about peace it is right, good, and a virtue. Life being like a dome, its nature is also domelike. Disturbance of the slightest part of life disturbs the whole and returns as a curse upon the person who caused it; any peace produced on the surface comforts the whole, and thence returns as peace to the producer.

This is the philosophy of the reward of good deeds and the punishment of bad deeds given by the higher powers.

Chapter 12

HARMONY

Harmony is the source of manifestation, the cause of its existence, and the medium between God and man.

The peace for which every soul strives and which is the true nature of God and the utmost goal of man is but the outcome of harmony; this shows that all life's attainments without a sense of harmony are but vain. It is the attainment of harmony that is called heaven, and it is the lack of it that is termed hell. The master of it alone understands life, and he who lacks it is foolish in spite of all other knowledge that he may have acquired.

The Sufi gives great importance to the attainment of harmony, believing that light is for angels and darkness for the devil, but that harmony is necessary for a human being in order to keep a balance in life.

There are three aspects of harmony: eternal, universal, and individual.

Eternal harmony is the harmony of consciousness. As it is in itself eternal, all things and beings live and move in it; yet it remains remote, undisturbed, and peaceful. This is the God of the believer and the God of the knower. All vibrations from the finest to the grossest are held together by this harmony, as well as each atom of manifestation, and both creation and destruction take place in order to uphold it. Its power ultimately attracts each being towards the everlasting peace.

Man is drawn in two opposite directions by the power of harmony: towards the infinite and towards manifestation. He is less conscious of the former than of the latter, and by facing towards one direction he loses sight of the other. The infinite, being the essential spirit of all, finally attracts all to itself. The Sufi gives the greatest importance to harmony with the infinite, which he realizes by resignation to the will of God, the Beloved.

The existence of land and water—the land for the water and the water for the land—and the attraction between the heavens and the earth demonstrate the universal harmony. The attraction of the sun and moon to each other, the cosmic order of the stars and the planets, all connected and related with each other, moving and working under a certain law; the regular rotation of the seasons, the night following the day and the day in its turn giving place to the night; the dependence of one being on another; the distinctiveness, attraction, and assimilation of the five elements—all prove the universal harmony.

The male and female, beast and bird, vegetable and rock, and all classes of things and beings are linked together and attracted to each other with a chord of harmony. If one being or thing, however apparently useless, were missing in this universe of endless variety, it would be as it were a note missing in a song. As Sa'adi says, "Every being is born for a certain purpose, and the light of that purpose is kindled within his soul." All famines, plagues, and disasters such as storms, floods, volcanic eruptions, wars, and revolutions, however bad they may appear to man, are in reality for the adjusting of this universal harmony.

There is a story told in India of how once all the inhabitants of a village that had suffered from drought gathered together before the temple of their god, praying that for this year an abundance of rain might fall.

A voice from the unseen replied, "Whatever We do is for the betterment of our purpose. Ye have no right to interfere with our work, oh ye men." But they again cried for mercy, and continued to do so more persistently. Then came the answer saying, "Your prayers, fastings, and sacrifices have induced Us to grant for this one year as much rain as ye desire." They all returned home rejoicing. In the autumn they worked vigorously on their farms, and after having prepared the ground and sown the seed, they prayed for rain. When they considered that sufficient had fallen they again had recourse to prayer, and the rain ceased. In this way an ideal crop of corn was produced and all the inhabitants of that country made merry over it. This year more corn was grown than ever before. After the crops were gathered in, however, all those who ate the corn died, and many were the victims. In perplexity the survivors again sought the god, bowing low before the temple, crying, "Why hast Thou shown such wrath to us, after having shown so great a mercy?" The god replied, "It was not our wrath but your folly for interfering with our work. We sometimes send a drought and at other times a flood so that a portion of your crops may be destroyed, but We have our reasons for so doing. For in this way all that is poisonous and undesirable in them is also destroyed, leaving only what is beneficial for the preservation of your life."

The villagers prostrated themselves in humble prayer saying, "We shall never again try to control the affairs of the universe. Thou art the Creator and Thou art the Controller. We are Thine innocent children, and Thou alone knowest what is best for us." The Creator knows how to control His world, what to bring forth and what to destroy.

There are two aspects of individual harmony: the harmony between body and soul, and the harmony between individuals.

The soul rejoices in the comforts experienced by the external self, yet man becomes so engrossed in them that the soul's true comfort is neglected. This keeps man dissatisfied through all the momentary comforts he may enjoy, but not understanding this he attributes his dissatisfaction to some unsatisfied desire in his life. The outlet of all earthly passions gives a momentary satisfaction yet creates a tendency for more. In this struggle the satisfaction of the soul is overlooked by man, who is constantly busied in the pursuit of his earthly enjoyment and comfort, depriving the soul of its true bliss. The true delight of the soul lies in love, harmony, and beauty, the outcome of which is wisdom, calm, and peace. The more constant they are, the greater is the satisfaction of the soul.

If a person in his daily life would examine every action that had reflected a disagreeable picture of himself upon his soul and caused darkness and dissatisfaction, and if on the other hand he would consciously watch each thought, word, or deed that had produced an inward love, harmony, and beauty, and each feeling that had brought him wisdom, calm, and peace, then the way of harmony between soul and body would be easily understood, and both aspects of life would be satisfied, the inner as well as the outer. The soul's satisfaction is much more important than that of the body, for it is more lasting. In this way the thought, speech, and action can be adjusted, so that harmony may be established first in the self by the attunement of body and soul.

The next aspect of individual harmony is practiced in one's contact with another. Every being has an individual ego produced from his own illusion. This limits his view, which is led in the direction of his own interest, and he judges good or bad, high or low, right or wrong in relation to himself and others through his limited view, which is generally partial and imaginary rather than true. This darkness is caused by the overshadowing of the soul by the external self. Thus a person becomes blind to his own infirmities as well as to the merits of another, and the right action of another becomes wrong in his eyes while the fault of the self seems right. This is the case with mankind in general, until the veil of darkness is lifted from his eyes.

The *nafs*, the ego of an individual, causes all disharmony with the self as well as with others, thus showing its unruliness in all aspects of life. The lion, the sovereign among all animals, most powerful and majestic, is always unwelcome to the inhabitants of the forest, and he is even unfriendly to his own kind. Two lions will never greet one another in a friendly way, for their *nafs* is so strong; and although the lion is the ruler of all other animals, he is a slave to his own passions, which make his life restless. The *nafs* of herbivorous animals such as sheep and goats is subdued; for this reason they are harmless to one another and are even harmonious enough to live in herds. The harmony and sympathy existing among them makes them mutually partake of their joys and sorrows, but they easily fall victim to the wild animals of the forest. The masters of the past like Moses and Muhammad have always loved to tend their flocks in the wilderness, and Jesus Christ spoke of himself as the Good Shepherd, while Saint John the Baptist spoke of the lamb of God, harmless and innocent, ready for sacrifice.

The *nafs* of the bird is still milder. Therefore upon one tree many and various kinds can live as one family, singing the praise of God in unison and flying about in flocks of thousands.

Among birds are to be found those who recognize their mates and who live together, harmoniously building the nest for their young, each in turn sitting on the eggs and bearing their part in the upbringing of their little ones. Many times they mourn and lament over the death of their mate. The *nafs* of the insects is still less: they walk over each other without doing any harm, and live together in millions as one family, without distinction of friend or foe. This proves how the power of *nafs* grows at each step in nature's evolution and culminates in man, creating disharmony all through his life unless it is subdued, producing thereby a calm and peace within the self and a sense of harmony with others. Every human being has an attribute peculiar to his *nafs*. One is tigerlike, another resembles a dog, while a third may be like a cat and a fourth like a fox. In this way man shows in his speech, thought, and feelings the beasts and birds. The condition of his *nafs* is akin to their nature, and at times his very appearance resembles them. Therefore his tendency to harmony depends upon the evolution of his *nafs*.

As man begins to see clearly through human life, the world begins to appear as a forest to him, filled with wild animals, fighting, killing, and preying upon one another.

There are four different classes of people who harmonize with each other in accordance with their different states of evolution: angelic, human, animal, and devilish.

The angelic seeks for heaven, and the human being struggles along in the world. The person with animal propensities revels in his earthly pleasures, while the devilish one is engaged in creating mischief, thereby making a hell for himself and for others. Man after his human evolution becomes angelic, and through his development in animality arrives at the stage of devil.

In music the law of harmony is that the nearest note does not make a consonant interval. This explains the prohibition of marriage between close relatives because of their nearness in quality and blood. As a rule harmony lies in contrast. Men fight with men and women quarrel with women, but the male and the female are as a rule harmonious with each other, and a complete oneness makes a perfect harmony. In every being the five elements are constantly working, and in every individual one especially predominates. The wise have therefore distinguished five different natures in man, according to the element predominant in him. Sometimes two elements or even more predominate in a human being in a greater or lesser degree.

The harmony of life can be learned in the same way as the harmony of music. The ear should be trained to distinguish both tone and word and the meaning concealed within, and to know from the verbal meaning and the tone of voice whether it is a true word or a false note; to distinguish between sarcasm and sincerity, between words spoken in jest and those spoken in earnest; to understand the difference between true admiration and flattery; to distinguish modesty from humility, a smile from a sneer and arrogance from pride, either directly or indirectly expressed. By so doing the ear becomes gradually trained in the same way as in music, and a person knows exactly whether his own tone and word as well as those of another are false or true. One should learn in what tone to express a certain thought or feeling, as in voice cultivation. There are times when one should speak loudly, and there are times when a soft tone of voice is needed; for every word a certain note, and for every speech a certain pitch is necessary. At the same time there should be a proper use of a natural, sharp, or flat note, as well as a consideration of key.

There are nine different aspects of feeling, each of which has a certain mode of expression: mirth, expressed in a lively tone; grief, in a pathetic tone; fear, in a broken voice; mercy, in a tender voice; wonder, in an exclamatory tone; courage, in an emphatic tone; frivolity, in a light tone; attachment, in a deep tone; and indifference, in the voice of silence.

An untrained person confuses these. He whispers the words that should be known and speaks out loudly those that should be hidden. A certain subject must be spoken of in a high pitch, while another requires a lower pitch. One should consider the place, the space, the number of persons present, the kind of people, and their evolution and speak in accordance with the understanding of others. As it is said, "Speak to people in their own language." With a child one must have childish talk; with the young only suitable words should be spoken; with the old one should speak in accordance with their understanding. In the same way there should be a graduated expression of our thought so that everybody may not be driven with the same whip. It is consideration for others that distinguishes human beings from the animals.

It must be understood that rhythm is the balance of speech and action. One must speak at the right time; otherwise silence is better than speech. A word of sympathy with the grief of another, and a smile at least when another laughs. One should watch the opportunity for moving a subject in society, and never abruptly change the subject of conversation, but skillfully blend two subjects with a harmonious link. Also one should wait patiently while another speaks and keep a rein on one's speech when the thought rushes out uncontrollably, in order to keep it in rhythm and under control during its outlet. One should emphasize the important words with a consideration of strong and weak accent. It is necessary to choose the right word and mode of expression, to regulate the speed and to know how to keep the rhythm. Some people begin to speak slowly and gradually increase the speed to such an extent that they are unable to speak coherently. The above applies to all actions in life.

The Sufi, like a student of music, trains both his voice and ear in the harmony of life. The training of the voice consists in being conscientious about each word spoken, about its tone, rhythm, meaning, and appropriateness for the occasion. For instance words of consolation should be spoken in a slow rhythm, with a soft voice and sympathetic tone. When speaking words of command a lively rhythm is necessary, and a powerful and distinct voice. The Sufi avoids all unrhythmic actions; he keeps the rhythm of his speech under the control of patience, not speaking a word before the right time, not giving an answer until the question is finished. He considers a contradictory word a discord unless spoken in a debate, and even at such times he tries to resolve it into a consonant chord. A contradictory tendency in man finally develops into a passion, until he contradicts even his own idea if it be propounded by another.

In order to keep harmony the Sufi even modulates his speech from one key to another; in other words, he falls in with another person's idea by looking at the subject from the speaker's point of view instead of his own. He makes a base for every conversation with an appropriate introduction, thus preparing the ears of the listener for a perfect response. He watches his every movement and expression, as well as those of others, trying to form a consonant chord of harmony between himself and another.

The attainment of harmony in life takes a longer time to acquire and a more careful study than does the training of the ear and the cultivation of the voice, although it is acquired in the same manner as the knowledge of music. To the ear of the Sufi every word spoken is like a note that is true when harmonious and false when inharmonious. He makes the scale of his speech major, minor, or chromatic as occasion demands, and his words—sharp, flat, or natural—are in accordance with the law of harmony. For instance, the straight, polite, and tactful manner of speech is like his major, minor, or chromatic scale, representing dominance, respect, and equality. Similarly he takes arbitrary or contrary motions to suit the time and situation by following step by step, by agreeing and differing, and even by opposing, and yet keeping up the law of harmony in conversation. Take any two persons as two notes: the harmony existing between them forms intervals either consonant or dissonant, perfect or imperfect, major or minor, diminished or augmented as the two persons may be.

The interval of class, creed, caste, race, nation, or religion, as well as the interval of age or state of evolution, or of varied and opposite interests, shows the law here distinctly. A wise person would be more likely to be in harmony with his foolish servant than with a semi-wise person who considers himself infallible. Again, it is equally possible that a wise person may be far from happy in the society of the foolish, and vice versa. The proud person will always quarrel with the proud, while he will support the humble. It is also possible for the proud to agree on a common question of pride, such as pride of race or birth.

Sometimes the interval between the disconnected notes is filled by a middle note forming a consonant chord. For instance the discord between husband and wife may be removed by the link of a child, or the discord between brothers and sisters may be taken away by the intervention of the mother or father. In this way, however inharmonious two persons may be, the forming of a consonant chord by an intervening link creates harmony. A foolish person is an unpliable note, whereas an intelligent person is pliable. The former sticks to his ideas, likes, dislikes, and convictions, whether right or wrong, while the latter makes them sharp or flat by raising or lowering the tone and pitch, harmonizing with the other as the occasion demands. The keynote is always in harmony with each note, for it has all notes of the scale within it. In the same way the Sufi harmonizes with everybody, whether good or bad, wise or foolish, by becoming like the keynote.

All races, nations, classes, and people are like a strain of music based upon one chord, where the keynote, the common interest, holds so many personalities in a single bond of harmony. By a study of life the Sufi learns and practices the nature of its harmony. He establishes harmony with the self, with others, with the universe, and with the infinite. He identifies himself with another, he sees himself, so to speak, in every other being. He cares for neither blame nor praise, considering both as coming from himself. If a person were to drop a heavy weight and in so doing hurt his own foot, he would not blame his hand for having dropped it, realizing himself in both the hand and the foot. In like manner the Sufi is tolerant when harmed by another, thinking that the harm has come from himself alone. He uses counterpoint by blending the undesirable talk of a friend and making it into a fugue.

He overlooks the faults of others, considering that they know no better. He hides the faults of others, and suppresses any facts that would cause disharmony. His constant fight is with the *nafs,* the root of all disharmony and the only enemy of man. By crushing this enemy one gains mastery over himself; this wins for him mastery over the whole universe, because the wall standing between the self and the Almighty has been broken down. Gentleness, mildness, respect, humility, modesty, self-denial, conscientiousness, tolerance, and forgiveness are considered by the Sufi as the attributes that produce harmony within one's own soul as well as within that of another. Arrogance, wrath, vice, attachment, greed, and jealousy are the six principal sources of disharmony. *Nafs,* the only creator of disharmony, becomes more powerful the more it is indulged; that is to say, the more its desires are gratified, the more it is pleased. For the time being it shows its satisfaction at having gratified its demands, but soon after it demands still more, until life becomes a burden. The wise detect this enemy as the instigator of all mischief, but everybody else blames another for his misfortunes in life.

Chapter 13

THE VOICE

The voice is not only indicative of man's character, but it is the expression of his spirit. The voice is not only audible but also visible to those who can see it; the voice makes impressions on the ethereal spheres, impressions that can be called audible but are visible at the same time. On all planes the voice makes an impression, and those scientists who have made experiments with sound and have taken impressions of sound on plates will find one day that the impression of the voice is more living, deeper, and has a greater effect than any other sound. Other sounds can be louder than the voice, but no sound can be more living. Knowing this, the Hindus of ancient times said that singing was the first art, playing the second art, and dancing the third art which make music. Having found out that by these three different aspects of music one attains spirituality much sooner than by any other way, the Hindus discovered that the shortest way to attain to spiritual heights is by singing. Therefore the greatest prophets of the Hindus were singers like Narada and Tumbara. Narada inspired Valmiki, who wrote the Ramayana and the Mahabharata, the great Hindu scriptures.

There are three principal kinds of voices: the *jelal* voice, the *jemal* voice, and the *kemal* voice. The *jelal* voice indicates power; the *jemal* voice indicates beauty; the *kemal* voice indicates wisdom. If you take careful notice in everyday life, you will find that sometimes before a person has finished his sentence, you have become annoyed. It is not because of what he has said, but it is his voice. And you will also notice—perhaps not every day in your life but sometimes—that you have heard a person say something only once, and it has always remained with you, giving all the time a beautiful feeling, remaining always soothing, healing, uplifting, inspiring.

A doctor coming to see a patient may frighten him and make him more ill if his voice is not harmonious; and another doctor may, by his voice, treat the patient so that before the medicine is brought he is already feeling better. The doctor gives a medicine, but it is the voice with which he comes to the patient that counts. In the history of the world, have not men marched hundreds of miles with strength and vigor, not knowing what they were going to face, on hearing the voice of their commander: "Quick march!"? It seemed that all fear, all anxiety, were taken away and vigor and courage were given to them as they were going to march. And have you not heard also of commanders who have given the order "Fire!" and the soldiers have turned back and fired at them? That is the voice too.

The voice therefore is a wine. It may be the best wine, or it may be the worst liquor. It may make a person ill, or it may uplift him. It is told that Tansen, the great singer of India, performed wonders by singing. Tansen was a yogi, a yogi of singing, and he had mastered sound. Therefore the sound of his voice became living, and because he had made his voice living, everything he wanted happened. Very few in this world know to what extent phenomena can be produced by the power of voice. If there is any real trace of miracle, of phenomenon, of wonder, it is in the voice.

There are five qualities of the voice that are connected with the particular character of a person. The earth quality of the voice is hope-giving, encouraging, tempting; the water quality is intoxicating, soothing, healing, uplifting; the fire quality is impressive, arousing, exciting, horrifying, and at the same time awakening. Very often warning is given in the voice of fire quality. The "tongues of flame" spoken of in the New Testament tell of that voice and the word that was the warning of coming dangers; it was alarming for people to awaken from their sleep, to awaken to a greater, a higher consciousness.

Then there is the air quality of the voice, which is uplifting, taking one far away from the plane of the earth. The ether quality of voice is inspiring, healing, peace-giving, harmonizing, convincing, appealing, and at the same time most intoxicating. Every *jelal* voice, *jemal* voice, or *kemal* voice has one or another of these five qualities predominant in it, and according to that quality it creates an effect.

The most wonderful thing in the study of voice is that from the voice you can find out the stage of a person's particular evolution. You do not need to see him; just his voice will tell you how far he has evolved. There is no doubt that the character of a person is evident in his voice. And at every age—infancy, childhood, youth, and more advanced age—the pitch of the voice changes. Advanced age is an expression of what a person has gained, and so the voice is also indicative of his attainment. As with everything else in a person's life, there comes also a change in the voice with every step forward in spiritual evolution. Every experience in life is an initiation; even in worldly life one takes a step forward, and this experience changes the voice of a person.

There is another wonderful thing to be found in the science of voice: it is that the fortunate person has a different voice from the one who is not so fortunate. If you gather five persons who have really proved to be very fortunate and you listen to their voices, you will find how great the difference is between their voices and the ordinary voice. When you compare the voices of great people, no matter what their line may be, with the voices of others, you will find that there is a difference.

But what is meant here is only the speaking voice. In singing it is quite different, because today the art of singing has become as artificial as can be. The whole modern idea is to train the voice and make it different from what it is naturally. The training of the voice does not aim at developing what is natural in it; mostly it aims at bringing into it something that is not natural to it. Therefore, when a person sings according to the method of the day he has a voice which is not his own. He may have great success, he

may be audible to thousands of people, but at the same time he
is not singing in his natural voice, and you cannot find the stage
of his evolution in his voice. The real character of a person is to
be found in his speaking voice.

A third thing to be understood is the softness and the loudness
of the voice; there are times when the voice is softer and others
when the voice is louder. That shows the natural condition of the
spirit at that particular time, because sometimes the spirit is tender, and with the tenderness of the spirit the voice becomes softened. Sometimes the spirit is harder, and then the voice becomes
hardened. In order to scold someone you do not need to affect a
hard voice; the voice becomes hard naturally. In order to sympathize with a person, in order to express your gratitude, your love,
your devotion, your affection to someone, you do not need to
soften your voice; your voice is soft before you can feel it, before
you can think about it. This shows that the voice is the expression
of the spirit. If the spirit is soft, the voice is soft; if the spirit is hard,
the voice is hard; if the spirit is powerful, then the voice has power;
if the spirit has lost its vigor, then the voice loses its power.

Inspiration chooses its own voice. And when a speaker has to
change his voice in accordance with the hall where he is speaking,
then inspiration is lost; because when inspiration begins to feel, "It
is not my voice," it does not come. Then the speaker has to struggle twice: one struggle is that he must speak without inspiration,
and the other struggle is that he must be audible to everyone
present. That cannot be done.

Nowadays a new method has been developed called elocution.
Someone who has learned elocution can shout as loudly as ten
people and everyone will think it wonderful. But what impression
does it make? None. Also, a loudspeaker that enlarges the voice
twenty times is all right for trade and business purposes, but when
you come to life itself, to conversation and speaking to your
firends, it is a different thing. It is an occasion of great psychological significance when one speaks to one person or to many persons,
because it has its echo in the cosmos. No word spoken is ever lost.
It remains and it vibrates; and it vibrates according to the spirit put
into it. If a person makes his voice artificial in order to convince
people, it only means he is not true to his spirit. It cannot be. It

is better that one is natural in one's speech with individuals and with the multitude than that one becomes artificial. Very often people think that when they have to recite they must affect a different voice, become a different being, and they do not want to remain what they are. But there is nothing more beautiful, nothing more convincing and appealing and impressive, than reciting in one's own natural voice.

As to singing, there are certain things that must be retained in the voice. However much the voice may be developed, however great may be its volume, and however far-reaching it has been made by practice, one must yet feel responsible for preserving one's natural voice unharmed through every stage of development. This does not mean that one should not have a far-reaching voice, a voice of a larger volume, or that one should not have a voice with vigor and flexibility. Everything that enriches the voice is necessary and must be developed by practice. But at the same time one should always keep in view that one must not sacrifice the natural quality of one's voice. For every person must know that there is no other voice like his, and if that peculiarity belonging to the voice of each soul is lost, then nothing is left to it. Besides this, every person is an instrument in the orchestra that is the whole universe, and every voice is the music that comes from one of its instruments, each instrument being made distinct and particular, so that no other voice can take the place of that particular voice. If, then, with the instrument that God has made and the music that God intended to be played in the world, one does not allow that music to be played and develops a voice that is not one's own, this is naturally a great loss to oneself and to others.

There is a mechanical way to train the voice and a natural way. The mechanical way is from instruments. But there is a natural way that the ancient people understood. They recognized the thunder and other sounds of nature, they made the seven notes out of them, and they saw the comparison between human beings and the notes of nature. That is why in ancient Indian music there are notes that are nature's notes. And the tuning fork from which these notes can be regulated is the sound of animals.

For those on the spiritual path—thinkers, students, and meditative souls—it is of the greatest importance to know the condition of their spirit from time to time by consulting their voice. It is the barometer. From morning till evening one can watch the weather created by oneself, whether it is warm or cold, or whether it is spring or winter. One's voice is the instrument, the barometer that shows us what is coming, because what will come is the reaction, the result of what is created, and the voice is indicative of it. Those who think still more deeply on this subject will be able, if only they consult their voice, to see how step by step they are progressing in the spiritual path. Every step in the spiritual path brings about a small change. When you study it, you will find by the change in your voice that you have gone so much further, or that you have gone backward again; the voice will tell you.

Another thing that is most wonderful about the voice is that once you have worked with the voice and have cultivated and deepened and widened it, you may leave it for months and years; the voice may take a different shape and appearance, but at the same time what you have once developed remains with you somewhere. It is just like a deposit kept in a bank. You have forgotten it perhaps, yet it is there. The day when you touch it again it will come back in the same way, and it will take very little to complete the work.

If the voice has developed a spiritual quality and one finds later that that quality has been lost, one must not be discouraged or disappointed. One must correct oneself and try to go forward again, and be sorry for having gone backward. But never be discouraged, never be without hope, because it is there, it needs only a little touch. It is just like a candle that has gone out: once you strike a match you can light it again, for it remains a candle just the same. The voice is a light. If the light becomes dim, it has not gone out; it is there. It is the same with the voice. If it does not shine, it only means that it has not been cultivated; you must cultivate it again and it will shine once more.

Chapter 14

TUNING ONESELF
TO A DESIRED RHYTHM
(RELAXATION)

Mystic relaxation is of the greatest importance, for the whole spiritual culture is based and built upon this one subject, and yet there is so little spoken and written about it. It has been experienced and studied by the seekers after truth of all ages, and it was by the full understanding of this subject that they attained to greater power and inspiration.

Life is rhythm. This rhythm may be divided into three stages, and at every stage this rhythm changes the nature and character of life. One rhythm is mobile, another is active, and the third is chaotic. The mobile rhythm is creative, productive, constructive, and through that rhythm all power and inspiration are gained and peace is experienced. The further stage of this rhythm, the active rhythm, is the source of success and accomplishment, of progress and advancement, the source of joy and fulfillment. And the third stage of this rhythm, the chaotic rhythm, is the source of failure, of death, of disease and destruction, the source of all pain and sorrow.

The first kind of rhythm is slow, the second kind is faster, and the third is faster still. The direction of the first is direct, of the second even, and of the third zigzag. When one says that a person is wise and thoughtful, it means that he is in the first rhythm; when one says that a person is persevering and successful, he is in the second rhythm; and when it is said that this person has lost his head and has gone astray, he is in the third rhythm. He is either digging his own grave or the grave of his affairs; he is his own enemy. Everything he wants to accomplish, however much he wants to advance or progress, all goes down in destruction because he has taken this third rhythm, the chaotic and destructive rhythm. Therefore it is up to us to tune ourselves either to the first, to the second, or the third rhythm, and accordingly this will become our condition in life.

Have planetary influences, then, nothing to do with our life? Yes, they have, but how do even planetary influences work on us? If we have put ourselves in a particular rhythm, these influences have no power to bring about success or failure; if we only put ourselves in that rhythm there will be a similar result, and also the environment will react in the same way. If we are in favorable or in unfavorable, in congenial or uncongenial surroundings, it all means that we have put ourselves in that particular rhythm. When we experience success, good luck or bad luck, good or bad fortune, it is according to the rhythm we have brought about.

Where is this power to be found; how is it to be realized? If a person thinks about it, he can very easily realize it physically, mentally, and spiritually. There is a time when the body is in a perfectly calm condition, and there is a time when the body is excited, when the breath has lost its rhythm, is irregular, uneven; that is a chaotic condition. When the body has a regular circulation and proper rhythm and even breath, then a person is capable of doing things, accomplishing things. When the body is restful, comfortable, relaxed, we are able to think; inspirations and revelations come; we feel quiet; we have enthusiasm and power. In Sanskrit the first rhythm is called *sattva,* the second *rajas,* and the third *tamas.* It is from the middle rhythm that the word *raja* has come, which means, "the one who has persevered with his sword and made a kingdom." His rhythm is the middle rhythm. The first rhythm is sometimes called *sand,* which makes one think of the English *saint.* From this rhythm comes goodness.

In our life at a certain time one rhythm prevails, at another the second rhythm, and at still another the third; and yet in our life one rhythm is predominating through all changes, whether a person has the third, the second, or the first rhythm.

One who has the first rhythm has always power to accomplish things. As it is with the body, so it is with the mind. Body and mind are so closely connected that whatever rhythm the mind has, the body has. And the rhythm that is predominating in body and mind, that same rhythm is the rhythm of one's soul.

There was a king who when a certain problem was brought to him by his ministers, used to say, "Read it again," and the minister would read it again. Maybe after four lines he would stop him and say, "Read it again," and the minister would do so. After he had heard it three times, his answer would be perfect. But what do we sometimes do when we converse with people? Before the conversation has stopped, we have answered them. So impatient are we, eager to answer, and excited about it, that only one in a hundred people stops to listen to what another has to say.

It is the wrong rhythm, the chaotic rhythm, that brings about chaotic results. Where does war come from? From chaotic action. When there is chaotic action, nations become involved in war; by chaotic action the whole world may be involved in war. People doubt the religious belief that Christ saved the whole world; they cannot understand it. They say that man saves himself. But they do not realize that one person can ruin the whole world and that one person can save it. It is by rhythm that he can save the whole world. When there is a chaotic influence it works like an intoxicating drink in thousands of people, like a germ of disease, spreading from one person to another through the whole country. If that is true mechanically, then psychologically it can be true that one person's chaotic influence can put the whole world in despair, though it is very difficult for ordinary people to understand this.

The Turkish nation was greatly depressed on every side, and wars had made the country very poor. With nothing but disappointment all the time it had gone down and down. Then there came one man, Kemal Pasha, and his rhythm put life into thousands and thousands of dead souls who were waiting for some result, hungry from lack of food, disappointed with every effort.

One man brought cheer to them all and picked up the whole country.

This is only the outer plane; in the spiritual plane the effect is still more powerful, only those who work on the spiritual plane do not manifest to view. What happens in the political world is known, but in the spiritual world great things happen and they are not known. But their influence is most powerful because of their rhythm.

We see this in the life of Napoleon. Some appreciate his life and some do not. But nevertheless during his wars he was the inspiration and power and backbone of the whole country. It was all Napoleon's spirit. And always, even during the greatest anxieties of war, he used to have moments of silence, even sometimes on horseback; and while he was having this silence he would recuperate all the strength lost in the continual responsibilities of war, and he would feel refreshed after having closed his eyes. What was it? He had the key of relaxation. It is tuning oneself to a desired rhythm.

We should not be surprised or laugh at sages who keep one hand raised up, or stand perhaps on their heads with their feet up, or sit in one posture for a long time. There is some reason for it. Those artists who know the different ways of the art of relaxation know how to bring about a relaxed condition in the body and mind. Continually for about twelve years I myself had only three hours' sleep at night, and sometimes not even that. And all those twelve years I was never ill. I had all the strength necessary and was perfectly well because of the practice of relaxation.

The question is, how does one relax? It is not by sitting silent with closed eyes, for when the mind is giving attention to the body by thought or feeling, then the body is not relaxed, because the mind is torturing the body. And when feeling is giving attention to the mind, then the mind is tortured. This torture—even if the eyes are closed, even if we are sitting in a certain posture—does no good. With relaxation one should consider three points of view: the point of view of the physical body, the point of view of the mind, and the point of view of the feeling. The point of view of the physical body is that one must accustom oneself to get power over or to have influence on one's circulation and pulsation, and one can do that with the power of thought and with the power of will, together with breath. By will power one can bring about a certain condition in one's body so that one's circulation takes a certain rhythm. It is decreased according to will. One can do the same in regulating one's pulsation by the power of will. No sooner has the will taken in hand the circulation and the pulsation of the body than the will has in hand a meditation of hours. It is for this reason that sages can meditate for hours on end, because they have mastered their circulation; they can breathe at will, slower or quicker. And when there is no tension on one's nervous or muscular system, then one gets a repose that ten days' sleep cannot bring about. Therefore to have relaxation does not mean to sit quiet, it is to be able to remove tension from one's system—from one's circulation, one's pulsation, and one's nervous and muscular systems.

How does one relax the mind? The method for relaxation of the mind is first to make the mind tired. He who does not know the exercise for making the mind tired can never relax his mind. Concentration is the greatest action one can give to one's mind, because the mind is held in position on a certain thing. After that it will relax naturally, and when it relaxes it will gain all power.

Relaxation of feeling is achieved by feeling deeply. The Sufis in the East in their meditation have music played that stirs up the emotions to such a degree that the poem they hear becomes a reality. Then comes the reaction, which is relaxation. All that was blocked up, every congestion, is broken down; and inspiration, power, and a feeling of joy and exaltation come to them.

It is by these three kinds of relaxation that one becomes prepared for the highest relaxation, which is to relax the whole being: the body in repose, the mind at rest, the heart at peace. It is that experience which may be called *nirvana*, the ideal of thinkers and meditative souls. It is that which they want to reach, for in it there is everything. In that condition each person becomes for the time as a drop that is assimilated or submerged in its origin. And being submerged for one moment means that all that belongs to the origin is attracted by this drop, because the origin is the essence of all. The drop has taken from its origin everything it has in life. It is newly charged and has become illumined again.

Chapter 15

THE SILENT LIFE

When we look at the universe, we find there are two aspects of existence: first, life; second, the condition which compared with what we call life seems to be lifeless. The one aspect of existence we call life, the other aspect we overlook. We divide it into periods and call it time, or we compare it with objects and call it space.

We say that an object is alive when it shows some activity and consciousness, meaning that it can move and see and think. An object that cannot see and is not active we call dead. Whatever seems to be devoid of activity and consciousness is called a thing; when it has consciousness and activity, it is called living.

What is the source of this consciousness and activity? The circulation of the blood, the energy of the movements of the body, the activity of the nerves and muscles—if we could only know what it is that keeps them in action! A person may say that it all goes on mechanically, like a clock, but the clock is not the source of the movement. The mind is the source of the clock: the mind has made the clock, has thought about it, has wound it; it continues to depend upon man to keep it going. Therefore behind clock is man. Even if it only wants winding once a year, still there is man behind it, whom we do not see.

It is the same with the whole mechanism of nature: all is mechanical and runs according to certain laws, and yet there is a source or origin of things hidden behind it all. As the artist is hidden behind his art, as the scientist is hidden behind his invention, as the mind is hidden behind the body, as the cause is hidden behind the action, so there is always one aspect of life that is hidden behind that other aspect which alone is recognized as life.

Both science and religion show that consciousness has evolved through different stages, from mineral to vegetable, from vegetable to animal, and from animal to humanity. It is regarded as the achievement of modern science that this thought has been reached, but its source lies in the traditions of the past. Rumi's *Masnavi* tells us the experience of consciousness from the mineral up to the plant:

> I died as a mineral, and rose a plant,
> I died as a plant, and rose again an animal,
> I died as an animal, and rose a man.
> Why then should I fear to become less by dying?
>
> I shall die once again as a man,
> To rise an angel, perfect from head to foot.
> Again, when I suffer dissolution as an angel,
> I shall become what passes the conception of man.

Science today stops at man, but the poem says that from man I shall rise to be an angel, and from angel I shall ascend to that stage of being which passes man's comprehension. This poem was written in the thirteenth century.

This proves Solomon's saying, "There is nothing new under the sun." When man discovers something today, he in reality only brings to light something that existed in the past, either as history or as tradition. Even before Rumi one finds this idea in the Qur'an.

What can we learn from this? Every activity that we call "life" has sprung from a source that is silent and will always be silent; and every activity, however different in aspect, peculiar to itself, and unlike others in its effect, is still the activity of a tiny part of that life which is as wide as the ocean. Call it world, universe, nation, country, race, community, one individual, or only a particle, an atom—its activity, its energy springs in each case from one inseparable and eternal silent aspect of life. And not only has it sprung from it, but it also resolves itself into it. One throws a pebble into water that is still and calm; there comes an activity for one moment, and then it vanishes. Into what does it vanish? It vanishes into the same silence in which the water was before. Water is a substance that is active by nature, and the silence, the stillness, the calmness that it shows is just the original state, the effect of its original source. This means that the natural inclination of every thing and every being is silence, because it has come from silence; and yet it is active, because it is activity that produces activity. And its end is silence.

Therefore sages, mystics, and philosophers who have probed into the depths of life have seen that what we call life is death, and that what we call no life is the real life.

A Hindustani poet says, "Raise your eyes, friend, from what you call life to that which perhaps you do not recognize as life, and then you will find that what you had once called life is nothing but death, and what you thought was nothing is really life."

When one comes to the essence of the teachings of Christ, one will see that from beginning to end the whole attitude of the master is to tell mankind that there is a life beyond, which is higher than this that one calls life and that yet is not life; that is to say, higher in quality, not beyond in time.

The life one recognizes is only the mortal aspect of life. Very few have ever seen or been conscious of the immortal aspect at all. Once one has realized life, that which one had hitherto called life is found to be only a glimpse or shadow of the real life that is beyond comprehension. To understand it one will have to raise one's light high from under the cover that is hiding it like a bushel. This cover is man's mind and body; it is a cover that keeps the light active on the world of things and beings. "Do not keep your light under a bushel" means that we are not to keep the consciousness absorbed in the study of the external world and in its pleasures and enjoyments.

Man is always apt to say that the religious thinker is a dreamer, lost in vague ideals, having no proof of what he believes, and far from what he himself would call the reality. He never thinks that what he calls "real" has in its turn become unreal to the one to whom the silent life has become reality. Can you call this life real which is subject to such changes every moment? Every activity and the object of everyone's life—riches, power, love, friendship, childhood, youth, health, pleasure, displeasure, happiness, and poverty—all change sooner or later. Can anybody think that such things are reality? What can one call all this that is subject to change, whose source is unseen and whose end is unseen, and which is subject to death and destruction, after which it is seen no more? Is that reality? Or are not the realities perhaps really behind the scene, from whence everything came and to which everything goes?

Perhaps many of us have experienced at some time or other, in our own home or in a church, a temple, or some other religious place, how there is a kind of silence as we sit there. Compared with a bazaar, a market, or a factory, there is no activity. If under such circumstances we noticed the condition of our own self, of our mind, of our thoughts, of our body, and have felt any comfort, have we then asked ourselves why we felt comfort and rest? Then take another experience: we may be a few moments or a few hours in the woods, away and apart from everybody. It may seem as if even the trees and the leaves are keeping silence. The feelings that we have at such a time cannot be expressed in words. These feelings cannot be called pleasure, because what we are accustomed to in pleasure or in joy is not the same. We can only say, "That peculiar pleasure, that peculiar joy." There is no name for it, and yet it is a true experience of the soul.

Then there is a still greater and deeper experience: when a person is in a wilderness, near rocks in the desert, where there is no sound even of birds or beasts, when there is absolute silence. In the East, did not all the prophets from the time of Abraham, Moses, David, and in the time of Christ and Muhammad, all the prophets of the Old Testament and the New, and of the Qur'an, receive their inspiration from the same source? The history of Moses on Mount Sinai, the Prophet of Nazareth in the wilderness, the Prophet Muhammad in Ghar-e Hira, did they not all drink from the silent life? Though God is in all activities and forms and names, it is His other aspect, solid, firm, eternal, all-sufficient and-powerful, all-intelligent, undivided and inseparable, from which the inspiration came as a perfect inspiration, so that the world could take it as the sacred word in all ages and in all times.

Then, coming to the cause of idol worship, a person might wonder about the old custom of Brahmans and Buddhists, who went into the temple of Buddha or Krishna and sat before an idol that neither spoke to them nor took notice of them. One might think, "What could they gain? It has a mouth and speaks not; it has hands yet cannot move." And so people mocked at them, scoffed at them, and called them "heathen" and "pagan." But they did not know of this silence that was impressed upon the worshipper. This human form sitting before them, silent and quiet, not speaking or hearing or thinking, absolutely quiet—just think what it means.

When a person is among friends he may get tired. Sometimes he enjoys their society, but when he does not enjoy it, he thinks, "I am drained of all vitality." Why is this? It is the impression of their minds that has been produced in his mind. Perhaps someone has insulted him or snubbed him or told him this or that, and he goes among his friends bringing all his troubles with him. Then he leaves, still saying, "I am tired." If he is working in a factory, it is reasonable to be tired in body; but why should he be tired in society where people are laughing and chatting? It is because their condition of mind is not like his.

But before the idol there is perfect harmony. See, here is someone sitting quiet. A quiet human form that does not speak—what rest! It may not help, but it does not disturb. It keeps the worshipper silent; that was the idea.

What do we learn from this? Every effort was made by the teachers of religion to waken people to that aspect of life that is overlooked in ordinary life, which they call "life." The purpose of concentration, contemplation, meditation, all that is the essence of religion or mysticism or philosophy, is nothing but this one thing: to attain to that depth which is the root of our life.

A Marathi poet has said, "O mind, my restless mind, my mind with its thoughts of a thousand things that it supposes will make it happy, saying, 'If I had that, I should be happy; if I had this, I should feel life was not wasted.'! O my mind, will you tell me who in this world is happy?" The mind says, "If I had the wealth that

I see others have, I should be happy." But are these others happy? They in their turn say they would be if they had something still higher!

The secret of happiness is hidden under the veil of spiritual knowledge. And spiritual knowledge is nothing but this: that there is a constant longing in the heart of man to have something of its origin, to experience something of its original state, the state of peace and joy that has been disturbed, yet is sought after throughout its whole life and never can cease to be sought after until the real source has at length been realized. What was it in the wilderness that gave peace and joy? What was it that came to us in the forest, the solitude? In either case it was nothing else but the depth of our own life, which is silent like the depths of the great sea, so silent and still. It is the surface of the sea that makes waves and roaring breakers; the depth is silent. So the depth of our own being is silent also.

This all-pervading, unbroken, inseparable, unlimited, ever-present, omnipotent silence unites with our silence like the meeting of flames. Something goes out from the depths of our being to receive something from there, which comes to meet us; our eyes cannot see and our ears cannot hear and our mind cannot perceive it because it is beyond mind, thought, and comprehension. It is the meeting of the soul and the spirit.

Therefore the idea of understanding the spiritual ideal is to attain to that state of being, of calm and peace and joy and everlasting happiness, which neither changes nor ceases to exist. It is to realize what is said in the Bible, "Be ye perfect even as your Father in heaven." Those words do not tell us to remain imperfect as everybody on earth. No, they mean the idea of all perfection, all unity, no separation. It is the opposite of the idea that religion should keep part of humanity separate, saying, "You do not belong to our church, our mosque, our temple!" It is the opposite of loyalty to this particular sect or community or to that particular sacred book, to this particular teaching or to that particular truth. Is not the source of all truth hidden in every man's heart, be he Christian, Muslim, Buddhist, or Jew? Is not each one part of that life which we call "spiritual" or "divine"? To be just this or that is the same as not going further than this or that. The bliss found in solitude is hidden within every human being; he has inherited it from his heavenly Father. In mystical words it is called "the all-pervading light." Light is the source and origin of every human soul, of every mind.

The Sufi looks upon life as one life, upon all religions as his religion: call him a Christian and he is that; call him a Muslim or a Hindu and he is that; call him whatever you like, he does not mind. A Sufi does not think about what people call him. Who calls him Sufi? It is not he. But if he does not call himself something, someone else is sure to find a name for him. Cats and dogs do not declare their names; it is man that gives them a name. If you call yourself "New Thought," it will be made into the name of a new sect someday; if you call yourself "Higher Thought," that will be a sect one day. Call yourself what you will—philosophy, theosophy, religion, mysticism—it is only the one thing, it is nothing but the constant longing of the soul of the human being. After experiencing all the different aspects of the life of activity, the longing to attain to that state of peace or calm seems in the end to be the only object that the soul wishes to achieve.

A person may keep thinking that perhaps he will be happy when he is a king, or rich, or an officer; then he will gain his desire, and as long as he has not got it, the sweetness of the thought lies only in the hope. As long as there is hope there is sweetness; after the desire is fulfilled, the hope has gone. Then he hopes for something else. It is hope that is sweet, not the object. The object is never sweet; it is the sweetness of the hope that makes the object seem sweet.

"If I could reach that height!" a person says. So long as he has not reached that height, the dream of reaching the height, of one day experiencing that position, experience, or imagination, the dream of being comforted by it—so long he has the sweetness of the hope. But when it has come, the sweetness is finished. Then begins a new hope, always hoping, hoping. Still behind it all is that one inclination, common to all, the inclination of which he does not know the nature. No person would live did he not have the hope of something for which he was waiting.

Hope is the only food of life. Then reason says, "Yes, I am looking forward to my change from this place to the next; to getting my inheritance someday; then I shall be all right. I shall be all right when I get that position, that house, that comfort." Man has always something before him, imagining, building, preparing and holding it in the mind all the time—and yet when he does get it, there is always another hope.

It is only those who are blessed by perceiving the origin and source of all things who awaken to the fact that the real inclination of every life is to attain to something that cannot be touched or comprehended or understood. The hidden blessing of this knowledge is the first step to perfection. Once awake to this fact, one sees there is something in life that will make one really happy and give one one's heart's desire. One can say, "Though there are many things in life that I need for the moment and for which I shall certainly work, yet there is only that one thing, around which life centers, that will satisfy me: spiritual attainment, religious attainment, or, as one may even call it, the attainment of God." Such a one has found the key to all happiness, and has found that all the things he needs will be reached because he has the key to all. "Seek, and ye shall find; knock, and it shall be opened unto you. . . . Seek ye first the kingdom of God, and all these things shall be added unto you." This kingdom of God is the silent life; the life inseparable, eternal, self-sufficient, and all-powerful. This is the life that the wise contemplate. It is the face of this life that they long to see; it is the ocean of this life that they long to swim in. As it is written, "In Him we live and have our being."

These are the ones who are really happy, who are above all unhappiness, above death and the destruction of life.

There is a saying that words are valuable but silence is more precious. This saying will always prove true. The more we understand the meaning of it, the more we realize its truth. How many times during the day do we find that we have said something that would have been better left unsaid! How many times do we disturb the peace of our surroundings, without meaning to, by lack of silence! How often do we make our limitation, our narrowness, our smallness come out, which we would rather have concealed, because we did not keep silent! How very often, though desiring to respect others, we cannot manage to do so because we do not keep silent! A great danger lies in wait for a person in the life of this world, the danger of confiding in someone in whom he did not wish to confide. We run that danger by not keeping silent. That great interpreter of life, the Persian poet Sa'adi, says, "What value is sense, if it does not come to my rescue before I utter a word!" This shows us that in spite of whatever wisdom we may have, we can make a mistake if we have no control over our words. We can easily find examples of this truth: those who talk much have less power than those who talk little. For a talkative person may not be able to express an idea in a thousand words which those who are masters of silence express in one word. Everyone can speak, but not every word has the same power. Besides, a word says much less than silence can express. The keynote to harmonious life is silence.

In everyday life we are confronted with a thousand troubles that we are not always evolved enough to meet, and then only silence can help us. For if there is any religion, if there is any practice of religion, it is to have regard for the pleasure of God by regarding the pleasure of man. The essence of religion is to understand. This religion we cannot live without having power over the word, without having realized the power of silence. There are so very many occasions when we repent after hurting friends, which could have been avoided if there had been control over our words. Silence is the shield of the ignorant and the protection of the wise. For the ignorant does not prove his ignorance if he keeps silent, and the wise person does not throw pearls before swine if he knows the worth of silence.

What gives power over words? What gives the power that can be attained by silence? The answer is, it is will power that gives control over words; it is silence that gives one the power of silence. It is restlessness when a person speaks too much. The more words are used to express an idea, the less powerful they become. It is a great pity that man so often thinks of saving pennies and never thinks of sparing words. It is like saving pebbles and throwing away pearls. An Indian poet says, "Pearl shell, what gives you your precious contents?" "Silence; for years my lips were closed."

For a moment it is a struggle with oneself; it is controlling an impulse; but afterwards the same thing becomes a power.

Now coming to the more scientific, metaphysical explanation of silence. There is a certain amount of energy spent by words, and breath, which has to bring new life into the body, is hindered in its regular rhythm when one speaks all the time. It is not that a nervous person speaks too much, but much speaking makes him nervous. Where did the great power attained by yogis and faqirs come from? It was gained by having learned and practiced the art of silence. That is the reason why in the East, in the houses where faqirs meditated and even at the court, there was silence. There were times during different civilizations of the world when people were taught, whenever they were collected together for a feast, to keep silence for a certain time. It is the greatest pity that at this time we have so neglected that question; we think so little about it. It is a question that affects health, that touches the soul, the spirit, life. The more we think about this subject, the more we see that we are continually involved in a kind of action. Where does it lead us and what is the result of it? As far as we can see, it leads us to greater struggle, competition, disagreeableness. If we think of the result, we see that it leads us to greater care, worry, and struggle in life. There is a saying of the Hindus, "The more one seeks for happiness, the more unhappiness one finds." The reason is that when happiness is sought in a wrong direction, it leads to unhappiness. Our experience in life is sufficient to teach us this, yet life is intoxicating; it absorbs us in action so that we never stop to think of it.

It seems that the world is awakening to spiritual ideals, but in spite of this there is more activity, not only outer activity, but also activity of mind. In reality mankind has shattered his nerves by the lack of silence, by the overactivity of body and mind. When the body is resting, man calls it sleep. But his mind is going on, on the same record as during the day. In this world of competition everyone is a hundred times more busy than he ever was. Naturally his life needs rest and quietude and peace more than that of people who live in the forest, who call all the time their own. When activity is increased and the art of silence is lost, then what can we expect?

Where do we learn thoughtfulness? In silence. And where do we practice patience? In silence. Silence practiced in meditation is something apart, but silence means that we should consider every word and every action we do; that is the first lesson to learn. If there is a meditative person, he has learned to use that silence naturally in everyday life. The one who has learned silence in everyday life has already learned to meditate. Besides a person may have reserved half an hour every day for meditation, but when there is half an hour of meditation and twelve or fifteen hours of activity, the activity takes away all the power of the meditation. Therefore both things must go together. A person who wishes to learn the art of silence must decide, however much work he has to do, to keep the thought of silence in his mind. When one does not consider this, then one will not reap the full benefit of meditation. It is just like a person who goes to church once a week and the other six days he keeps the thought of church as far away as possible.

A very devout Persian king was asked by his prime minister, "You are spending most of the night in meditation, and all day long you work. How can that go on?" The Shah said, "During the night I pursue God; during the day God follows me." It is the same with silence: he who seeks silence is followed by silence. So it is with all things we wish for; when we seek after them sufficiently, they follow us in time by themselves.

There are many who do not mind if they hurt anyone as long as they think they have told the truth. They feel so justified that they do not care if the other one cries or laughs. There is, however, a difference between fact and truth. Fact is that which can be spoken of; truth is that which cannot be put into words. The claim, "I tell the truth," falls flat when the difference is realized between fact and truth. People discuss dogmas, beliefs, moral principles as they know them. But there comes a time in a person's life when he has touched truth, of which he cannot speak in words; and at that time all dispute, discussion, argument ends. It is then that the person says, "If you have done wrong or if I have done wrong, it does not matter. What I want just now is to right the wrong." There comes a time when the continual question that arises in the active mind, what is what and which is which?, comes to an end, for the answer rises from the soul and is received in silence.

The general attitude of man is that of listening to all that comes from outside. And not only are the ears open to the external world, but even the heart is attached to the ears. The heart that is listening to the voices coming from the external world should turn its back on all that comes from there and wait patiently until it becomes capable of hearing the voice from within.

There is an audible voice and an inaudible voice, from the living and from those who are not living, from all life. What one can say in words always expresses little. Can one speak about gratefulness, about devotion, about admiration? Never; there will always be a lack of words. Every deep feeling has its own voice; it cannot be expressed in outer words. This voice comes from every soul; every soul is only audible to the heart. And how is the heart prepared? Through silence.

We need not be surprised that some have sought the mountains and the forest and preferred the wilderness to the comforts of worldly life. They sought something valuable. They have passed on something of the experience gained by their sacrifice. But it is not necessary to follow them to the forest or to the caves of the mountains. One can learn that art of silence everywhere; throughout a busy life one can maintain silence.

Silence is something that consciously or unconsciously we are seeking every moment of our lives. We are seeking silence and running away from it, both at the same time. Where is the word of God heard? In silence. The seers, the saints, the sages, the prophets, the masters have heard that voice which comes from within by making themselves silent. I do not mean by this that because one has silence one will be spoken to; I mean that once one is silent one will hear the word that is constantly coming from within. When the mind has been made still, a person also communicates with everyone he meets. He does not need many words: when glances meet he understands. Two persons may talk and discuss all their lives and yet never understand one another; and two others with still minds look at one another and in one moment a communication is established between them.

Where do the differences between people come from? From within. From their activity. How does agreement come? By the stillness of the mind. It is noise that hinders a voice that we hear from a distance, and it is the troubled waters of a pool that hinder our seeing our own image reflected in the water. When the water is still it takes a clear reflection, and when our atmosphere is still then we hear that voice which is constantly coming to the heart of every person. We are looking for guidance; we all of us search for truth, we search for the mystery. The mystery is in ourselves; the guidance is in our own souls.

Chapter 16

MUSIC: THE VOICE OF BEAUTY

Music, the word we use in our everyday language, is nothing less than the picture of our Beloved. It is because music is the picture of our Beloved that we love music. But the question is, what is our Beloved and where is our Beloved? Our Beloved is that which is our source and our goal. What we see of our Beloved before our physical eyes is the beauty that is before us; and that part of our Beloved not manifest to our eyes is that inner form of beauty of which our Beloved speaks to us. If only we would listen to the voice of all the beauty that attracts us in any form, we would find that in every aspect it tells us that behind all manifestation is the perfect spirit, the spirit of wisdom.

What do we see as the principal expression of life in the beauty visible before us? It is movement. In line, in color, in the changes of the seasons, in the rising and falling of the waves, in the wind, in the storm, in all the beauty of nature there is constant movement. It is movement that has caused day and night and the changing of the seasons, and this movement has given us the comprehension of what we call "time.". Otherwise there would be no time, for actually there is only eternity. This teaches us that all we love and admire, observe and comprehend is the life hidden behind it, and this life is our being.

It is owing to our limitation that we cannot see the whole being of God; but all that we love in color, line, form, or personality belongs to the real beauty, the Beloved of all. When we trace what attracts us in this beauty that we see in all forms, we shall find that it is the movement of beauty; in other words the music. All forms of nature, for instance the flowers, are perfectly formed and colored; the planets and stars, the earth, all give the idea of harmony, of music. The whole of nature is breathing; not only the living creatures but all nature. It is only our tendency to compare that which seems living with what to us is not so living that makes us forget that all things and beings are living one perfect life. The sign of life given by this living beauty is music.

What makes the soul of the poet dance? Music. What makes the painter paint beautiful pictures, the musician sing beautiful songs? It is the inspiration that beauty gives. Therefore the Sufi has called the beauty *Saki,* the divine Giver who gives the wine of life to all. What is the wine of the Sufi? Beauty in form, in line, in color, in imagination, in sentiment, in manner; in all this he sees the one beauty. All these different forms are part of the spirit of beauty that is the life behind them, a continual blessing.

As to what we call music in everyday language, to me architecture is music, gardening is music, farming is music, painting is music, poetry is music. In all the occupations of life where beauty has been the inspiration, where the divine wine has been poured out, there is music. But among all the different arts, the art of music has been specially considered divine, because it is the exact miniature of the law working through the whole universe. For instance, if we study ourselves we shall find that the beats of the pulse and the heart, the inhaling and exhaling of the breath are all the work of rhythm. Life depends upon the rhythmic working of the whole mechanism of the body. Breath manifests as voice, as word, as sound; and the sound is continually audible, the sound without and the sound within ourselves. That is music; it shows that there is music both outside and within ourselves.

Music inspires not only the soul of the great musician but every infant, who the instant it comes into the world begins to move its little arms and legs with the rhythm of music. Therefore it is no exaggeration to say that music is the language of beauty, of the

One whom every living soul has loved. When one realizes this and recognizes the perfection of all beauty as God, our Beloved, one understands why the music we experience in art and in the whole universe should be called the divine art.

Many in the world take music as a source of amusement, a pastime, and to many music is an art and a musician an entertainer. Yet no one has lived in this world and has thought and felt who has not considered music as the most sacred of all arts. For the fact is that what the art of painting cannot clearly suggest, poetry explains in words, but that which even a poet finds difficult to express in poetry is expressed in music. By this I not only say that music is superior to art and poetry, but in point of fact music excels religion, for music raises the soul of man even higher than the so-called external forms of religion.

By this it must not be understood that music can take the place of religion, for every soul is not necessarily tuned to that pitch where it can really benefit by music, nor is every music necessarily so high that it will exalt a person who hears it more than religion will. However, for those who follow the inner path, music is essential for their spiritual development. The reason is that the soul who is seeking for that is in search of the formless God. Art no doubt is most elevating, but at the same time it contains form; poetry has words, names, suggestive of form; it is only music that has beauty, power and charm and at the same time can raise the soul beyond form.

That is why in ancient times the greatest of the prophets were great musicians. For instance, among the Hindu prophets one finds Narada, the prophet who was musician at the same time, and Shiva, a godlike prophet who was the inventor of the sacred vina. Krishna is always pictured with a flute.

There is also a well-known legend of the life of Moses which says that Moses heard a divine command on Mount Sinai in the words; *Muse ke*, "Moses, hark". The revelation that thus came to him was of tone and rhythm, and he called it by the same name, *musik*. Words such as *"music"* and *musique* have come from that word. David's song and verse have been known for ages; his message was given in the form of music. Orpheus of the Greek legends, the knower of the mystery of tone and rhythm, had by this knowledge power over the hidden forces of nature. The Hindu goddess of beauty, of knowledge, whose name is Sarasvati, is always pictured with the vina. What does it suggest? It suggests that all harmony has its essence in music. Besides the natural charm music possesses, it has also a magic charm that can be experienced even now. It seems that the human race has lost a great deal of the ancient science of magic, but if there remains any magic it is music.

Music, besides power, is intoxication. When it intoxicates those who hear it, how much more must it intoxicate those who have touched the perfection of music and have meditated upon it for years and years! It gives them an even greater joy and exaltation than a king feels sitting on his throne.

According to the thinkers of the East there are five different intoxications: first the intoxication of beauty, youth, and strength; then the intoxication of wealth; third, that of power, command, the power of ruling; and the fourth intoxication is the intoxication of learning, of knowledge. But all these four intoxications fade away just like stars before the sun in the presence of the intoxication of music. The reason is that it touches the deepest part of man's being. Music reaches further than any other impression from the external world can reach. The beauty of music is that it is both the source of creation and the means of absorbing it. In other words, by music the world was created, and by music it is withdrawn again into the source that created it.

In this scientific and material world we see a similar example. Before a machine or mechanism will run, it must first make a noise. It first becomes audible, and then shows its life. We can see this in a ship, in an airplane, in an automobile. This idea belongs to the mysticism of sound. Before an infant is capable of admiring a color or form, it enjoys sound. If there is any art that can most please the aged it is music. If there is any art that can charge youth with life and enthusiasm, emotion and passion, it is music. If there is any art in which a person can fully express his feeling, his emotion, it is music. At the same time it is something that gives man that force and that power of activity which make the soldiers march with the beat of the drum and the sound of the trumpet. In the traditions of the past it was said that on the Last Day there will be the sound of trumpets before the end of the world comes. This shows that music is connected with the beginning of the creation, with its continuity, and with its end.

The mystics of all ages have loved music most. In almost all the circles of the inner cult, in whatever part of the world, music seems to be the center of the cult or the ceremony. And those who attain to that perfect peace which is called *nirvana,* or in the language of the Hindus *samadhi,* do this more easily through music. Therefore Sufis, especially those of the Chishtia school of ancient times, have taken music as a source of their meditation. By meditating thus they derive much more benefit than those who meditate without the help of music. The effect that they experience is the unfoldment of the soul, the opening of the intuitive faculties; and their heart, so to speak, opens to all the beauty which is within and without, uplifting them, and at the same time bringing them that perfection for which every soul yearns.

Chapter 17

THE ALCHEMY OF VIBRATIONS

Music, literature, and philosophy are akin to our souls, whatever be our faith or belief or our way of looking at life. India, in the history of the world, represents a country and a people engaged in the search for truth through the realm of music, philosophy, and poetry at a time when the rest of the world had not yet begun to do so. It is therefore necessary to study Indian music, philosophy, and poetry in order to understand their foundation. Linguists today agree that the Sanskrit language was the origin or mother of many languages; the origin of the science of music is also to be found in Sanskrit.

It is a fact that not only art but even science has its source in intuition. This seems to have been sometimes forgotten, but undoubtedly even the scientist is helped by intuition, although he may not always recognize the fact. Scientists who have delved deeply into their science will admit this. Intuition working in answer to the need of the mind and the body, inventing through matter things of daily use, and gaining a knowledge of the nature and character of things, is called science. Intuition working through the beauty that is produced in the form of line and color and rhythm is called art. Therefore the source of both science and art is intuition.

Realizing this source, the Hindus based their music on intuition, and the practice of Indian music has been a culture of stimulating intuition, awakening the faculty of appreciating beautiful sounds and often words, and expressing itself in beautiful forms.

In India life has always begun with the soul; therefore science, art, philosophy, and mysticism were all directed to one and the same goal. Not only arts and sciences, but even professions and commerce were not without a religious view. One can imagine how in a country where even business and professional people had a spiritual outlook, the musician's life was full of religious thought.

No part of the world, East or West, can really deny the divinity of music. In the first place music is the language of the soul, and for two people of different nations or races to unite there is no better means than music. For music not only unites man to man, but man to God. Now the question comes: when is it that music unites man with God, and how? Belief in God has two aspects. One belief in God is when a person thinks, "Perhaps there is a God," or "As others believe I believe too." He does not know God by reason, nor does he see God before him. God for him is perhaps in heaven. Whether He exists or does not exist he does not know. From one who has this kind of belief, a little confusion or disappointment or injustice takes it away. It is for this reason that thousands and thousands of people who worshipped God have given up their belief in Him.

There is another aspect of belief, and it is gained through the realization of God's presence not only in the heavens, but in one's own surroundings. When a person arrives at this point, this belief becomes a living identity. To him God is not only a judge or a sustainer; to him He is a friend who hears the cry of his soul in solitude and knows the best and greatest secret he has in his heart, a friend upon whom one can always rely in good and bad experiences and even in the hereafter. For a musician, music is the best way to unite with God. A musician with a belief in God brings to God the beauty and the perfume and the color of his soul.

From the metaphysical point of view there is nothing that can touch the formless except the art of music, which in itself is formless. There is another point of view: that the innermost being of man is the *akasha,* which means capacity. Therefore all that is directed from the external world to the world within can reach this realm, and music can reach it best. A third point of view is that all creation has come from vibrations, which the Hindus have called *nada;* and in the Bible we can find it as the word, which came first of all. On this point all the different religions unite. Man, therefore, loves music more than anything else. Music is his nature: it has come from vibrations, and he himself is vibration.

There are two aspects of life: the first is that man is tuned by his surroundings, and the second is that man can tune himself in spite of his surroundings. This latter is the work of the mystic. The Sufis in the East work for years together to tune themselves. By the help of music they tune themselves to the spheres where they wish to be, as the yogis do. Therefore the beginning of music in India was at the time of Shiva, lord of the yogis. The great yogi teacher taught to the world the science of breath. Among the Sufis there was a great saint, Moinuddin Chishti of Ajmer. At his grave music is played, and Hindus and Muslims go there on pilgrimage. This shows that the religion of the knowers of truth is the religion of God. The prayer of the greatest devotee rises from his heart into the realm of music. All the various methods of bringing about calm and peace can be attained through the help of music.

The music of India can be divided into four periods: the Sanskrit period, the Prakrit period, the Moghul period, and the modern period. The Sanskrit period is on mystical lines. The Prakrit period is expressive of emotions of different sorts. In the Moghul period music was influenced by Persia and Arabia, and it developed into the modern music. Besides this the two different races in India, the Dravidians and the Aryans, each had their own tradition of music; the Dravidians or Karnatic race produced the music of southern India, and the Aryans or Hindus produced the music of northern India.

The science of Indian music has come from three sources: mathematics, astrology, and psychology. We find this in western music also, for the entire science of harmony and counterpoint is based on mathematics. In Sanskrit the science of Hindu music is called *prestara,* which means mathematical arrangement of rhythm and modes.

In the Indian system there are a great many modes and rhythms which are used in everyday music. The modes are called *ragas,* and they are grouped in four classes. One class has seven notes, as in the natural scale of western music. Then there are the modes of six notes, where one note of the seven-note raga is omitted; that gives quite another effect to the octave and has a different influence on the human mind. There are also ragas of five notes, omitting two notes of the scale. In China they use a scale of four notes, but not in India.

Some say that the origin of the scale of four or five notes lies in the natural instinct that man shows in his discovery of instruments. The first instrument was the flute, symbolical of the human voice. It seems natural that after taking a piece of reed from the forest, one would make four holes in that reed at distances where he could place the tips of his fingers without effort, and would then make one hole below. That made the raga of five notes. It was only later that scientists arrived at the knowledge of vibrations; but this scale comes naturally when a person places his hand on the reed, and a great psychological power seems to be attached to it. It has a great influence on human nature, and this shows that the power of anything deriving directly from nature is much greater than when man has made changes and alterations in order to create a new form in art.

The science of astrology was based on the science of cosmic vibrations, for everything depends on vibratory conditions, including the position of the stars and the planets and of individuals, nations, races, and all objects. A great deal of secret power that the Hindus found in the science of music was derived from the science of astrology. Every note of the Hindu music corresponds with a certain planet, and every note reflects a certain pitch of the animal world.

In the ancient Vedas the science of the elements fire, water, air, and ether is to be found, but these words should not be taken as meaning the same as in everyday language. The element of water, for instance, signifies a liquid state; fire signifies heat or warmth. Through this science the Hindus have been able to arrange ragas or modes to be sung or played at a certain time of day or night. And undoubtedly those who knew the alchemy of vibrations have worked wonders by the power of music. After songs have been sung for thousands of years, the race has developed such a sense of appreciation of these ragas that even an ordinary person in the street cannot bear to hear a morning raga sung in the evening. He may not know the notes, but to his ears it sounds disagreeable; he cannot stand it. It is like taking a stroll on a midsummer morning wearing an evening dress! We may say it is a matter of habit, and that is true, but at the same time a mode that should be sung in the middle of the night loses its beautiful influence if we sing it at noon.

Every planet has a certain influence, and there must be a certain mode to answer it. If this is not taken into consideration music may become a pastime, but it does not do the work for which it is designed.

To an Indian music is not an amusement or only for enteraintment. It is something more than that: it answers the deepest demands of his soul. The human being is not only a physical body, he has a mind too. The body hungers for food, and what generally happens is that man only ministers to his bodily needs and gives no attention to his inner existence and its demands. He experiences momentary satisfaction, but then he hungers again, not knowing that the soul is the finest of his being. And so that unconscious craving of the soul remains.

In the undeveloped person that silent craving of the soul becomes something disagreeable and makes him restless or irritated. He does not feel contented with anything in life; he feels like quarreling and fighting. In the person of fine feeling, this hunger of the soul expresses itself in depression or despair. He finds some satisfaction in love of reading or love of art.

The soul feels buried in the outer, material world, and the soul feels satisfied and living when it is touched with fine vibrations. The finest matter is spirit, and the grosser spirit is matter. Music, being the finest of the arts, helps the soul to rise above differences. It unites souls, because even words are not necessary. Music is beyond words.

Hindu music is unique in character, for the player and singer are given perfect freedom in expressing their souls through their art. The character of the Indian nature can be understood by the spirit of individualism. The whole education tends to individualism, to express one's self in whatever form one is capable of. Therefore in some ways to their disadvantage, but in many ways to their advantage, they have to express their freedom. Uniformity has its advantages, but it very often paralyzes progress in art.

There are two ways in life, uniformity and individualism. Uniformity has its strength, but individualism has its beauty. When one hears an artist, a singer of Hindu music, the first thing he will do is to tune his *tambura,* to give one chord; and while he tunes his tambura he tunes his own soul, and this has such an influence on his hearers that they can wait patiently, often for a considerable time. Once he finds he is in tune with his instrument, with that chord, his soul, mind, and body all seem to be one with the instrument. A person with a sensitive heart listening to his song, even a foreigner, will perceive the way he sings into that chord, the way he tunes his spirit to that chord. And by that time he has become concentrated; by that time he has tuned himself to all who are there. Not only has he tuned the instrument, but he has felt the need of every soul in the audience and the demands of their souls, what they want at that time. Not every musician can do this, but the best can. And when he synthesizes, and it all comes automatically as he begins his song, it seems that it touches every person in the audience, for it is all the answer to the demand of the souls that are sitting there. He has not made a program beforehand; he does not know what he will sing next, but each time he is inspired to sing a certain song or to play a certain mode. He becomes an instrument of the whole cosmic system, open to all inspiration, at one with the audience, in tune with the chord of the tambura, and it is not only music but spiritual phenomena that he gives to people.

The traditional ancient songs of India composed by great masters have been handed down from father to son. The way music is taught is different from the western way. It is not always written, but it is taught by imitation. The teacher sings and the pupil imitates, and all the intricacies and subtleties are learned by imitation.

It is the mystical aspect of music that has been the secret of all religions. The great ones of this world, such as Christ, Buddha, and others, have come from time to time to be examples for the people, and to express that perfection which is the object of every soul.

The secret that was hidden behind all these great religions, and in the work of these teachers, was that man should reach that utmost height which is called perfection. It is the principle which is taught from the first lesson the musician gives to his pupils. The pupil imitates not only the teacher, but he focuses his spirit upon the spirit of the teacher; and he not only learns, but he inherits from his teacher.

The lack we find today of spiritual awakening, the reason so many seekers after truth have not come to a satisfactory result, is that they always pursue it outwardly; they take it from a book or learn it from a teacher. There was a time in the East (and this still exists even now), when a little boy who went to a teacher to learn had a great regard for his teacher; his respect, his attitude towards his teacher was as it would be towards a priest. Therefore in this manner he learned to value and appreciate and respect the knowledge of the teacher. It is most wonderful to read about the lives of the great singers of India, how they imitated their teachers and how they sometimes became even greater than their teachers.

The object of Indian music is the training of the mind and the soul, for music is the best way of concentration. When you tell a person to concentrate on a certain object, the very fact of trying to concentrate makes his mind more disturbed. But music, which attracts the soul, keeps the mind concentrated. If one only knows how to appreciate it and give one's mind to it, keeping all other things away, one naturally develops the power of concentration.

Besides the beauty of music, there is the tenderness, which brings life to the heart. For a person of fine feelings, of kindly thought, life in the world is very trying. It is jarring, and it sometimes has a freezing effect. It makes the heart so to speak frozen. In that condition one experiences depression, and the whole of life becomes distasteful; the very life that is meant to be heaven becomes a place of suffering.

If one can focus one's heart on music, it is just like warming something that was frozen. The heart returns to its natural condition, and the rhythm regulates the beating of the heart, which helps to restore health of body, mind, and soul, and bring them to their proper tuning. The joy of life depends upon the perfect tuning of mind and body.

Chapter 18

SPIRITUAL DEVELOPMENT
BY THE AID OF MUSIC

The word "spiritual" does not apply to goodness or to wonder-working, the power of producing miracles, or to great intellectual power. The whole of life in all its aspects is one single music; and the real spiritual attainment is to tune oneself to the harmony of this perfect music.

What is it that keeps a person back from spiritual attainment? It is the denseness of this material existence, and the fact that he is unconscious of his spiritual being. His limitations prevent the free flow and movement that is the nature and character of life. Take for instance this denseness. There is a rock, and you want to produce sound from it, but it does not give any resonance; it does not answer your desire to produce sound. String or wire, on the contrary, will give an answer to the tone you want. You strike them and they answer. There are objects which give resonance; you wish to produce a sound in them, and they respond. They make your music complete. So it is with human nature. One person is heavy and dull; you tell him something, but he cannot understand; you speak to him, but he will not hear. He will not respond to music, to beauty, or to art. What is it? It is denseness.

There is another person who is ready to appreciate and understand music and poetry or beauty in any form, in character or in manner. Beauty is appreciated in every form by such a person, and it is this that is the awakening of the soul, which is the living condition of the heart. It is this that is the real spiritual attainment. Spiritual attainment is making the spirit alive, becoming conscious. When a person is not conscious of the soul and spirit but only of his material being, he is dense; he is far removed from spirit.

What is spirit and what is matter? The difference between spirit and matter is like the difference between water and ice: frozen water is ice, and melted ice is water. It is spirit in its denseness that we call matter; it is matter in its fineness that may be called spirit. Once a materialist said to me, "I do not believe in any spirit or soul or hereafter. I believe in eternal matter." I said to him, "Your belief is not very different from mine, only that which you call eternal matter I call spirit; it is a difference in terms. There is nothing to dispute about, because we both believe in eternity. So long as we meet in eternity, what difference does it make if the one calls it matter and the other calls it spirit? It is one life from beginning to end."

Beauty is born of harmony. What is harmony? Harmony is right proportion, in other words right rhythm. And what is life? Life is the outcome of harmony. At the back of the whole creation is harmony, and the whole secret of creation is harmony. Intelligence longs to attain to the perfection of harmony. What we call happiness, comfort, profit, or gain, all we long for and wish to attain is harmony; in a smaller or greater degree we are longing for harmony. Even in attaining the most mundane things, we always wish for harmony. But very often we do not adopt the right methods. Very often our methods are wrong. The object attained by both good and bad methods is the same, but the way one tries to attain it makes it right or wrong. It is not the object that is wrong, it is the method one adopts to attain it.

No one, whatever his station in life, wishes for disharmony, for all suffering, pain, and trouble is lack of harmony.

To obtain spirituality is to realize that the whole universe is one symphony. In this every individual is one note, and his happiness lies in becoming perfectly attuned to the harmony of the universe. It is not following a certain religion that makes one spiritual, or having a certain belief, or being a fanatic in regard to one idea, or even becoming too good to live in this world. There are many good people who do not even understand what spirituality means. They are very good, but they do not yet know what ultimate is. Ultimate good is harmony itself. For instance all the different principles and beliefs of the religions of the world, taught and proclaimed by priests and teachers but which man is not always able to follow and express, come naturally from the heart of someone who attunes himself to the rhythm of the universe. Every action, every word he speaks, every feeling he has, every sentiment he expresses is harmonious; they are all virtues, they are all religion. It is not following a religion, it is living a religion, making one's life a religion that is necessary.

Music is a miniature of the harmony of the whole universe, for the harmony of the universe is life itself. Man, being a miniature of the universe, shows harmonious and inharmonious chords in his pulsation, in the beat of his heart, and in his vibration, rhythm, and tone. His health or illness, his joy or discomfort, all show the music or lack of music in his life.

What does music teach us? Music helps us to train ourselves in harmony, and it is this that is the magic or the secret behind music. When you hear music that you enjoy, it tunes you and puts you in harmony with life. Therefore man needs music; he longs for music. Many say that they do not care for music, but these have not heard music. If they really heard music, it would touch their souls, and then certainly they could not help loving it. If not, it would only mean that they had not heard music sufficiently, and had not made their hearts calm and quiet in order to listen to it and to enjoy and appreciate it. Besides, music develops that faculty by which one learns to appreciate all that is good and beautiful in the form of art and science, and in the form of music and poetry one can then appreciate every aspect of beauty.

What deprives man of all the beauty around him is his heaviness of body or heaviness of heart. He is pulled down to earth, and by that everything becomes limited. But when he shakes off that heaviness and joy comes, he feels light. All good tendencies, such as gentleness, tolerance, forgiveness, love, and appreciation, all these beautiful qualities come by being light—light in the mind, in the soul, and in the body.

Where does music come from? Where does the dance come from? It all comes from that natural and spiritual life that is within. When that spiritual life springs forth, it lightens all the burdens that man has. It makes his life smooth, as though floating on the ocean of life. The faculty of appreciation makes one light. Life is just like the ocean. When there is no appreciation, no receptivity; man sinks like a piece of iron or stone to the bottom of the sea. He cannot float like a boat, which is hollow and which is receptive.

The difficulty in the spiritual path is always what comes from ourselves. A person does not like to be a pupil, he likes to be a teacher. If one only knew that the greatness and perfection of the great ones who have come from time to time to this world was in their being pupils and not in teaching! The greater the teacher, the better pupil he was. He learned from everyone, the great and the lowly, the wise and the foolish, the old and the young. He learned from their lives, and studied human nature in all its aspects.

Someone learning to tread the spiritual path must become like an empty cup in order that the wine of music and harmony may be poured into his heart. When a person comes to me and says, "Here I am. Can you help me spiritually?" and I answer, "Yes," very often he says, "I want to know first of all what you think about life or death, or the beginning and the end." Then I wonder what his attitude will be if his previously-conceived opinion does not agree with mine. He wants to learn, and yet he does not want to be empty. That means going to the stream of water with a covered cup. He wants the water, and yet the cup is covered, covered with preconceived ideas.

But where have the preconceived ideas come from? No idea can be called one's own. All ideas have been learned from one source or another, yet in time one comes to think they are one's own. And for those ideas a person will argue and dispute, although they do not satisfy him fully; but at the same time they are his battle-ground, and they will continue to keep his cup covered. Mystics therefore have adopted a different way. They have learned a different course, and that course is self-effacement, or in other words, unlearning what one has learned. This is how one can become an empty cup.

In the East it is said that the first thing to be learned is how to become a pupil. One may think that in this way one loses one's individuality, but what is individuality? Is it not what is collected? What are one's ideas and opinions? They are just collected knowledge, and this knowledge should be unlearned.

One would think that the character of the mind is such that what one learns is engraved upon it; how then can one unlearn it? Unlearning is completing this knowledge. To see a person and say, "That person is wicked; I dislike him," that is learning. To see further and recognize something good in that person, to begin to like him or to pity him, that is unlearning. When you see the goodness in someone whom you have called wicked, you have unlearned. You have unraveled that knot. First one learns by seeing with one eye; then one learns by seeing with two eyes, and that makes one's sight complete.

All that we have learned in this world is partial knowledge, but when this is uprooted by another point of view, then we have knowledge in its completed form. This is what is called mysticism. Why is it called mysticism? Because it cannot be put into words. Words will show us one side of it, but the other side is beyond words.

The whole manifestation is duality, the duality that makes us intelligent. Behind the duality is unity. If we do not rise beyond duality and move towards unity, we do not attain perfection, we do not attain spirituality.

This does not mean that our learning is of no use. It is of great use. It gives us the power of discrimination and of discerning differences. This makes the intelligence sharp and the sight keen, so that we understand the value of things and their use. It is all part of human evolution and all useful. So we must learn first, and unlearn afterwards. One does not look at the sky first when one is standing on the earth. First one must look at the earth and see what it offers to learn and to observe. But at the same time one should not think that one's life's purpose is fulfilled by looking only at the earth. The fulfillment of life's purpose is in looking at the sky.

What is wonderful about music is that it helps one to concentrate or meditate independently of thought. Therefore music seems to be the bridge over the gulf between form and the formless. If there is anything intelligent, effective, and at the same time formless, it is music. Poetry suggests form; line and color suggest form; but music suggests no form. It creates also that resonance which vibrates through the whole being, lifting the thought above the denseness of matter. It almost turns matter into spirit, into its original condition, through the harmony of vibrations touching every atom of one's whole being.

Beauty of line and color can go so far and no further. The joy of fragrance can go a little further. But music touches our innermost being and in that way produces new life, a life that gives exaltation to the whole being, raising it to that perfection in which lies the fulfillment of human life.

Chapter 19

THE PSYCHOLOGICAL INFLUENCE
OF MUSIC

In the field of music there is much to be explored, and the psychological influence of music seems little known to modern science.
We are taught that the influence of music or of sound and vibration comes to us and touches the senses from without; but there
is one question that remains; What is the source of the influence
that comes from within? The real secret of the psychological influence of music is hidden in that source, the source whence sound
comes.

It is plain and easy to understand that the voice has a certain
psychological value, that one voice differs from another, and that
every voice expresses its psychological value and has its psychological power. Very often one feels the personality of one who is
talking at a distance over the telephone. A sensitive person can feel
the effect of the voice alone, without seeing the speaker. Many do
not depend so much on words as upon the voice that is speaking
the words. This shows that psychological development is expressed in speaking, and more especially in singing.

In Sanskrit breath is called *prana,* the very life. And what is
voice? Voice is breath. If there is anything in life, in the human

constitution, that may be called life, it is the breath. And the sound of the voice is breath manifested outwardly. Therefore a person can best express himself in song or in what he says. If there is anything in the world that can give expression to the mind and the feelings, it is the voice. Very often is happens that a person speaks on a certain subject with a thousand words, and it has no influence; yet another person who expresses a thought in a few words can make a deep impression. This shows that the power is not in the words, but in what is behind the words; that is, in the psychological power in the voice, which comes from *prana.* According to its strength it impresses the listener.

The same thing is found in the finger tips of the violinist and in the lips of the flute player. According to the influence coming from his thought, the musician produces that influence through his instrument. He may be very skillful, but if his finger tips do not produce a feeling of life, he will not be a success. Apart from the music he plays there is the value of the *prana* or psychological power that he gives to what he plays.

In India there are vina players who do not need to play a symphony in order to exert an influence, in order to produce a spiritual phenomenon. They only have to take the vina in their hand and strike one note. As soon as they strike one note it penetrates through and through; in striking one or two notes they have tuned the audience. The sound works on all the nerves; it is like playing on the flute that is in every heart. Their instrument becomes simply a source, the response to which is found in the heart of every person, friend and foe alike. Let the most antagonistic person come before a real vina player and he cannot keep his antagonism. As soon as the notes have touched that person, he cannot prevent the vibrations that are created in him, he cannot help becoming a friend. Therefore in India such players are often called, instead of musicians, "vina magicians." Their music is magic.

A really musical soul is someone who has forgotten himself in music, just as a real poet is someone who forgets himself in poetry, and a worldly soul is someone who has lost himself in the world. And godly is the soul who has forgotten himself in God. All the great musicians—Beethoven, Wagner, and many others—who have left to the world a work that will always be treasured would not have been able to do so if they had not forgotten themselves in their work. They altogether lost the idea of their own being, and in that way they deepened and became one with the thing they had come to give to the world. The key to perfection is to be found in forgetting the self.

There are different ways of listening to music. There is a technical state, when a person who is developed in technique and has learned to appreciate better music feels disturbed by a lower grade of music. But there is a spiritual way, which has nothing to do with technique. It is simply to tune oneself to the music; therefore the spiritual person does not worry about the grade of the music. No doubt the better the music the more helpful it is for a spiritual person. But at the same time one must not forget that there are lamas in Tibet who do their concentrations and meditations while moving a kind of rattle, the sound of which is not specially melodious. They cultivate thereby that sense which raises a person by the help of vibration to the higher planes. There is nothing better than music as a means for the upliftment of the soul.

No doubt the power of music depends upon the grade of spiritual evolution that a person has touched. There is a story of Tansen, the great musician at the court of Akbar. The emperor asked him, "Tell me, O great musician, who was your teacher?" He replied, "Your Majesty, my teacher is a very great musician, but more than that. I cannot call him 'musician,' I must call him 'music.'" The emperor asked, "Can I hear him sing?" Tansen answered, "Perhaps, I may try. But you cannot think of calling him here to the court." The emperor said, "Can I go to where he is?" The musician said, "His pride may revolt even there, thinking that he is to sing before a king." Akbar said, "Shall I go as your servant?" Tansen answered, "Yes, there is hope then."

So both of them went up into the Himalayas, into the high mountains, where the sage had his temple of music in a cave, living with nature, in tune with Infinite. When they arrived the musician was on horseback and Akbar walking. The sage saw that the emperor had humbled himself to come to hear his music, and he was willing to sing for him. And when he felt in the mood for singing, he sang. His singing was great; it was a psychic phenomenon and nothing else. It seemed as if all the trees and plants of the

forest were vibrating; it was a song of the universe. The deep
impression made upon Akbar and Tansen was more than they
could stand; they went into a state of trance, of rest, of peace. And
while they were in that state, the master left the cave. When they
opened their eyes he was not there. The emperor said, "Oh, what
a strange phenomenon! But where has the master gone?" Tansen
said, "You will never see him in this cave again, for once a person
has had taste of this, he will pursue it, even if it costs him his life.
It is greater than anything in life."

When they were home again the emperor asked the musician
one day, "Tell me what raga, what mode did your master sing?"
Tansen told him the name of the raga and sang it for him, but the
emperor was not content, saying, "Yes, it is the same music, but
it is not the same spirit. Why is this?" The musician replied, "The
reason is this: that while I sing before you, the emperor of this
country, my master sings before God. That is the difference."

If we study life today, in spite of the great progress of science,
the radio, telephone, gramophone, and all the wonders of this age,
yet we find that the psychological aspect of music, poetry, and art
does not seem to develop as it should. On the contrary, it is going
backward. If we ask what is the reason, the answer will be in the
first place that the whole progress of humanity today is a mechanical progress, and this hinders the progress of individualism.

A musician has to submit to the laws of harmony and counterpoint. If he takes one step differently from the others his music is
questioned. When in Russia I asked Taneiev, a very great musician, who was the teacher of Scriabin, what he thought of Debussy's music. He said, "I cannot understand it. " It seems that we are
restricted by uniformity so that there is no scope. And you will
find the same thing in the medical and scientific worlds. But in art
especially, where the greatest freedom is necessary, one is restricted by uniformity. Painters and musicians cannot get their
work recognized. They must follow the crowd instead of following the great souls. And everything that is general is commonplace,
because the great mass of the people are not highly cultured.
Things of beauty and good taste are understood, enjoyed, and
appreciated by few, and it is not easy for the artists to reach those
few. In this way, what is called uniformity has become a hindrance

to individual development.

What is necessary today is that in children's education the psychological value of music should be taught. That is the only hope, the only way in which we can expect better results as time goes on. Children learning music should not only know the music, but they should know what is behind it and how it should be presented.

The secret of all magnetism, whether expressed through personality or through music, is life. It is life that charms, that is attractive. What we are always seeking for is life, and it is lack of life that may be called lack of magnetism. If musical teaching is given on this principle, it will be most successful in its psychological results. It is on the health of the physical body, on thought, on imagination, and on the heart (which is very often cold and frozen) that psychology depends. And it is this life that one expresses through one's finger tips on the violin, through one's voice when singing.

What the world is seeking, what human souls yearn for, is that life, whether it comes through music, color, lines, or words. What everyone desires is life. It is life that is the real source of healing; music can heal if life is put into it. There is no great secret about this, if only a person is able to understand the truth in its simplicity. When a person plays mechanically, the fingers running about the piano or violin almost automatically, it may create a temporary effect, but it soon passes. Music that heals the soul is music with a soothing effect. One can produce a soothing effect or a harsh effect, and this depends not only on the musician, but upon the composer also, upon the mood that inspired him. A person aware of the psychological effect of music will find it easy to understand what mood the composer was in when he wrote. If he put life and beauty into his music it will still prove to be beautiful and life-giving, even after a thousand years. No doubt study and qualifications help him to express himself better but what is really needed is that life which comes from the expanded consciousness, from the realization of the divine light that is the secret of all true art and the soul of all mysticism.

Of course there are two sides to this question: outward conditions and the presentation of the art. Outward conditions may be

more or less helpful. Music or a song performed before two or
three people who are congenial, sympathetic, harmonious, understanding, and responsive brings quite a different vibration, creates
a different effect, from the same music or song played before five
hundred people. What does this mean? It means that some people
are like instruments: when good music is presented before them
they respond, they become attuned to it, they are all music. They
take a share in the music, and therefore a phenomenon is created.
This phenomenon can reach even the highest ideal that is to be
expected of music, which is the realization of the soul's freedom,
what is called *nirvana* or *mukti* (salvation) in the East and "salvation" in the Christian world.

For there is nothing in this world that can help one spiritually
more than music. Meditation prepares, but music is the highest for
touching perfection. I have seen wonders happen through the
psychological power of music, but only when there were congenial
surroundings. Five or six people, a moonlit night or dawn or sun-
set. It seems that nature helps to complete the music, and both
work together, for they are one.

PART III

THE KNOWLEDGE OF VIBRATION

Everything in life is speaking, is audible, is communicating, in spite of its apparent silence. Therefore the word is not only what is audible to us, but the word is all.

INSIGHT

The presence of man speaks of his past, present, and future. This shows that every individual has a tone, a rhythm. But as it wants the musician's ears to sense the overtone of a sound and the artist's eyes to recognize the form from its shadow, and as it requires a keen sight to distinguish the degree of the reflection of light, so it wants the soul of the seer to see through all things in life, to penetrate below the surface and find out what is hidden in all things.

Chapter 20

COSMIC LANGUAGE

There are some people who know beforehand the coming of floods, the coming of rain, or a change of weather—all the various changes in nature. What is it that makes them know this? No doubt there are signs that become words for those who can read them, and by those signs they can understand the coming events of nature. For such people these signs are the language of nature, but for those who do not understand them, it is all just gibberish.

What is it that those who know not only astronomy but also astrology can see in the movements of the planets and stars concerning people, their past, their present, and their future? It is simply that there are signs that indicate the past, present, and future just as words would indicate them, and from these they learn of coming events. There are phrenologists who can learn things from the shape of the head. There are also those who understand physiognomy and can read from a face things that no one has told them. There are others who know an unimportant science such as palmistry, but even here the signs of the hands speak to them as loudly as the form of a face.

Then there are the natural conditions, such as the mother understanding the language of the little child who is not yet able to speak. Its tears and smiles and its looks explain to the mother its

145

moods, its pleasures and displeasures, its aspirations and wants. The heart of the lover knows the pleasure and displeasure and the changing mood of the beloved, without one word having been spoken. There are physicians who through their experience of life have become so skillful that before the patient speaks one word they have already found out what is the matter. There are businessmen in whom business is so engraved that as soon as a person comes to their shop they know whether he will buy or whether he will leave without buying. What does this show to us? That whatever our walk in life, whatever our profession, our business, or our occupation, through it all there is a sense within us that can understand the language spoken without words.

There is also another point that is closely connected with this one, and it is that everything in life is speaking, is audible, is communicating, in spite of its apparent silence. What we call in our everyday language "word" is only the word that is audible; what we consider hearing is only what we hear with our ears; for we do not know what else there is to hear. In point of fact there is nothing that is silent; everything that exists in this world is speaking, whether it seems living or not. Therefore the word is not only what is audible to us, but the word is all.

The real meaning of the word is life; and is there anything that is not life, whether silent or not? Take for instance a person not knowing the secret of the planets, their influence, their nature, or their character; what can they tell him? Nothing. He knows that there are planets, and that is all. As far as the science of astronomy goes, a person who has studied it may say that the planets have a certain influence upon the weather and upon the seasons. The astrologer will perhaps hear the voice of the planets more clearly, and he may say that the planets have also a certain influence upon the individual and on his life. We understand by this that to one the planet does not speak, to another it speaks in whispers, and to another it speaks loudly.

It is the same with physiognomy; to one person a person is a mystery, another knows something about him, and to a third he is like an open book. One physician finds it necessary to make an examination of a patient with all kinds of instruments, another physician likes to ask the pateint about his condition, and a third physician just looks at the patient and knows perhaps more about him than the patient himself.

Is it not the same thing with art? We see that one person goes to a picture gallery, looks at different pictures and only notices different colors and lines. He is pleased to look at them and that is all; he knows nothing more about it. There is another person who sees the historical subject of the picture, and he is more interested than the first because the picture has spoken more to him. But here is a third person for whom the pictures are living. The picture that he sees, that he appreciates, communicates with him. He reads in it the meaning that was put into it by the artist; it is revealed to him by looking at it. Therefore, through the medium of the picture, the thought or the ideal of one person is known to another. In the same way to one person music is a noise, or perhaps a harmonious group of notes, a pastime and a kind of amusement. To another it gives some joy, some pleasure; he feels the music that is coming towards him. But there is a third person who sees the soul of the one who is performing the music and who sees the spirit of the one who wrote the music, even if it were written a thousand years ago.

Is not everything communicative? Whether it be in art or science or in whatever form, life expresses its meaning. If one were only able to understand this one could understand everything. The one who does not understand this will not understand anything. His sense is closed; it is just like being deaf. In the same way his sense of communicating with things has become dull; he does not understand. But if a person does not hear, he should not say that life is not speaking. In the same way, if a person cannot sense the meaning of life, he should not say that life has no meaning . The word is everywhere, and the word is continually speaking.

By "word" is not meant a word that is audible to the ears; by word is meant all that is conveyed, that is expressed, and that comes as a revelation. It means all that one hears with one's ear, that one smells with one's nose, that one tastes or touches with the different senses, all that becomes intelligible—that is a word. In other words, life's mission is to convey something, and everything that it conveys is a word, through whichever sense one experiences it.

It is not only upon the five senses—taste, hearing, seeing, smelling, and touching—that the word depends. We only call them by different names because we experience them through five different organs, but in reality there is only one sense, a sense that experiences life through the vehicle or medium of the five external senses. As life is experienced through these five different directions, the experience of life becomes divided into five different experiences. That is to say, the word or life becomes visible, tangible, audible, and can be smelled or tasted. But besides these five aspects in which we are accustomed to hear the word there is another way of hearing it, independently of the five senses, and this way of hearing the word is called the intuitive way. When you meet someone, whether you are satisfied with him or dissatisfied, whether he has attracted your sympathy or antipathy, you cannot say that by seeing or hearing that person you have recognized him. But you can say that you had a certain impression of him . This shows that there is a language that is beyond the senses, a language that we are capable of understanding if the one sense is open to a certain degree. Some people have never experienced it; some have experienced it more and others less. Some are conscious, some are unconscious; but when a disaster is coming, a sorrow, a failure, a success, one generally feels it.

No doubt someone with a tender heart, with great sympathy, with love awakened in his heart is more capable of experiencing this sentiment. It is this feeling that may be called intuition, something that does not depend upon the senses. A woman feels it more perhaps than a man. Very often a woman says to a man, "I feel it; I feel that it is going to be a success or a failure," and when he asks her for what reason, as a man is a very reasoning being, she will still only say, "I feel it." There is a language that she understands; a man will not hear it.

Then there is another experience. It is not only the experience of spiritual or very advanced people, it is also known to the artist, to the material person, to the inventor. He may not believe it, but the experience comes all the same: it is a sense of how to work out his invention or how to form his system, how to make a plan, how to write his poetry or to arrange something that he wants to arrange. People may attribute the achievements of the great inventors to their having studied mechanics and may feel that it is the result of this that gives them their ability, but there are thousands of students who have studied mechanics, yet not every one is an inventor.

The one who really accomplishes something surely accomplishes it by the help of inspiration. One may ask all kinds of artists,—a painter, a draftsman, a singer, a dancer, a writer, a poet —"Can you always do the work you wish to do as perfectly and as excellently as you are able to sometimes?" The answer will be "No, I never know when and how it will be done. Inspiration comes, and sometimes I am able to do it. It comes, but I do not know when or where." A poet may try for six months to write a poem that his soul is longing for and never be able to finish it, and yet it is finished in a few minutes if that moment of inspiration comes. The poet cannot imagine how such a thing can come in a few minutes, something that is wonderful and complete in itself, that gives him the greatest satisfaction and that is living. The great musicians too have not generally taken a long time to write their most beautiful compositions, their masterpieces. Much of what took them a long time to write is of less importance; it is what they wrote and completed in a few inspired moments that is living and will always live. It is the same with all aspects of art; creative art depends upon inspiration. Mechanical art may be developed, a person may be highly qualified, but it is a dead art. The only living art is the art that comes from a living source, and that living source is called inspiration.

What then is inspiration? Inspiration is the same word that has been spoken of all through this book. It is the hearing of that word that comes from within, and a person hears it and expresses it in the form of line, color, notes, words or in whatever other form. The most interesting and wonderful thing is that the same inspiration may come to several persons. It is the same word that is coming to these persons. One is drawing it in the form of a line, another is composing it in the form of notes, another writes it down in words, another paints it as colors. This shows that artistic inspiration, inventive genius, every form in which the meaning of life wishes to express itself, has another aspect besides what we see in the external life.

Then what is this inspiration, this word that is the soul of inspiration? It is beauty in itself, energy, wisdom, and harmony in itself. It is energy because it gives the greatest joy when expressed by an artist or by an inventor; it is wisdom because it brings an understanding of accomplishment; it is light because the thing that one wants to make becomes clear to one and there is no more obscurity; it is harmony because it is by harmony that beauty is achieved.

There is another form of this, which is attained by a greater enlightenment, by a greater awakening of the soul. This form can be pictured as a person going through a large room where there are all kinds of things exhibited, and yet there is no light except a searchlight in his own hand. If he throws its light on music, on notes and rhythm, the music becomes clear to him; if he throws his light on words the words become clear to him; if he throws his light on color, all color become distinct; if he throws his light on line, all lines in the most harmonious and beautiful form become clearly visible to him.

This searchlight may become greater still and may reach still further. It may be thrown on the past, and the past may become as clear as it was to the prophets of ancient times. It may be thrown on the future, and it is not only a sense of precaution that a person may gain by it, but also a glimpse into the future. This light may be thrown upon living beings, and the living beings may become like open books to him. It may be thrown on objects, and the objects may reveal to him their nature and secret. If this light were thrown within oneself, then the self would be revealed to him and he would become enlightened as to his own nature and his own character.

It is this form of experience, this way of knowing, that may be called revelation. Through it one accomplishes the purpose of life, or as the mystics have said, the word that was lost is found. Every child is born crying; his crying conveys that he has lost something. What has he lost? He has lost the word. This means that all he sees conveys nothing to him; he knows not what it is. He seems to be lost in a new country where he has been sent. But as he begins to recognize either his mother or those around him, the color and the lines and all the things of this world begin to communicate with him. He begins to know things with the hands, ears, nose, and mouth, and in this way he begins to know the word that is within.

It is this communication that is the sustenance of life. It is not food or drink which keeps a person alive, it is this communication through the different senses, to the extent that he understands what they have to say, that makes man live. When we think of our life, when we compare the pain we suffer in our life with the pleasure we have, the portion of pleasure is so small. Besides, what little pleasure there is also costs something, and therefore it resolves into pain. If that is the nature of life, how could we live in this life if there were not this communication, if there were not this word which, to a greater or lesser extent, we hear from all things and from nature itself?

The fulfillment of this communication is that no wall or barrier stands anymore between us, nor between the life within and without. This is the longing of our soul; it is in this that revelation comes; it is in this that lies the purpose of our life.

Chapter 21

INSIGHT

Insight shows itself in different aspects: in impression, intuition, inspiration, dream, and revelation.

How does one get impressions? All impressions reach the brain through the nerve centers. They are mostly taken in by the breath, but by this one does not mean the breath inhaled through the nostrils. He who is able to get an impression of a person need not wait to see how he will turn out; he knows it instantly. Very often one may have a feeling at first sight whether someone will be one's friend or prove unfriendly.

When someone comes and tells me, "I am very interested in your philosophy, but before I take it up I want to study it," he may study for a thousand years and he will not get to that insight. It is the first moment: either you are my friend or not my friend. When two persons meet a confidence is established; one does not need years in order to develop friendship.

Everyone receives an impression on seeing a certain person or looking at a certain situation. One may not believe that impression, but all the same it is there. The first impression tells a person whether he will be successful or not, whether a person is right or not, whether there will be friendship between two people ot not. When this faculty is developed, a person can get an impression of a place and of persons and of conditions. Impressions come to those whose minds are still; those whose minds are active cannot take impressions. For the mind is like water: when the pool of water is disturbed, one cannot see any reflection in it. Thus purity of mind is necessary. In which sense? All that is called wrong is not necessarily wrong; some things are called wrong because of a certain moral, a certain principle, originated by the mechanical action of the mind. When the mind is kept pure from all activity that disturbs it, then it becomes like pure water. Very often the water of the mind is polluted, but when the mind is in its pure condition, then naturally it can take impressions.

The mind may be likened to a photographic plate. If several impressions have been made upon it, then there can be no other impressions. That is why the mind should be kept pure from all undesirable impressions, in order that every impression may be clear.

Intuition is still deeper, for by intuition one gets a warning. Intuitively one feels, "This person will one day deceive me or turn against me; or he will prove faithful to me, sincere, to be relied upon. Or in this particular business I will have success or failure." One knows it. But the difficulty is in distinguishing the right intuition. That is the great question, for as soon as intuition springs up, reason, its competitor, rises also and says, "No, it is not so." Then there is conflict in the mind and it is hard to distinguish, because there are two feelings at the same time. If one makes a habit of catching the first intuition and saving it from being destroyed by reason, then intuition is stronger and one can benefit by it. There are many intuitive people, but they cannot always distinguish between intuition and reason and sometimes they mix then up, for very often the second thought, being the later, is more clear to one than the first. Therefore the intuition is forgotten and reason remembered. Then a person calls it intuition, and it is not so. Reason and intuition are competitors, and yet both have their place, their importance, and their value. The best thing would be first to try and catch the intuition, to distinguish and know and recognize it as intuition, and then to reason it out.

Besides, those who doubt intuition, their intuition doubts them. In other words, the doubt becomes a wall between themselves and their intuitive faculty. And there is a psychological action: as soon as intuition has sprung up, doubt and reason spring up too, so that the vision becomes blurred. One should develop self-confidence. Even if one proves to be wrong once or twice or thrice one should still continue; in time one will develop trust in one's intuition, and then intuition will be clear.

Women are naturally more intuitive than men. The reason is that a woman is more responsive by nature and more sympathetic; therefore she can perceive intuition more clearly. Very often a man may reason and think and yet not come to a conclusion, to a clear understanding, while a woman, or any more intuitive person, in one moment is clear about a certain question, a certain point. That comes from intuition. Intuition is a faculty of the heart that feels deeply, be it of a man or a woman; the quality of intuition belongs to a sympathetic heart.

The intuition of dogs and cats and of horses sometimes seems to be more clear than that of man. They know when there is going to be an accident, when death is going to occur in a family. They know beforehand and give people warning. But people are so busy in their daily occupations that they do not respond to the intuition of the animals. People in the East believe that small insects know about happenings and give a warning to those who can understand it, and it is true. Besides, birds always give a warning of storm and wind, and of rain and the absence of rain. Mankind is naturally more capable of intuition, but because his mind is absorbed by a hundred things, his deep feelings become so blunted in everyday life that he ignores the existence of intuition or inspiration, and so this faculty itself becomes blunted and he feels and knows less than the animals. The human body is a vehicle, a telescope, an instrument by which one can perceive the knowledge of oneself within, of conditions, of others, and of everything outside.

The question is, how does one develop this faculty of intuition? The first thing is self-confidence. When there is no self-confidence one cannot develop this faculty, because it comes more and more by one's belief in it. When a person doubts and says, "Is this an intuition, will this really help me, or shall I be deceived by my own intuition?" then naturally reason produces confusion in the mind and intuition is destroyed. There are many intuitive people, and their intuition has been destroyed only by this doubt that arises in their minds, whether their intuition is right or wrong. That is why they lose this faculty of intuition. Every faculty needs nurturing; if it is not nurtured it becomes blunted and destroyed and one can make no more use of it. Besides, a person may underestimate the value of this faculty in his life. He then naturally destroys it. This faculty disappears also by a too-speedy action of the mind. When a person thinks of a thousand things in a short time, the mind becomes too active and then one cannot perceive intuition, which needs a certain rhythm, a certain concentration.

A further aspect of insight is inspiration. The difference between inspiration and instinct is that what we recognize in the lower creation as instinct is the same as that which works through the human mind in the form of intuition or inspiration. One may say from a biological point of view that the lower creatures are born with certain instincts, such as the inclination to fly, to defend themselves with their horns, or to bite with their teeth. All the faculties they show are born with them. They are not only the heritage brought from their ancestors, they do not belong to their family only, they are a property of the spirit. From the spirit all living beings get guidance in the form of inclination. What we recognize as instinct in the lower creations is inspiration in mankind. Today, as science is increasing and as materialism prevails, humanity is forgetting the heritage that it has from the spirit and attributes all knowledge and experience to the material existence of the physical world. In this way we deprive ourselves of those gifts which could be called our own and without which we cannot live a fuller life.

Inspiration comes to poets, writers, inventors, scientists. Where does it come from, what is its source? Why does not the inspiration of a musician come to a poet; why does not a poet's inspiration come to a musician? Why should it reach the person to whom it belongs? The reason is that there is a mind behind all minds, that there is a heart that is the source of all hearts, and that there is a spirit that collects and accumulates all the knowledge that every living being has had. No knowledge or discovery that has ever been made is lost. It all accumulates and collects in that mind as an eternal reservoir. This is what is recognized by the seers as the divine mind. From this mind all vision can be drawn. The mind of the poet is naturally exalted; that is why it becomes enlightened by the divine mind. From the divine mind all that is needed manifests. It may be that a poet works without inspiration for six months on a poem, and it gives satisfaction neither to the poet nor to others, who find it mechanical. And there is another one who receives the inspiration in a moment and puts it down. He can never correct what he has written, he can never change it. No one can change it. If it is changed, it is spoiled. It is something that comes in a moment and it is perfect in itself. It is a piece of art, it is an example of beauty, and it comes so easily. That is inspiration.

Many have tried to imitate inspired people, in poetry or in scientific inventions. They tried, but they never reached that perfection which came in a moment's time. Those who were inspired never searched after it, it came in a mood. All that comes from inspiration is living; it always keeps its value. There are writings of such poets in the East as Rumi of Persia and Kalidasa of India, and now, after thousands of years, their writings are read by people and they are never old and people never tire of them. It is the same with Shakespeare. He has made a living world. The more time passes, the more it lives, the more it is appreciated. It is forever living. That is the character of inspiration. And it only comes to the one whose mind is still and whose thought is absorbed in the beauty of the work that he is contemplating. The mind of the musician who knows little of this world except music is concentrated and focused on the beauty of his art. Naturally he will draw inspiration. So it is with the poet. But when the mind is absorbed in a thousand things, then it is not focused, then it cannot receive inspiration.

How is inspiration developed? By concentration. An inspired poet is he whose mind is fully fixed on the idea he wishes to express; he is floating, so to speak, in the beauty of it. His mind becomes focused and inspiration mechanically comes to him. A person who troubles about inspiration, who wants to drag it towards him, cannot get it; it does not belong to him. In order to get it he must float in the idea, he must merge all his heart in its beauty. He must be so positively focused to that spirit of beauty that inspiration may naturally flow into him.

The dream or vision is another aspect of insight. Very often people consider a dream as an automatic action of the mind, but this is not always the case. There is no movement in the mind that is meaningless. Every motion and action has a meaning behind it, every motion is directed towards something, either with intention or without. There is no movement, there is no action that is not directed from some source or other.

There are three kinds of dreams. In the first a person sees his mind working along the same lines as it did during the day, at the same time suggesting the past, present, or future. Then there is another kind of dream when the mind sees in everything quite the opposite of what is going to happen. There is a third type of dream in which one sees something out of the past actually happening, or sees what is going to happen in the future. This proves that everything on the physical plane is first formed in the inner planes and then registered on the mind in the dream. When one is concentrated one sees the happening more clearly.

There is also a state of dream in which one sees a vision. This happens in a meditative condition. A vision is more communicative, more expressive; it may be a warning that is given for the future, or an incident of the past may be made known. In the vision one can go still further and communicate with the unseen world. But a vision only comes to those who are born with that faculty or have developed that faculty in the mind by becoming fully concentrated.

A dream may be symbolical, and this is the most interesting type of dream. The greater the person, the subtler the symbolism of his dream will be. When someone is gross the symbolism will be gross. The more evolved the person is, the more fine, artistic, and subtle the dream will be. For instance, for a poet there will be poetic symbols, and the dream of a musician will have musical symbols; in the dream of the artist there will be sumbols of art.

In the realistic dream one actually sees what is going to happen. All that we call accident is only our conception; because we did not know it beforehand we call it accident. This also gives us insight into what we call fate. But there is a plan: it is all planned out and known beforehand to the spirit and to those who know.

There are sages who know of their death a year before. There is no such thing as accident. When a person does not know, it means he does not see, but it is there.

Revelation is still greater. It is the perfection of insight. It means a higher development when one has revelation, and it begins when a person feels in tune with everybody, everything, and every condition. But in order to come to that stage one must develop according to it. The heart must be tuned to the stage and the pitch where one feels at-one-ment with persons, objects, and conditions. For instance, when one cannot bear the climate, it only means that one is not in harmony with the climate; when one cannot get on with persons, that one is not in harmony with them; when one cannot get on with certain affairs, that one is not in harmony with those affairs. If conditions seem hard, it shows that one is not in harmony with the conditions.

Revelation came to the saints and saviors of humanity. It is not just a tale when we hear that the saints spoke with trees and plants in the wilderness, that a voice from the sea rose and the saints heard it, that masters talked with the sun, moon, and stars. For the deeper a person dives into life, the more he is convinced that all is living, whether beings or objects, whether art or nature; whatever he sees, whatever he perceives through the senses, whatever he can touch, all that is intelligible to him. It may not be seen and it may not be known by anybody else, but everything is communicating. Once a person begins to communicate with nature, with art, he begins to have the proof of this, for everything begins to speak. As the great poet of Persia, Sa'adi, said, "Every leaf of the tree becomes a page of the Book when once the heart is opened and it has learned to read."

When revelation begins, a person does not need to converse. Before talking, he knows what the other wishes to say. The condition of the person or the persons before him is revealed; it is like reading a letter. The person may speak to him, but without his speaking he knows. This is not thought-reading, not telepathy, not psychometry or clairvoyance as people think. Revelation is all the phenomena there are. What is it? It is a fuller development of inspiration. When the intuitive faculty is fully developed, one receives revelation. All dumb creatures and mute things begin to speak. For what are words? Are they not covers over ideas? No feeling can ever be expressed in words, no idea can be put fully into verse. A true glimpse of ideas and feelings can only be perceived in that plane which is feeling itself.

Revelation depends upon purity of mind. Very often someone who is worldly-wise is not really wise. Intellectuality is one thing; wisdom is another thing. Not all the knowledge learned from books and from experiences in the world and collected in the mind as learning is wisdom. When the light from within is thrown upon this knowledge, then the knowledge from outer life and the light coming from within make a perfect wisdom; and it is that wisdom that guides man on the path of life.

Those who received revelation have given us sacred books such as the Bible, the Qur'an, and the Bhagavad Gita. Hundreds and thousands of years have passed and their sacred teachings remain alive even now. But at the same time we must know that what they have given in the form of preaching, in the form of teachings, is the interpretation of the living wisdom that cannot be fully expressed in words. One can only know that living knowledge when one has experienced it oneself by the opening of the heart. It is then that the purpose of life is fulfilled.

One can easily trace a person's past from what he says and from how he expresses it. The past is ringing in the heart of man like a bell. The heart of man is a gramophone record that goes on by itself. If it has finished talking, one has only to wind the machine; then it goes on again. Man's present is the re-echo of his past. If he has been through suffering, even if he is better he will vibrate the same; outer conditions will not change his inner being. If he has been happy, even in a troublous time his heart will vibrate the past. People who have been against one another, if by chance they become friends, will still feel in themselves the heating of the pulse of hostility in the past. Great kings who have been dethroned, imprisoned—still one can feel their past vibrating in their atmosphere.

The past lives, and one cannot easily destroy it, however greatly one may wish to close it. It gets hold of the human tongue to express itself. As every heart is eager to tell its story, so the past is more eager to sing its legend. It only seeks the way to express itself. A Sufi, therefore, does not need spirit communications to learn the past or astrological science to discover what has happened. To him every person explains his past without even one word spoken. But by the speech of a person about his past the Sufi can see what is hidden behind it, what is being said and what remains unsaid. He need not trace the past in history or in traditions. He who can read has but to open his eyes and all is written before him.

As there is a shadow of every form, as there is a re-echo of every sound, and as there is a reflection of every light, so there is a re-impression of everything one sees, hears, or perceives. But as it wants the musician's ears to sense the overtone of a sound, an artist's eyes to recognize the form from its shadow, and a keen sight to distinguish the degree of the reflection of light, so it wants the soul of a seer to see through all things in life. The seer's eye is in the heart of every soul, but it is the attitude that keeps everyone looking down to the earth instead of raising his eyes upwards. The average tendency is to see on the surface.

It is not true that the average person cannot see any further, but the average person does not think that there is anything further, so he does not take the trouble to see any further. There are many who are intelligent enough to perceive all that is behind things, but the first thing that makes their view limited is the narrow range of their interest. They are not interested enough to take trouble about things they neither know nor believe. They would be glad to have intuition if it came without their taking any trouble. There are many who can think, but they do not wish to take the trouble of thinking.

There are two things necessary in order to perceive: one thing is openness; the other thing is effort made in that direction. When contemplating anything the mind must be free from all that stands in the way; that is called openness. Also, one must arrive by the help of concentration at focusing one's mind on a certain object. The next thing is to be interested enough in all things that one comes in contact with and cares to know about that one may penetrate below the surface and find out what is hidden in all things. Every line that is deeply engraved on the surface of the mind may be likened to a vein through which the blood runs, keeping it alive. While the blood is running it is productive of offshoots of that deepset line. There are moments when a kind of congestion comes in a line where the blood is not running, and there are no offshoots. This congestion can be broken by some outer influence. When the congested line is touched by an outer influence related to that line, then this sets the blood running again and offshoots arising, expressing themselves in thoughts. It is just like a waking or sleeping state of the lines. As one note of music can be fully audible at a time, so one line of offshoots can be intelligible at a time, and it is the warmth of interest that keeps the blood running in that particular line. There may be other lines where the blood is alive also; still, if they are not kept warm by one's interest they become congested and thus paralyzed. Yet the blood is there, the life is there; it awaits the moment to awaken. The sorrows of the past, the fears of the past, the joys of the past can be brought to life after ages, and could give exactly the same sensation that one had experienced formerly.

The more one knows the mystery of this phenomenon, the more one learns to understand that there is a world in oneself, that in one's mind there is the source of happiness and unhappiness, the source of health and illness, the source of light and darkness, and that it can be awakened either mechanically or at will, if only one knew how to do it. Then one does not blame his ill fortune nor complain of his fellow man. One becomes more tolerant, more joyful, and more loving toward his neighbor, because one knows the cause of every thought and action and sees it all as the effect of a certain cause. A physician would not revenge himself on a patient in an asylum, even if the patient hit him, for he knows the cause. Psychology is the higher alchemy, and one must not study it only without practicing it. Practice and study must go together, which opens the door to happiness for every soul.

The modern psychologist adopts a system of psychoanalysis in order to investigate the state of mind of his patient, and the attorney in the law court cross-examines in order to investigate the truth of the case. These methods are more or less useful when they are rightly practiced, but the chief thing for getting to the mind of a person is to see the person, in his form, in his expression, in his movements, in his words, in his imagination, and in the way of his action. But the principal thing that helps in seeing the mind of another person is the light of intuition. Nothing else, neither rules nor studies nor standard of understanding, can help without the development of intuition. One thing must be remembered: that man shows the lines engraved upon his mind in his form, expression, in his movements, words, in his imagination and action, and it is possible to detect a person from his word before his action, or from his movement before his action, or from his expression before his words, or from his form before even he had time to imagine. Therefore, the knowledge of this can save a great deal of trouble in life, if one only knows beforehand how to act with different people.

The person who acts in the same manner with every person, however good or kind he may be, must always meet with disappointments. As the direction of the fire is upward and that of the water is downward, so the direction of one person is different from that of another. Therefore, if you expect a person who is going to the south to take your message to the north, you will find yourself mistaken in the end. Generally a person dealing with others thinks of the affair more than of the person. Really the person must be the chief object of study, not the affair, for the affair depends upon the person. In the East there is a superstition of a dog or a cat or a horse being lucky or unlucky for the person who possesses it, but the reality of this idea can be most seen in every human being with whom one comes in contact through one's everyday life. He must surely bring something with him: pleasure, displeasure, happiness, unhappiness, good or bad influence. Everyone in himself is a world, and every new contact is a new world opened before us.

Chapter 22

THE LEGEND OF THE PAST
(IMPRESSIONS)

The whole of manifestation in all its aspects is a record upon which the voice is reproduced, and that voice is a person's thought. There is no place in the world, neither desert, forest, mountain, nor house, town, nor city, where there is not some voice that, once engraved upon it, has continued ever since. No doubt every such voice has its limit: one voice may continue for thousands of years, another voice for several months, another for some days, another for some hours or moments. For everything that is created intentionally or unintentionally has a life; it has a birth and so it has a death. In fact it has a beginning and an end.

One can experience this by feeling the atmosphere of different places. Sitting upon rocks in the mountains one often feels the vibrations of someone who has been sitting there before; sitting in a forest, in a wilderness, one can feel what has been the history of that place. It may be that there was a city, that there was a house there, that people lived there, and now it has turned into a wilderness. One begins to feel the history of the whole place; it communicates with one.

Every town has its particular voice. It is, so to speak, telling aloud who lived in the town and how they lived, what was their life; it tells of their stage of evolution, it tells of their doings, it tells of the results produced by their actions. People perceive the vibrations of haunted houses. It is only because the atmosphere is stirred, it is intense and therefore it is often felt distinctly. But there is no town, there is no place which does not have its own voice.

By this is meant the voice that has been engraved upon it, so that it has become a reproducing record of what has been given to it consciously or unconsciously. Where many people have lived there is a dominating voice, which is more distinct than other voices. But at the same time, as one feels what a composer wishes to convey through the whole music he writes, with all the different instruments, so even the different voices that are going on together make one result. And that result is like a symphony to the person who can hear them together.

A collective thought comes especially when one can perceive it in a town, in a new city. It is a kind of voice of the past and a voice of the present, a voice of all as one voice, and it has its peculiar and particular effect. The whole tradition is in that voice. One who can hear it clearly feels as if the city is speaking about its past, about its present.

In remote places sometimes the voices have become buried, and there is a kind of overtone that is most gentle and soothing. For the voices have gone, and the vibration remains as an atmosphere. If that place has always been a desert it is still more elevating, because it has its own natural atmosphere, and it is most uplifting. Yet if some travelers have passed through it, it brings their voice to us. Even that is much better than what one perceives and feels in cities, in towns, because in nature man is quite a different person. The more he is in nature, the more what is artificial falls away from him, and he becomes more at one with nature. Therefore his predisposition, which is nature and truth, which is goodness, all comes up and makes life a kind of dream for him, a romance, a lyric. And even his thought there, as a human thought, begins to sing through nature.

When Abraham returned from Egypt after his initiation into the mysteries of life, he arrived at Mecca. A stone was set there in memory of the initiation that he had just received from the ancient esoteric school of Egypt, and the voice that was put into it by the singing soul of Abraham continued and became audible to those who could hear it. Prophets and seers since that time have made pilgrimages to this stone of *ka'bah*; the voice continued and still exists. A place like Mecca, a desert with nothing of interest, where the ground was not fertile nor the people very evolved, where no science or art was cultivated and no business or industry flourished, has had an attraction for millions of people who only went for one purpose, and that was pilgrimage. What was it and what is it? It is the voice that has been put into the place in a stone. A stone has been made to speak, and it speaks to those whose ears are open.

The thought of a person who is evolved has a greater power than what the thought contains because the person is the life of that thought, the thought is the cover over that life. Perhaps Abraham would not have been able to engrave any other stone with that impression which he had at that moment, when he came with his first impression after his initiation. Perhaps at that time the impression was more intense than at any other time in his life before or after. As he said, "That stone I set here as a memory of initiation, of God to be understood as One God, that this stone shall remain forever as a temple." Abraham was not a rich man; he could not build a temple other than that stone. But that stone has remained for a much longer time than many other temples built with riches.

This is only one example, but there are numberless examples to be found. For instance, the atmosphere of Benares and the vibrations of Ajmer, where Khwaja Moinuddin Chishti lived and meditated and died. There is a tomb of the saint, and there is a continual vibration going on, a vibration so strong that a person who is meditative can sit there and would like to sit there forever. It is in the midst of the city, but it has a feeling of wilderness, because in that place the saint sat and meditated on *saut-e sarmad*, the cosmic symphony. Through his hearing that cosmic music continually, there has been produced cosmic music.

The thought of the people coming after would not prolong the thought, it would add to it. For instance, if there is a flute, then the clarinet, the trumpet, or the trombone added to it makes up the volume of sound, but there is always one instrument which plays the first part. The main voice stands as a breath, and all the other voices attracted to it build a form around it. The breath remains as life. The form may compose and decompose, yet the breath remains as life.

There was a wonderful experience during the lifetime of the Khwaja of Ajmer. To visit this saint, a great master, Khwaja Abdul Qadir Jilani came from Baghdad, who was also an advanced soul. A remarkable meeting took place in Ajmer, the two coming together. Now the latter was very strict in his religious observances, and the religious people where he came from would not have music. So naturally in order to respect his belief the Khwaja of Ajmer had to sacrifice his daily musical meditation. But when the time came the symphony began by itself, and everybody began to listen. Khwaja Abdul Qadir felt that music was going on without playing. He said to the saint, "Even if religion prohibits it, it is for others, not for you."

Every place where a person sits and thinks a moment on any subject takes up the thought of that person. It takes the record of what has been spoken, so that no one can hide his thought or feeling; it is recorded even in the seat he has been sitting on while thinking. Many who are sensitive by sitting in that place begin to feel it. Sometimes the effect is quite contrary. When a person sits down on a certain seat, the moment he does so he may have a thought quite foreign to him, a feeling that does not belong to him. This is because on that seat there was that thought, that feeling, vibrating. As a seat can hold the vibrations of the thought for a much longer time than the life of the person who has thought or spoken, so an influence remains in every place where one sits, where one lives, where one thinks or feels, where one rejoices or where one sorrows; and thus it continues for an incomparably longer time than the life of the person who has spoken or thought.

Also, the ancient people made the tomb of a person where his seat had been, where there was his atmosphere, where he had lived. The tomb was a mark to show that he used to sit there. Very often in India, where cremations take place, they make a seat as a mark of the place where the one who died had produced his vibrations. He may not be buried there, but they have made a mark just the same.

The secret of the idea of a blessing to be found in the holy places lies in this principle, that the holy place is no longer a place; it has become a living being. The prophets having proclaimed for ages the name of God. The law of the divine Being in the Holy Land makes it still living, and it has attraction for the whole world. They say that on Sa'adi's grave roses have sprung up for ages, that his grave has never been without roses. It is credible, for he wrote his *Rose Garden* in the thought of beauty. Although the mortal body of Sa'adi has passed, yet the beauty of his thought, once voiced, is still continuing, and if it maintained roses in the place of his burial for centuries it would not be surprising.

Often people wonder why the Hindus, who have such a great philosophical mind and deep insight into mysticism, should believe in such a thing as a sacred river. It is true that it is symbolical, but besides this there is another meaning to it. The great mahatmas lived on the heights of the Himalayas where the Ganges and Jumna streams rise, which then take different directions till they again unite and become one. This is really a phenomenon deep in its symbolism as well as in its actual nature. In its symbolism the rivers begin as one and then turn into duality, and after the two have been separated for many miles they are attracted to one another and they meet in a place that is called *Sangam,* at Allahabad, a place of pilgrimage. This gives us in its interpretation the ideal of the whole of manifestation, which is one in the beginning, dual in its manifestation, and unites in the end. But besides this the thoughts of the great Mahatmas, flowing with the water, combined with this living stream of Ganges, coming into the world. It brought the vibrations of the great ones, and it spoke as a voice of power, of wakening, of blessing, of purity, and of unity to those who heard it.

Those unconscious of the blessing have also been blessed by bathing in the same river. For it was not only water; it was a thought besides, a most vital thought, a thought of power and with life in it. Those who have perceived that have perceived its secret. For in many poems in the Sanskrit language one reads how in the waves of the Ganges and of the Jumna seers heard the voice of the evolved souls and felt their atmosphere as a breath current of those advanced beings coming through the water.

There is a tank in Mecca, a tank from which the prophets of all ages have drunk water. This tank is called *Zemzem.* They not only drank water, they received from it what had been put into it, and then they charged it with what they had to give to it. Even now pilgrims go there and receive the water as a blessing.

In India there is a place where a great healer, Miran Datar, used to sit. Throughout his life he healed thousands of patients; many he healed instantly. In the same place his grave was made, and till this day people are attracted to his tomb, and many who touch this place are healed instantly.

There is a story told in the East of five brothers who were traveling. Each of them was gifted in some way, but when they arrived at a certain place they suddenly found that they had lost their talents. They were confused, disappointed, and they were wondering about the reason of such an experience until the wisest among them, by the power of concentration, found in the end that it was the effect of the place. The place had lost its life, it was a dead place. Everyone who came there felt as if he had no life in him; the inner life had gone. We see the same happen in land, which after having been used for many thousands of years has lost the strength, the vitality of the earth. If externally the land can lose it, then internally also the vitality, the breath of the land can be lost. Often one feels most inspired in one place, in another place most depressed; in one place confused, in another place one feels dull, one finds nothing of interest, nothing to attract one. One may think it is the effect of the weather, but there are places outwardly most beautiful in nature, with wonderful climates, and yet you do not feel inspired there. If an artist is born in a dead country, his talent cannot be developed there. There is no nourishment, his artistic impulse will become paralyzed. Even a plant is not sufficient in itself; it must have air, sun, water. Yet a prophet can inspire a dead land by just passing through it.

Jelaluddin Rumi said centuries ago that before man fire, water, earth, air, are objects; before God they are living beings that work at His command. The meaning of what Rumi has said is that all objects, all places are as phonograph records: what is put into them they speak. Either your soul hears it or your mind, according to your development.

It seems that people are now beginning to believe in what they call psychometry. What is it? It is learning the language that objects speak, that apart from the color or form an object has, there is something in that object that speaks to you. Either it belongs to that object or it belongs to the one who has used it, but it is in the object.

Sometimes one may bring an object into the house, and the moment one has brought it there, other objects begin to break. As long as the object is there, there is always a kind of loss. It can bring disharmony in the house; it can bring illness; it can bring bad luck. Therefore those who knew the psychological effect that comes from objects always avoided getting old objects, however beautiful and precious; they always bought a new object for their use.

Besides this there is an effect upon one's health, on one's condition of mind, on one's feeling from what one wears. If it is a jewel, it may have the voice of thousands of years. As old as a jewel is, so much tradition it has behind it; it explains it. Intuitive persons who are sensitive and feeling can consciously perceive the vibrations of old stones; it seems as if they speak to them. Also, with all one gives to another in the form of food or sweet or drink or fruit or flower, one gives one's thought, one's feeling; it has an effect. Among the Sufis in the East there is a custom of giving to someone either a piece of cloth or a flower or a fruit, some grains of corn, and there is a meaning behind it. It is not what is given in that object, but what is given with it.

How little we know when we say, "I believe in what I see." If one can see how the influence works, how thought and feeling speak, and how objects partake of them and give them to another, how thought and feeling, life and influence, are conveyed by the medium of an object, it is most wonderful.

There are many ancient places where one finds stones engraved or roots carved with artistic designs. Sometimes there are letters engraved on the rock of a mountain, on a stone; letters today no one can read. Yet one endowed with the gift of intuition can read them from the vibrations, from the atmosphere, the feeling that comes from them. They are engravings outwardly; inwardly they are a continual record, a speaking record that is always expressing what is written upon it. No traveler with his intuitive faculties open will deny the fact that in the lands of ancient traditions he will have seen numberless places, so to speak, sing aloud the legend of the past.

One sees the same in the atmosphere of the trees in the forests, in the gardens, which also express the past, the impressions that have been given to them by those who sat under them. Very often people have superstitions about a tree being haunted, and this one finds very much more in the East. Actually a vibration has been created, consciously or unconsciously, by someone who has lived there, who has taken the shelter of the tree and pondered upon a certain thought, upon a certain feeling, which the tree has taken up and is expressing. Perhaps the person has forgotten and the tree is still repeating what has been given to it. For the tree can express the voice that has been put into it more clearly than a rock. In the tropical countries, where in ancient times people used to travel on foot through the forests and woods and take shelter under a certain tree, all that they thought and felt has been taken up by the tree. Those with intuitive faculties open have heard it more clearly than one would hear it from a living person.

One finds the same thing among the pet animals who live and partake of thought and feeling through their contact with people. There exists a superstition about horses especially. Those who know are very particular in buying a horse that has good vibrations, besides considering the health and breed of the horse. Very often a horse of a very good breed and perfectly sound may prove to be unlucky. The reason is that the disappointment of someone who has been riding upon this horse has been left there, recorded upon the heart of the horse. Perhaps the condition of that person is changed, but that which the horse has kept of it is still continuing.

I was myself once very impressed in Nepal by seeing a horse and an elephant that were kept only for the maharajah of Nepal to ride on. It seemed as if those two animals were conscious of that rider. You could see from their dignity that they knew that they belonged to the maharajah. In every movement that the horse would make, in the look that the elephant would give, you could feel the presence of a maharajah. And not only that, but all that belonged to the maharajah, as pain or pleasure, as life and expression all seemed to have been recorded upon the elephant. The most surprising thing was this: the elephant was not larger than other elephants (and most often it is its size that gives dignity to the elephant); nor was the horse larger than other horses. But the size did not count; it was the spirit, a life that you could see in those animals, expressing the feeling they had in their hearts.

This wakens us again to another field of thought, and that is what an association can create in someone, the association of a sad person or of a happy one, of a foolish or of a wise person; the association of a noble-minded person or of one who is low. The associate partakes of the one he associates with and vibrates what he partakes of, and you can almost hear it spoken in the atmosphere of that person, in his expression, in his speech and action. A person, however happy, will have a line or melody of wretchedness if he has associated with someone who is miserable. It continues, it sings its song separate from the whole symphony. It has its peculiar tone; you can always distinguish it. A wise person who has associated with a foolish one has kept a line. It is quite a different melody, it is in a different key, it has a different pitch from his original song. In a person who has associated with someone who is noble-minded, of high quality, in spite of all his shortcomings you will see a line marked, distinctly audible to the hearts that listen.

It is not a thing of little importance to consider association. It is of great importance from a psychological point of view; it makes all the difference. For a wise person is not always positive against a foolish person, nor is a good person always positive against a wicked one. The one who is positive cannot always be positive; he has his times when he must be negative for a change. Therefore association certainly brings to one that which is received by the contact. Thus there is a great wisdom in the saying that a person is known by his associates. In the East much thought has been given to it, especially from a spiritual point of view. For those who seek after the spiritual truth the association with friends in the same Path is more precious than anything in the world. Everything else comes after; an association is held as the first and most important thing.

Chapter 23

THE VOICE OF THOUGHT
(VIBRATORY POWER)

In preparing anything one not only puts one's magnetism into it, but the voice of one's soul is produced in the thing one prepares. For instance, it is not difficult for an intuitive person to find in the food that comes before him the thoughts of the cook. It is not only the grade of evolution that the cook has but also what the cook is thinking at that particular time that is produced in it. If the cook is irritated while cooking, if she is grumbling, if she is sighing, if she is miserable, wretched, all that comes before you with the food she prepares. It is the knowledge of this fact that made the Hindus engage as cooks high-caste Brahmans, whose evolution was great, whose life was pure, whose thoughts were elevated. It is not the custom of the past, it is the custom of today that a Brahman who is sometimes the guru, the teacher of other castes, may also be the cook. Besides this, in the ancient times when human personality was keenly observed in everything one did, every person, what-

173

ever his rank or position in life, was qualified in cooking and preparing dishes for himself and for his friends. A great mark of appreciation and affection was shown by people who invited some relations or friends to come to their house and placed before them dishes that they themselves had prepared. It was not the dish that mattered, it was the thought that was put into it.

Life at the present time seems to have taken away many considerations of personal character. But whether in the East or in the West, there was a time when the craft of knitting or weaving clothes was known by every little girl, and to give one's brother or sister or beloved or relation some little thing made by one's own hand was the custom. Now a thing is easily bought at the shop; no one knows who made it, nor whether it was made grudgingly, or with grumbling, or how. Especially at this time, when the working man is in revolt, what the workman has put into the objects he has made for you is a question. In sewing for the one she loves, a thought naturally has gone with every stitch that a girl has made. If it is done with love and affection, every stitch produces a new thought; it completes that living thought of love, thus giving inwardly that help that every soul is in need of.

Then also, the wagons, carriages, and ships that are used at the risk of man's life, by whom are they made? Who knows what was the condition of mind of the builders of the *Titanic*? Was there a peacemaker teaching them to keep a certain rhythm of mind while making her?

Everything that is made has a magical influence in it. If it is made with a thought quite contrary to what is needed, it only means dangers awaiting the ship, the train, the wagon, the car. Very often without apparent cause you find a boat in danger, something breaking without a substantial reason. In its make-up the thought of destruction has been given. It is working through it; it is something more living than the object itself. So it is when a house is built. The thoughts given to it by the one who was building it, or by those who worked on it, all count.

The thought attached to things is a life power. In order to define it, it may be called a vibratory power. In a mystic's conception vibrations may be considered to have three aspects: audible, visible, and perceptible. The vibrations put into an object are never audible and visible; they are only perceptible. Perceptible to what? To the intuitive faculty of man. But it is not meant by this that the one who lacks intuitive faculty does not perceive it. He perceives it too, but unconsciously. In short, we understand by this that there is a thought attached to all things made either by an individual or by the multitude, and that that thought will give results accordingly.

The influence put into things is according to the intensity of the feeling, as a note resounds according to the intensity with which you strike it. You may strike a note on the piano, and it will continue to resound for so long. If you strike it with less intensity it resounds for a shorter time. At the same time it is according to the strength with which you strike and the instrument on which you strike. There may be one instrument the string of which will continue to vibrate for a very long time; there is another instrument whose string will not vibrate for very long, and then it will quiet down. So it is also according to the medium that you take in striking vibrations that the effect is made.

In all things there is God, but the object is the instrument, and man is life itself. Into the object a person puts life. When a certain thing is being made, it is at that time that life is put into it which goes on and on like breath in a body. This also gives us a hint that when we take flowers to a patient and we bring a healing thought with them, the flowers convey the thought of healing. As the patient looks at the flowers, he will receive from the flowers the healing that has been put there. Any eatable or sweet, anything that we take to a friend with a thought of love, may create a harmonious, a happy result with him. Therefore every little thing given and taken in love, with a harmonious and good thought, has a greater value than the object itself. For it is not the object, it is what is behind it. Does it not teach us that it is not always the doing or preparing of things in our everyday life but that it is giving these things with a harmonious, constructive thought that counts, so that our work may become a thousand times greater in effect and in its real value?

This also teaches us that while doing a certain thing we should be accomplishing something very great if we did it with this attitude, with this idea at the back of it: that we are not making a thing only, but that we are making it so that it lives. Does it not open before us a vast field of work that we could do easily, without much cost or effort? In its results that work could be of a much greater importance than anyone could think or imagine. Is it not at the same time a great blessing to be able to do a thing of great importance without any outward pretense? Even while writing a letter a person sometimes puts into it what words cannot explain, and yet the letter conveys it. There may be one word written with a loving thought behind it; that word will have a greater effect than perhaps a thousand others. Do we not almost hear a letter speaking? It is not always what is written in it; it brings the one who wrote it to us, and what mood he was in, his evolution, his pleasure, his displeasure, his joy, and his sorrow. The letter conveys more than what is written in it.

Consider the great souls who have come to the earth at different times. Conditions opposed them, and they found difficulties at every move in accomplishing what they wanted to do. Yet they have produced the voice, a living voice. That living voice continued long after they had left, and spread in time thrughout the whole universe, accomplishing what they had once wished. The effect of that one moment of thought took perhaps centuries to build something, but it was something worthwhile, something beyond man's comprehension.

If we could only understand what spirit is, we should esteem the human being much more than we do now. We trust man so little, we believe in man so little, we respect man so little, we esteem his possibilities so little. If we only knew what is at the back of every strong and weak soul, we should know that there is every possibility, and we should never underestimate anyone, nor fail to respect anyone in spite of all he may lack. We should recognize that it is the Creator creating through all the different forms, but it is one Creator; and that all that is built and prepared and made and composed is made by that One Being working through this world of variety.

Chapter 24

THE LIFE OF THOUGHT AND FEELING
(ELEMENTALS)

God is omniscient, omnipotent, all-pervading, and the Only Being. This suggests to us that the Absolute is a living being, that
there is no such thing as death, that there is no such thing as an
end, that every thing, every being, every particle has a continuity
because life is continuous.

End or death is only a change. Therefore every thought that has
once crossed the mind, every feeling that has once passed through
the heart, every word that is once spoken and perhaps never
thought about any longer, every action once done and forgotten,
is given a life, and it continues to live. It is just like a traveler who
is journeying, and on his way he has some seeds in his hands and
throws them on the ground. When the plants grow in that place
he never sees them; he just threw the seeds and they are there. The
earth has taken them, the water has reared them, and the sun and
the air have helped them to grow.

This life is an accommodation, and in it everything—as thought
or word or action or feeling—once given birth, is taken care of and
is raised and brought to fruitfulness. One would hardly think that
it could be so. One thinks something is spoken and gone, or done

and finished with; or it was felt, and now it is no longer there. But it is only a change, a change of which we are conscious. We know of something and then it is no longer before us and we think it is gone, but it is there still. It remains and it pursues its course, for it is life, and in everything there is a life. Life lives, and as all is life, there is no death.

No doubt birth and death, beginning and end, are the names of the different aspects of this mechanical working of the whole universe. It is a kind of automatic working that gives us an idea of something beginning and something ending. When you ring the bell the action takes only a moment, but the resonance lasts. It lasts to our knowledge only as long as it is audible. Then it passes on further and it is no longer audible to us, but it exists somewhere; it goes on.

If a pebble thrown into the sea puts the water in action, one hardly stops to think to what extent this vibration acts upon the sea. What one can see in the little waves and circles that the pebble produces before one, one sees only these. But the vibration that it has produced in the sea reaches much further than one can ever imagine. What we call "space" is a much finer world. If we call it "sea," it is a sea with the finest fluid. If we call it "land," it is a land that is incomparably more fertile than the land we know. It takes in everything, and it brings it up; it rears and it allows to grow that which one's eyes do not see, one's ears do not hear.

Does this thought not make us responsible for every movement we make, for every thought that we think, for every feeling that passes through our mind or heart? For there is not one moment of our life wasted, if we only know how to utilize our action here, how to direct our thought, how to express it in words, how to further it with our movement, how to feel it, so that it may make its own atmosphere. What responsibility! The responsibility that every person has is greater than a king's responsibility. It seems as if everyone has a kingdom of his own for which he is responsible, a kingdom that is in no way smaller than any kingdom known to us, but incomparably larger than the kingdoms of the earth. This teaches us to be thoughtful and conscientious and to feel our responsibility at every move we make. But every person does not feel this; he is unaware of himself, he is unaware of the secret of life. He goes on like a drunken man walking in a city. He does not know what he is doing, either for himself or against himself.

How can a thought live? In what way does it live? Has it a body to live in, has it a mind, has it a breath? Yes. The first thing we should know is that a breath that comes directly from the source seeks a body, an accommodation in which to function. A thought is like a body, that thought which comes from the source as a ray of that spirit which may be likened to the sun.

This makes the thought an entity; it lives as an entity. It is these entities that are called in the Sufi terms *muwakkals,* which means "elementals." They live; they have a certain purpose to accomplish. They are given birth by man, and behind them there is a purpose to direct their life. Imagine how terrible it is if in a moment's absorption a person expresses his wrath, his passion, his hatred; for a word expressed at such a moment must live and carry out its purpose. It is like creating an army of enemies around oneself. Perhaps one thought has a longer life than the other; it depends on what life has been given to it. If the body is stronger, then it lives longer. On the energy of mind the strength of the body of that thought depends.

Once someone asked me what the elementals are like. I answered, "Elementals look exactly like your thoughts. If you have the thoughts of human beings, then the elementals have human forms; if you have the thoughts of birds, then the elementals have the forms of birds; if your thoughts are of the animals, then the elementals have the form of animals. For elementals are made of your thought."

Elementals are created by man. When the winds blow and storms rage and create all destruction, one looks at it as a mechanical action of nature. But it is not only mechanical action, it is directed by people's feelings, by the intense feelings of human beings. These feelings turn into huge beings, the beings that direct. They push as a battery behind winds and storms and floods and volcanoes. So it is that those thoughts which call for blessing, such as rainfall, must bring the mercy of God on others. In the East they call rain "the divine mercy." The sunshine when the sky is clear and all other blessings of nature—the pure air that is exhilarating, the spring, good crops, fruits, flowers, and vegetables—all these different blessings, which come to us from the earth or heaven, are also directed by forces behind them. As the mechanical working of nature raises the vapors to the sky and they all form together in clouds and cause rain, so the thoughts and feelings and words and actions have their mechanical work to do also, and that work directs the action of the universe. This shows to us that it is not only a mechanical work of nature, but human intelligence mechanically working, directing the whole working of nature.

This gives one the idea that humanity's responsibility is greater than that of any other being in the world. It is told in the Qur'an that God said, "We offered our trust to the heavens and the earth and the mountains, and they did not dare to receive it; but man accepted our trust." This trust is our responsibility, not only our responsibility to those around us, to those whom we meet in everyday life, to the work that we are engaged in, or to the interest that we have in life, but our responsibility towards this whole creation what we contribute to this creation and whether it is something agreeable to bring about better and harmonious conditions in the sphere, in the world, on the earth. If we do so, then we know our responsibility; if we are unaware of it, we have not yet known the purpose of our being here.

There is childhood, when a child knows nothing. He destroys things of value and beauty owing to his curiosity, his fancy, but when the child is grown up he begins to feel his responsibility. The sign of maturity is the feeling of responsibility, so when a soul matures it begins to feel its responsibility. It is from that moment a person begins his life; it is from that moment that the soul is born again. For so long as the soul is not born again it will not enter the kingdom of God. The kingdom of God is here, but as long as person is not conscious of his responsibility he does not know the kingdom of God. It is his becoming conscious of his responsibility that wakens him to the kingdom of God in which is the birth of the soul.

Furthermore, in support of this idea there is a word that is used for the God-conscious people in the Sanskrit language, and that word is *Brahman,* creator. No sooner has a soul realized this idea than he begins to know that every moment of his life is creative, either outwardly or inwardly. And if he is responsible for his creation, he is responsible for every moment of his life. Then there is nothing in life that is wasted. Whatever be the condition, however helpless or miserable, yet his life is not wasted, for there is the creative power working through every move that he makes, every thought that he thinks, every feeling that he has. He is always doing something.

There is another word in Sanskrit for Brahman, which is *Dwija,* meaning "the soul who is born again." For the moment one has realized all this, the soul is born again because one's realization of life is different then, one's plan of life becomes different, one's action becomes different.

Now going a little further, there are souls who sometimes seem to be doing nothing; and a person thinks, "Yes, they are most spiritual people, I suppose. But what are they doing?" because what we know about doing is hustling and bustling and being busy all the time. However unimportant, yet something must be done; that is the thought. But when a person is evolved, even if outwardly he may not seem to be doing anything, he is doing, and he can do, much greater works inwardly than one can notice outwardly.

There is a story of a *madzub.* A *madzub* is a person who is not considered as an active person in the world; many think of him as someone who is not quite balanced. In the East there are some who know about such beings, and they have regard for them. There used to be a *madzub* in Kashmir some centuries ago, and he was allowed by the maharajah to roam about in the palace and the gardens wherever he wanted to, and was given a piece of ground where he could dwell. He was allowed to walk everywhere in the maharaja's gardens. There was a miniature toy cannon in the garden, and sometimes this *madzub* used to get a fancy to play with it. He used to take this gun and he would turn it either to the south or to the north or elsewhere. Then he would turn it again and he would make all sorts of gestures, and after making those gestures he would be delighted. It used to seem as if he were fighting, and as if after that fighting, he was now victorious and delighted. Every time he acted this way maharajah Ranjit Singh used to give orders to his army to prepare for war, and there was success. The war had been going on for many, many years, and it was going slowly and nothing had happened, but every time the *madzub* played with the cannon results were achieved.

There was in Hyderabad a *madzub* whose habit it was to insult everybody, to call people such names that they would go away from him. But still one man dared go there in spite of all the insults. The *madzub* said, "What do you want?" He said, "My case is coming on in the courts six days from now, and I have no money, no means. What shall I do?" The *madzub* said, "Tell me what is the case about, but tell me the truth." So the man told him all. This *madzub* listened to it, and on the ground he wrote, "There seems to be nothing in this case, so it must be dismissed." Then he said, "Go, it is done." The man went to the court. From the opposite party many barristers and pleaders were there; on his part there were none, because he was a poor man. The judge heard the case from both sides and then spoke the same words that the *madzub* had written on the ground.

What does it mean? It only explains to us the words Christ spoke, "Enter the kingdom of God": that every soul has in himself a kingdom of God. To become conscious of this mystery of life is to open one's eyes to the kingdom of God. Then whatever one does has a meaning, an influence; it is never lost. If it is not materialized, it does not matter; it is spiritualized. Nothing is gone, nothing is lost here. If it has not been produced on this plane it has been produced on another plane. But still it reflects on this plane, because there is always action and reaction between the two planes. It only means that what one does, if it is not materialized on this plane, is reflected from the other plane onto this plane and then materialized, that is all. If a person thinks, "I have not materialized it," it only means that the time and conditions have not allowed it to materialize. But if it is once sent out, it must ultimately be materialized.

Chapter 25

THE INFLUENCE OF WORKS OF ART

Works of art that have been made, independently of the skill that has been put into them and the ideas they convey to us, have a feeling in them and behind them. When I was visiting Berlin I saw around the kaiser's palace statuary: everywhere around was some work of art suggestive of horror, of terror, of destruction. As soon as I saw it I said, "No wonder things happened as they did, for this statuary was produced beforehand." A work of art may be beautiful to look at, it may have great skill in it, and yet the mind of the artist is working through it. The effect that the picture has is not what it suggests outwardly, but what it speaks aloud as the voice of its heart. In every picture, in every statue, in every artistic construction one can see this: there is a voice hidden in it, continually telling for what purpose the work of art was created.

Sometimes an artist is unaware of what he is creating. He is following his imagination. He may be working against his own work of art; he may be bringing about an effect that he had not desired for himself or for the person to whom that work of art was to be given. Once I went to see a temple. I could not call that temple beautiful, but it was wonderful, unique of its kind. No sooner did my eyes fall on the color scheme and the pictures that stood there as its prominent features, than I was surprised to think how such a temple could possibly have existed so long; it should have been destroyed long ago. Not long after that I heard that the temple had been destroyed. The idea is that the constructor of that temple was so absorbed in his scheme that he forgot the harmony of spirit that was to make the plan of it; and so it resulted in failure.

Once a friend took me to see some pictures made by her husband. No sooner did I see them than it brought to me the whole history of the person, how his soul went on through life, the agonies through which it went; the whole thing was expressed in the pictures. And what was the condition of the possessor of those pictures? Nothing but sorrow and depression.

It is better an artist should be afraid of making a work that might produce something undesirable, because then he will be careful; and if he tries to know the effect, then he will know it. It is very easy to enjoy a picturesque idea, but one never stops to think that it is not only the idea that is important, but also the outcome of it: is it destructive, is it constructive? For instance in steamers, especially in the English Channel, as soon as you go into the cabin the first thing you see is a picture of a person about to sink and putting on his lifebelt. It is the first thing you are impressed with, as the first omen. Certainly it is instructive; but it is not a psychological instruction. If there is some instruction needed, it would be better to circulate picture cards after the ship has started, after people are accustomed to it. Also it is more than unwise—one should use some other word for it—to place in a schoolroom or a chapel scenes of death, even of saints and masters, especially in connection with saints and masters who, being immortal, never died.

And so it is with poetry. Among the Hindus there is a psychology of poetry that is taught to the poet before he is allowed to write poetry. For it is not only the rhythm and the swing of mind and thought that are to be expressed, but to write poetry means to construct something, to make something or to mar something. Poetry has sometimes an effect upon the prosperity or the decline of great ones in whose praise it has been made. It has a science attached to it. A person may speak highly of a personality in poetry, yet the construction of words or the idea behind it may be harmful. It not only harms the person for whom it was made, but sometimes, if that personality is strong, it falls upon the poet, thus destroying him forever.

One may say, "Then do not drama and tragedy do harm?" There are many things that harm us, but there are many things that at the same time are interesting. Besides this, there are minds that are more attracted to tragedy than to anything else. It is natural, because sometimes there is a sore, and that sore feels alive for the moment, a sensation which is perhaps agreeable. It may be called a pain, but at the same time it is an agreeable pain when the sore is scratched. No doubt too much tragedy is not desirable for anybody, but an artistic nature, a person who loves poetry, finds something in tragedy. It would be depriving oneself of a great joy not to read Shakespeare. But when people write poetry in connection with some personality, a king or a sovereign or anyone, then it has a direct effect; the poetry of Shakespeare is general. However, a play has an effect, and a serious effect too.

The above is according to the psychological point of view; it is not meant that it is the point of view of the Sufi. For Sufis are very fond of poetry, and their passion for poetry sometimes goes very far in expressing the sentiment of longing, yearning, heartbreak, disappointment. But even that is not psychological; according to psychology it is not right.

And so it is with music. It may be very interesting for a musician to make a kind of magical music, describing how the flood came and the city was destroyed and everybody who lived in the city. For the moment it might seem to him an amusement, a queer imagination, but it has its influence.

The most interesting thing is that through art, poetry, music, or through the movements made in dance, a thought or feeling is created, the effect of which is the outcome of the whole action; the art, so to speak, is a cover. On every plane the cover of that plane is required in order to express the life on the plane. So music is a world; poetry is a world; art is a world. A person who lives in the world of art, he it is who knows art, who appreciates art; and so the person who lives in the world of music knows music and he appreciates music. In order to have an insight into music one must live in it and observe this world more keenly. In other words, it is not sufficient that a person should be musical and that he should occupy his heart and soul with music, but he must also develop intuition so that he may see more keenly.

How wonderful it is to notice that art in its every aspect is something living, speaking either good or evil. It is not only what meaning one sees in the frescoes in the old houses in Italy and what art is produced in the statuary of ancient times, but these works of art almost speak to you of the history of the past. They tell you of the artist who made them, his stage of evolution, his motive, his soul, and the spirit of that time. This teaches us that unconsciously our thought and feeling are produced in all things we use: a place, a rock, a tree, a seat, in things that we prepare. But in art an artist completes the music of his soul, of his mind. It is not automatic; it is very often a conscious effect, an effect that results in another effect. This shows that it is not enough for us to learn art or to pursue it, but in order to complete it we must understand the psychology of art, through which one accomplishes the purpose of one's life.

Chapter 26

THE NATURE OF THE MIND

The mind has five aspects, but the aspect that is best known is that for which we use the word "mind." Mind means the creator of thought and imagination. Mind is a soil upon which, in the form of thoughts and imaginations, plants grow. They live there, although as there is continual fresh growth, those plants and trees which have been created before are hidden from one's eyes, and only the new plants springing up there are before one's consciousness. It is because of this that one does not think much about thoughts and imaginations that are past, nor are they before one. But at the same time, whenever one wishes to find a thought which has once been shaped by one, it is immediately to be found, for it still exists there.

That part which consciousness does not see immediately is called subconsciousness. What is called consciousness remains on the surface, making clear to us that part of our thoughts and imaginations which we have just had and which we are still busy looking at. Nevertheless, once a person has had an imagination, a thought, it still exists.

In what form does it exist? In the form that the mind has given it. The soul takes a form in this physical world, a form that is borrowed from this world. So the thought takes a form that is borrowed from the world of mind. A clear mind, therefore, can give a distinct life, a distinct form to the thought; a mind that is confused produces indistinct thoughts. One can see the truth of this in dreams: the dreams of the clear-minded are clear and distinct; the dreams of those of unclear mind are confused. Besides, it is most interesting to see that the dreams of the artist, of the poet, of the musician, who live in beauty, who think of beauty, are beautiful; the dreams of those whose minds have doubt or fear or confusion are the same character as their minds.

This gives proof that the mind gives a body to the thought; the mind supplies form to each thought, and with that form the thought is able to exist. The form of a thought is not only known to the person who thinks it, but also to the one who reflects the thought, in whose heart it is reflected. Therefore there is a silent communication between people, the thought forms of one person reflecting in the mind of another. These thought forms are more powerful and clearer than words. They are very often more impressive than a spoken word, because language is limited, while thought has a greater scope of expression.

Imagination is an uncontrolled thought. One might ask if it is good to have a strong imagination. It is good to be strong oneself. If one has strength, then imagination is strong, thought is strong, and one is strong oneself. Furthermore, a strong imagination means strength going from oneself, reaching out without one's control. Therefore a strong imagination is not always promising; it is strength of thought that is desirable. For what is thought? Thought is self-directed and controlled imagination.

But if thought has a body, is it then bound to a place, or does it spread equally throughout the whole universe? This is a subtle question. In the first place, if a person is in a prison, is his mind also in prison, or can it reach beyond, can it go out of the prison? Certainly it can. It is the body of the person which is in the prison, his mind can reach anywhere. Perhaps a thought produced in the mind world is made captive by its object or motive, by its source, or by its application in a sphere, within a horizon where it is working out its destiny. Nevertheless it is thought, and it is capable of reaching every part of the universe in a moment's time.

There is another most interesting aspect in studying the nature of mind: that every mind attracts and reflects thoughts of its own kind, just as there is a part of the earth that is more suitable for flowers to grow in, another part of the earth more suitable for fruits, and yet another part of the earth where weeds grow. Thus a reflection that falls from one mind upon another mind only falls upon the mind that attracts it. This is the reason why like is attractive to like. If a robber or a thief goes to Paris, he will certainly meet with a thief. He will easily find out where the thief lives; he will see him at once, because his mind has become a receptacle of the same kind of thoughts. As soon as their glances meet there is a communication established; their thoughts are alike.

One sees in everyday life how like attracts like. The reason is that the mind has developed a certain character, and the thought pictures of that particular character appear in it. It is so very interesting for anyone who sees this phenomenon in ordinary life that there is not one moment when he does not see the truth of it.

High minds will always reflect and attract higher thought. From wherever it comes, it will come to them; it will be attracted by the ground of mind which is prepared for it. An ordinary mind is attracted to ordinary things. For instance, a person who has a habit of criticizing people is very eager to open his ears to criticism, because that is the subject that interests him; his pleasure is there. He cannot resist the temptation of hearing ill of another because it is most dear to his heart, for he speaks of it himself. To the ears of the person to whom that thought does not belong, it is a foreign note that he does not want to hear. His heart has no pleasure in it; it wants to throw off anything that is inharmonious. Therefore the mind world is man's kingdom, his property. Whatever he sows, that he reaps; for whatever purpose he keeps that property, that is produced in it.

Now going into the deeper metaphysics, what is it that forms the thought picture? It is a very subtle question. A materialistic scientist will say that there are thought atoms that group and make the form; joining together they compose the thought form. If he wants to make it more objective, he will say that in the brain there are little thought pictures just like moving pictures, and that moving successively they complete a form. For this person does not see further than his body, and so he wants to find out the secret of the whole of life in his body and in the physical world.

In reality the brain is only an instrument to make thoughts more clear; thought is greater, vaster, deeper, and higher than the brain. The picture of thought is made by the impressions of the mind. If the mind had had no impressions the thought would not be clear. For instance, a blind person who has never in his life seen an elephant will not be able to form an idea of an elephant, because his mind has not the form ready to compose at the command of the will. The mind must know it first in order to compose it. Therefore the mind is a storehouse of all the forms that a person has ever seen. But cannot a form be reflected upon a blind person's mind? Yes, but it will remain incomplete. If a thought is projected on a blind person, he takes only half of it; for he will not have that part which he should take from his own mind, and so he only takes the reflection that is projected upon him. Therefore he has a vague idea of the thing, but he cannot make it clear to himself because his mind has not yet formed that idea.

The form of a thought that the mind holds is reflected upon the brain. The brain may be likened to a photographic plate. The thought falls upon the brain just as a reflection falls upon the photographic plate, both one's own thought and the thought of another. But there is another process, and that is that the thought is developed like the photographic plate. What is it developed with? Is there some solution in which the photographic plate is to be put? Yes, and that is the intelligence; through one's own intelligence it is developed and made more clear to the inner senses. By "inner senses" is meant the inner part of the five senses. For outwardly it is these five organs that give us an idea of five senses, but in reality there is only one sense. Through five different outer organs we experience different things, and this gives us the idea of five senses.

There are visionary people who have conceptions of the different colors of thoughts and imaginations and feelings, and different imaginary forms of thoughts and feelings. No doubt this is symbolical rather than actual. The color of a thought corresponds with the condition of the mind. It shows the element to which the thought belongs, whether the thought belongs to the fire element, to the water element, or to the earth element. This means that it is, for instance, fire that is behind the thought; that fire produces its color around the thought as an atmosphere surrounding it. When such visionary people see the thought form in the form of color, what surrounds the thought is according to the character belonging to that thought.

A thought connected with earthly gain is of the earth element; a thought of love and affection represents the water element, spreading sympathy; a thought of revenge and destruction and hurt and harm represents fire; a thought of enthusiasm, courage, hope, aspiration represents air; a thought of retirement solitude, quiet, peace represents ether. These are the predominant characteristics of thoughts in connection with the five elements.

There is no superiority of one element over another. The superiority of thought is according to the outlook of the mind. For instance, a person standing on the ground sees a horizon before him. This is one outlook. Another person is standing on the top of a tower, and from there he is looking at the wide horizon; his outlook is different. It is according to the outlook that the thought is superior or inferior. Besides, no one can take a thought, any thought picture, and say, "This is an inferior thought," or, "This is a superior thought." Thought is not an earthly coin that is inferior or superior. What makes it inferior or superior is the motive behind it.

The form of thought also has its effect upon the form and expression of someone. For a thought has a particular language that manifests in a kind of writing, if one could read it. This language can be read in the face and form of a person. Everyone reads this to a certain extent, but it is difficult to define the letters, the alphabet of this language. There is one mystery that opens a door into thought language, and that is the vibrations and what direction the vibrations take. A thought works upon and around a person's form and becomes manifest to the eyes upon his visible being. There is a certain law that governs its work, and that law is the law of direction: if the forces are going to the right, or to the left, or upward, or downward. It is this direction of the vibrations of thought that produces a picture, so that a seer can see this picture as clearly as a letter. No doubt for a seer it is necessary to read the thought from the visible form of a person, because he cannot be a seer if he is not open to a reflection, so that every thought is reflected in him, which makes things even more clear. Besides that, he need not see the picture of the thought on the visible form in order to know it; the atmosphere tells him. The thought itself calls out, "I am this thought," whatever it may be, because thought has a language, a voice; thought has a breath and has life.

Chapter 27

MEMORY

Memory is a mental faculty as distinct as mind, a recording machine that records all that falls upon it through the five senses. What one sees, hears, smells, touches, tastes is recorded upon the memory. A form, a picture, an image once seen sometimes remains in the memory for the whole life, if it is well recorded by the memory. In the life of the world one hears so many words during the day, and yet some words that the memory has recorded remain for the whole life, as living as ever. So it is with music. Once a person has heard wonderful music and it is recorded on his mind, it remains for ever and ever. Memory is such a living machine that you can produce that record at any time; it is there. A good perfume once experienced, once perceived is remembered; the feeling of taste remains; the feeling of touch, memory holds.

Things do not remain in the memory as in a notebook, for as the notebook is dead, so what remains in the notebook is dead. But memory is living, and so what remains in the memory is living also, and has a living sensation. A record of pleasant memory is sometimes so precious that one wishes to sacrifice this objective world for such a record. I was very touched once by seeing a widow whose relations wished me to tell her to go into society, to mix with people, to live a more worldly life. I went to advise her on that subject. But when she told me gently, "All the experiences of this world's life, however pleasant, do not afford me pleasure. My only joy is the memory of my beloved. Other things give me unhappiness, other things make me miserable. If I find joy, it is in the thought of my beloved,' I could not say one word to change her mind. I thought it would be a sin on my part to take her away from her joy. If the memory had been a misery for her, I would have spoken to her otherwise, but it was a happiness for her, it was the only happiness. I thought that here was the living *sati.* I had only a great esteem for her, and could not speak one word.

In memory the secret of heaven and hell is to be found. As Omar Khayyam has said in his *Rubaiyat,* "Heaven is the vision of fulfilled desire, and hell the shadow of a soul on fire." What is it? Where is it? It is only in the memory. Therefore memory is not a small thing. It is not something that is hidden in the brain. It is something living, and it is something so vast that a limited mind cannot conceive of it; it is something that is a world in itself.

But people might ask, "What is it, then, if a person has lost his memory? Is it caused by a disorder in the brain?" In the first place no one really loses his memory. A person may lose his memory, but it does not lose him, because the memory is one's own being. What happens is that the disorder of the brain makes it incapable of distinguishing what the memory contains. Therefore a person who has lost his memory owing to a disorder in the brain still has a memory just the same. That memory will become clearer to him after death. For the mind is quite distinct from the body; it is something apart, standing independent of the body. The mind is dependent on the body for perceiving the outer experiences that it takes in through the senses, but the mind is independent of the body for holding the treasures that it has collected through the outer world and retaining them.

As we are accustomed to experience everything through the vehicle of this body, even our feelings, this makes us dependent for some time upon the body. But it does not mean that we cannot experience all that belongs to mind without the help of the body. Also, if a person lifted himself from his objective being, he would find his memory intact. Only, the memory cannot function in the brain that is out of order, but the impressions during the time that a person has lost his memory are still recorded; they come back later on. Only at the time when a person has lost his memory, the memory is not actively taking the record of things given to it.

To have a good memory is not only a good thing it is a bliss. It is a sign of spirituality because it shows that the light of the intelligence is clear and is illuminating every particle of the brain. A good memory is a sign of great souls. Besides, memory is the treasure where one's knowledge has been stored. If a person cannot draw the knowledge he has collected from his memory, then his dependence upon the book is of little worth.

One day, six months after I had been received by my murshid as his pupil, he began to speak on metaphysics. Being metaphysically inclined myself, I eagerly welcomed the opportunity. During those six months I was never impatient, I had never shown any eagerness to know more than I was allowed to know. I was quite contented at the feet of the master; that was everything to me. Nevertheless, it was a great stimulus to my mind to hear from him something about metaphysics. But as soon as I took out my notebook from my pocket my murshid ended the subject. He said nothing, but from that day I learned a lesson: "By this he means that my notebook must not be the storehouse of my knowledge. There is a living notebook, and that is my memory, a notebook that I shall carry with me all through life and through the hereafter."

No doubt we always write on paper things belonging to the earth, figures and other facts. But things pertaining to the spiritual order of things, to the divine law, are of much greater importance. The notebook is not made for them, it is in the memory that they must be treasured. For memory is not only a recording machine, it is at the same time a fertile ground, and what is put there is continually creative; it is doing something there. Therefore you not only possess something that you have deposited, there is its interest also.

At the same time we learn in the Sufi path how to erase from the record a living memory of something in the past; that is the work that we accomplish by concentration and meditation. It is not an easy thing; it is the most difficult, but also the most valuable, thing there is. This is why we keep our teachngs free from speculations and beliefs and doctrines and dogmas, for we believe in actual work with ourselves. What if you were told a thing one day and you believed it one day, and next day you doubted and did not believe? If you were told there is a house in the seventh heaven and a palace, what would it do for you? It would only answer your curiosity; it would take you nowhere. It is therefore by the way of meditation that we attain to those things. We can erase from the memory what we wish to, and in this way we are able to make our heaven ourselves. The whole secret of esotericism lies in controlling the mind and in working with it as an artist would work on a canvas and produce whatever he liked.

How can one destroy undesirable thoughts? Must they always be destroyed by the one who has created them? Yes, it is the creator of the thought who must destroy it, and it is not in every person's power to destroy it. Yet the same mind that has reached mastery, which can create as it wishes, can also destroy. When we are able to produce on the canvas of our heart all that we wish and to erase all we wish, then we arrive at that mastery for which our soul craves; we fulfill that purpose for which we are here. Then we become the masters of our destiny. It is difficult, but that is the object that we pursue in life.

Sometimes memory is weakened by too great a strain upon it. When one tries to remember, it puts a strain upon something that is natural. It is the nature of memory to remember. But when you put a strain upon it—"You must remember"—then it will forget. For the very fact that you have strained it will make it forget.

One must not try to impress one's mind more deeply than it naturally becomes impressed. It is not necessary to use the brain when trying to remember something, because by using the brain one only strains it. The memory is at the command of a person. If he wants to know about something, without his straining the brain it must come instantly. It is an automatic machine; it must bring before you instantly all that you wish to know.

If it does not work in that way, there is something wrong with it. Certainly, association of ideas helps. It is just as when a person has lost the thought of the horse from his mind, and the stable reminds him. Your attention is quite enough; will power must not be used to remember things. It is a wrong method that people are applying at present when they say that in order to remember things one must will it. By willing one weakens. Besides this, a balance between activity and repose is necessary.

Memory is never lost. What happens is that when the mind is upset the memory becomes blurred because it is the stillness of mind that makes one capable of distinguishing all that one's memory contains. When the mind is upset, when a person is not tranquil, then naturally one is not able to read all that the memory has recorded. It is not true that memory gives away what is stored in it. It is only that man loses the rhythm of his life by overexcitement, nervousness, weakness of nerves, anxiety, worry, fear, confusion. It is that which causes a kind of turmoil in the mind, and one cannot distinctly feel things that have been once recorded in the memory. For instance, a person who cannot easily learn by heart, in order to better this condition must make his mind tranquil as the first thing. That is the mental way. But a physical way of making the memory better is to eat less and sleep normally, not work too much, not worry very much, and to keep all anxiety and fear away. One need not work with memory in order to make it clear; what is required is to make oneself tranquil and rhythmical and peaceful in order to make memory distinct.

THE SCIENCE OF BREATH

...Therefore the Yogis regulated the rhythm of the circulation, of the heart, and of every action of the breath by the
help of the vibration of music, of both tone and rhythm.
This brought them from the audible vibrations to the inward
vibrations; that is to say from sound to breath. For this the
Hindus have one and the same word: *sura,* a name for both
sound and breath. It is the breath of an object that may be
called sound and it is the audibility of the breath that may
be called voice. Therefore breath and voice are not two
things; even breath and sound are not two things, if one
could understand that both have the same basis.

Chapter 28

THE SECRET OF BREATH

As the books, precepts, and doctrines of his religion are important
to the follower of a religion, so the study of the breath is important
to the mystic. We ordinarily think of the breath as that little air
that we feel coming and going through our nostrils. But we do not
think of it as that vast current which goes through everything, that
current which comes from the Consciousness and goes as far as the
external being, the physical world. In the Bible it is written that
first the word was, and from the word all things came. Before the
word was the breath, which made the word. We see that a word
can make us happy; a word can make us sorry. There is a story told
that once a Sufi was healing a child that was ill. He repeated a few
words, and then gave the child to the parents saying "Now he will
be well." Someone who was antagonistic to this said to him, "How
can it be possible that by a few words spoken anyone can be
healed?" From a mild Sufi an angry answer is never expected, but
this time he turned to the man and said, "You understand nothing
about it. You are a fool." The man was very much offended. His
face was red. He was hot. The Sufi said, "When a word has the
power to make you hot and angry, why should not a word have
the power to heal?"

Behind the word is the much greater power, the breath. If a person wishes to study the self, to know the self, what is important is not the study of the mind, of the thought, the imagination, nor of the body, but the study of the breath. The breath has made the mind and the body for its expression. It has made all, from the vibration to the physical atom, from the finest to the grossest. Breath is audible; it is a word in itself, for what we call a word is only a more pronounced utterance of breath fashioned by the mouth and tongue. In the capacity of the mouth breath becomes voice, and therefore the original condition of a word is breath. If we said, "First was the breath," it would be the same as saying, "In the beginning was the word."

The mystery of life does not concern only the material plane, but goes much further. This mystery resides also in the breath, for it is the continuation of breath and pulsation that keeps the mechanism of the body going. It seems that the people of ancient times had a greater knowledge of this mystery than those of today. For what is meant by the lute of Orpheus? It means the human body, which is a lute and is meant to be played upon. When this lute is not realized, when it is not understood, when it is not used for its proper purpose, then this body remains without the use for which it was created and has not fulfilled the purpose for which it was made. The beating of the heart and head, the pulse, all these things keep a rhythm. Man very rarely thinks about what depends upon this rhythm. The whole of life depends upon it. This breath which one breathes is certainly a secret in itself; it is not only a secret but it is the expression of all mystery, something upon which the psychology of life depends.

It is clear even to those who do not know medical science that the whole mechanism of the body stops when the breath has departed. That means that however perfect the mechanism of the body may be, in the absence of breath the body is a corpse. In other words, what is living in the body, or what makes it living, is breath. How few of us realize this fact! We go on day after day, working, busy with everyday life, absorbed in the thoughts we have, occupied with business, pursuing motives, and yet ignoring the principle upon which the whole of life is based. If someone says, "Prayer is a very important thing," people may think, "Yes, perhaps." If one says, "Meditation is a great thing," people may say, "Yes, it is something." But when one says, "Breathing is a great secret," the reaction is, "Why, I have never thought about it. What is it really?"

As far as science goes, breathing is known to be air breathed in and breathed out. When it is breathed in one gets oxygen from space, and when it is breathed out one throws carbonic acid gas into space. When one goes still further one knows that breathing keeps the lungs and the organs of breath going, that digestive gases are drawn in, and that one gets a greater digestive power. On the basis of that principle people are beginning to use breathing in physical exercises to make the body healthier. For some years now voice producers have given greater importance to breath. In reality the breathing itself is voice, and the whole voice construction depends upon breathing. Then again some physicians are beginning to see that many illnesses of the nerves, of the lungs, or of different nervous centers can often be helped by breathing. There seems to be a general awakening to the science of breath. Those who have practiced breathing in connection with physical culture or for the improvement of their particular condition, illness, or weakness have found wonderful results. It is thus far that the science of breath has reached.

But when we come to the mystery of breath, it is another domain altogether. The perceptible breath that the nostrils can feel as air drawn in and air going out is only an effect of breathing. It is not breath. For the mystic breath is that current which carries the air out and brings the air in. The air is perceptible, not the current; the current is imperceptible. It is a kind of ethereal magnetism, a finer kind of electricity, the current of which goes in and comes out, putting the air into action. This is what the mystic calls "nafs," which means "the self." Breath is the self, the very self of man. Also "atman" means the soul, and in German the same word is used for "soul" and for "breath." This shows that if there is any trace of the soul, it is to be found in breath.

Naturally, breath being the self, it is not only the air that one exhales but it is a current which, according to mystics, runs from the physical plane into the innermost plane; a current that runs through the body, mind, and soul, touching the innermost part of life and also coming back; a continual current perpetually moving in and out. This gives quite a different explanation of the breath and shows the importance of something that very few people consider important. It makes one understand that the most important part of being is breath, which reaches the innermost part of life and also reaches outwards to the surface, which means touching the physical plane. But the direction of breath is in a dimension that the science of today does not recognize, a dimension that is recognized by mystics as being the dimension "within."

One day I was lecturing in England and among the audience was a well-known scientist. After the lecture he came to me and said, "I am very interested, but there is one thing that puzzles me. I cannot understand the word within. What do you mean? Within the body? We can only understand inside the body." This shows the difficulty of reaching a common understanding between science and mysticism, but one day it will be overcome. It is only a temporary difficulty.

To give a philosophical explanation of this dimension, one can take as an example the simile of the eyes: what is it in these eyes of ours that can accommodate a horizon of so many miles? The size of the eyes is so small, and they can accommodate such a large horizon. Where is it accommodated? It is accommodated within. That is the only example one can give. It is a dimension that cannot be measured, but that is accommodating, that is an accommodation. The accommodation of the eye is not a recognized dimension, yet it is a dimension. In the same way there is a dimension of mind. One can think deeply and feel profoundly; one can be conscious of life and be more deeply conscious still. But one cannot point to it, because this dimension is abstract. If there is any word, it can only be called "within." Through that dimension a current runs from the innermost plane to the physical plane, and there it keeps life living. That is why one can say that breath is the soul and soul is the breath. It is important to understand that one does not inhale like a straight line, going in and coming out the same way, as one imagines it to be. The real action is that of a wheel, a circle; from the nostrils the breath makes a circle, and the end of the circle is again in the nostrils.

The third point to understand about breath is that, just like an electric wire, it shows a glow. As the heat and light are not confined to that glow but are around it too, in the same way the radiance of this circle of breath that goes on through the body touches every part of the body.

Another rule to be observed is that with every direction in which the current of breath goes it causes a different action and a different result. For instance, contracting, stretching, blinking—all these actions are the play of the breath going in different directions. So it is with every natural action one does during the day. Also coughing, yawning, heaving a deep sigh, all these are different actions of breath. Besides, the ability to eat and drink, the ability to expel all that one has in the body, are all results of different directions through which breath works. If the breath does not work in one direction, then that particular activity of the body is stopped. It is a science that has yet to be explored by scientists and physicians. And the more it is explored, the less necessity there will be for operations and many other dreadful things that doctors have to do or to give to their patients. Also the tendency to lung diseases, the pain of childbirth, early death—all these will be avoided when the science of breath is well understood by the scientists of the day and practiced by the generality.

The picture of God and of souls is that of the sun and its rays. The rays are not different from the sun; the sun is not different from the rays. Yet there is one sun and many rays. The rays have no existence of their own; they are only an action of the sun. They are not separate from the sun, and yet the rays appear to be many different rays. The one sun gives the idea of one center. So it is with God and man. What is God? The spirit that projects different rays, and each ray is a soul. Therefore the breath is that current which is a ray, a ray that comes from that sun which is the spirit of God. This ray is the sign of life. What is the body? The body is only a cover over this ray. When this ray has withdrawn itself from this cover the body becomes a corpse.

Then there is another cover, which is the mind. The difference between mind and heart is like that between the surface and the bottom. It is the surface of the heart that is mind, and it is the depth of the mind that is heart. The mind expresses the faculty of thinking, the heart of feeling. This is an inner garb, a garb worn by the same thing that is called breath. Therefore, if the ray that is the breath has withdrawn itself from the body, it still exists, for it has another garb, it has a garb within. The outer garb was the body; the inner garb is the mind. The breath continues to exist, and if it is lost in that garb which is called mind, then there is another garb finer still, called the soul. Breath runs through all three: body, mind, and soul.

Seeing from this point of view one will realize that man has never been separated from God, that with every breath man touches God. He is linked with God by the current of breath, just as people draw water from a well, the rope in their hands and the jug of water in the well. The jug has the water, but the rope is in the hand. Insofar as our soul is in the spirit of God, it is the ray of the divine sun, while the other end of it is what we call breath. We only see it reaching so far and no further because it is only the higher part of the physical body that touches different planes. The breath goes there, but we do not see the action of breath. The action of breath in our body is limited; but in reality this current, this breath, connects the body with the divine spirit, connecting God and man in one current.

The central current of our mind is also breath. That is why we do not breathe only through the body, but also through the mind, and through the soul too. Furthermore, death is only the departing of the body from this main current that we call breath. But when the body has departed the mind still adheres to it, and if the mind is living, the person is living also. This is what gives us the proof of the hereafter. Many will say, "How uninteresting to live after death not as an individual, a body, but as a mind!" But it is the mind that has made this body; the mind is more self-sufficient than we can imagine. The mind is in a sphere in which it has its own body, just as this physical body belongs to the physical sphere. The body of the mind is as sufficient as and even more concrete than the body we have in the physical world, for the reason that the physical body is very limited and subject to death and decay. The body of the mind which is ethereal lasts long, being less dependent upon food and water; it is maintained more by breath than by anything else. We are maintained even in this physical world chiefly by breath, although we recognize bread and water and other food as our sustenance. If we only knew that bread and water are not even a hundredth part of our sustenance compared with what breath does in our life! We cannot exist five minutes without breath; we can be without food for some days.

Since breath has such great importance, the greatest possible importance, it is clear that the way to bring order and harmony to our body, to bring order and harmony to our mind, to harmonize mind with body, and to harmonize body and mind with soul, is by the breath. It is the development of breath, knowledge of breath, practice of breath that help us to get ourselves straightened out, to put ourselves in tune, to bring order into our being. There are many who without proper guidance and knowledge practice breath. Year after year they go on and very little result is achieved. Many go out of their minds, and very often the little veins of the brain and chest are ruptured by wrong breathing. There are many who have experienced this by not knowing how to breathe. One has to be extremely careful; one must do breathing practices rightly or not do them at all.

One cannot speak fully of all that can be accomplished with the help of breath. If there are people living in the world today who while standing on the earth witness the inner planes of existence, if there are any who really can communicate with the higher spheres, if there are any who can convince themselves of the life in the hereafter and of what it will be like, it is the masters of breath, and not the students of intellectual books.

The yogis have learned very much about the secret of breath from the serpent; that is why they regard the serpent as the symbol of wisdom. Shiva, the lord of yogis, has a serpent around his neck as a necklace. It is the sign of mystery, of wisdom. There are cobras in the forests of tropical countries, especially in India, which sleep for six weeks. Then one day the cobra wakens, and it breathes because it is hungry; it wants to eat. Its thoughts attract food from wherever it may be; food is attracted from miles away by its thoughts. The breath of the cobra is so magnetic that the food is helplessly drawn: a fowl, a deer, or some other animal is drawn closer. It is so strongly drawn that it even comes down from the air and falls into its mouth. The snake makes no effort. It just breathes, it opens its mouth, and its food comes into its mouth. Then it rests again for six weeks.

The serpent, too, is so strongly built that without wings it flies and without feet it walks. Also, if there is any animal that can be called the healthiest animal of all, it is the serpent. It is never ill; before it becomes ill it dies, yet it lives a very long time. It is said by those living in tropical countries that cobras can take revenge after as much as twelve years. If you once hit a cobra, it will always remember. That shows its memory, its mind. Music also appeals to the cobra, as music appeals to intelligent people. The more unintelligent the person, the less music appeals to him; music is closely related to intelligence. This shows that every sign of intelligence, of wisdom, and of power is to be seen in the cobra.

The mystics have studied the life of the cobra and they have found two wonderful things. One is that it does not waste energy. Birds fly until they are tired; animals run here and there. The cobra does not do so. It makes a hole where it lives and rests. It knows the best way of repose, a repose that it can continue as long as it wishes. (We cannot do this. We human beings, of all creatures, know least about repose. We only know about work, not about repose. We attach every importance to work, but never to rest. This is because we do not find anything in rest, but everyting in work. The work of rest we do not see.)

Besides, the natural breathing capacity of the cobra is such as no other creature shows. That capacity goes as a straight line throughout its body. The current that it gets from space and that runs through it gives it lightness and energy and radiance and power. Compared with the cobra all other creatures are awkwardly built. The skin of the cobra is so very soft and of such silky texture, and in a moment's time it can shed its skin and be new, just as if born anew. The mystics have learned from it. They say, "We must go out of our body just as the cobra goes out of its skin; we must go out of our thoughts, ideas, feelings, just as the cobra does with its skin." They say, "We must be able to breathe as rhythmically, to control our breath as the cobra does. We must be able to repose and relax in the same way as the cobra can. Then it will be possible to attain all we desire." As Christ has said, "Seek ye first the kingdom of God and all things shall be added unto you." The same things that are added to the cobra, all that it needs, could be added to man also if only he did not worry about them. As Sa'adi has said, "My self, you worry so much over things that you need, but know that the One who works for your needs is continually working for them. Yet you worry over them because it is your disease, your passion that makes you worry all the time!"

When we look at life more keenly, we see it is the same. Our worry about things seems to be our nature, our character; we cannot help it. It becomes such a part of our nature to worry that if we had no worry we would doubt if we were really living! Mystics, therefore, for thousands of years have practiced control of the breath, its balance, its rhythm, the expanding, lengthening, broadening, and centralizing of the breath. By this great phenomena have been accomplished. All the Sufis in Persia, in Egypt, in India have been great masters of breathing. There are some masters who are conscious of their spiritual realization with every breath they inhale and exhale. With every breath comes the consciousness of their plane of realization.

For a person who really knows how to work with breath, if he is not lazy, there is nothing he cannot accomplish; he cannot say of anything that it is impossible. Only it requires work. It is not only a matter of knowing the theory, but it requires the understanding of it. That is why the adepts, the mystics do not consider breathing only as a science or as an exercise; they consider it as the most sacred thing, as sacred as religion. In order to accomplish this breathing a discipline is given by a teacher.

But there is a great difficulty. I have found sometimes in my travels, when I have been speaking about these things, that people come with preconceived ideas. They are willing to learn, but they do not want discipline. But in the army there is discipline; in the factory, in the office there is a certain discipline; in study at the university, everywhere there is discipline. Yet in spiritual things people do not want it; when it comes to spiritual things they make difficulties. They think so little of it that they do not want to make any sacrifice. Because they do not know where it leads to, they have no belief. Besides, there are false methods that are taught here and there, and people are commercializing that which is most sacred. In that way the highest ideal is brought down to the lowest depth. It is time that the real thing should be introduced, seriously studied, experienced, and realized by practice.

From the mystical point of view it is evident that there is some strength, some current, some affinity that runs through and binds togther all the trees and plants in a forest, and also causes the desert to be without them; that causes the coal mine to have coal, the gold mine to have gold, the sulphur mine to have sulphur in it. This strength, or force, draws all these elements together.

So it is too with the tides of the sea. It accounts for the waters running in the same direction, whether at first they tended towards the south, the east, the west, or the north; it accounts for the surface of the waves keeping a rhythm. Wherever we look, be it the changes of the seasons, the changes of the weather, or even the constant circles that the earth describes on its journey, all these show the same underlying current, the current of the whole of nature, which is the real breath. The whole universe is going on with a certain rhythm; there is a current that keeps the whole universe going. It is one breath, and yet it is many breaths.

There is a tide that has a cycle of forty days, a tide that has a cycle of seven days, and another of thirty days. Yet at every moment waves are rising and falling. There is a wave under the wave, and a wave over the wave. There is a tide that turns twice a day, and also a tide that turns once a month. So is it with breath: one breath, and yet many breaths.

Then consider how the trees keep together. There is one tree, and yet its branches and its fruits and its flowers all turn in different directions. Every branch takes a different direction, and yet all keep together. What is it that directs the vigor and the strength of one branch and not the others in that direction—for they are all attached to the same tree stem? Is it not that life current which runs through it that directs their ways? As long as it runs through a tree it produces fruit and flowers.

So it is with animals and birds and people. The same current of life runs through all. Man is the ideal being, as the scripture says.

He is ideal because intelligence is given to him to perceive the secret of this breath, whereas from animals and birds it is hidden. The life of all creatures is mysterious and full of wonder, but man alone is blessed with the intelligence that conveys the power of understanding the secret of the breath. If there is anything more lasting than our transitory life it is this, the secret of our being. It is by this that man is able to master life both here and in the hereafter.

Having understood this truth, mystics have been able to teach that the religion of all religions is the knowledge of self, for the knowledge of self brings the knowledge of life. This life current that runs through the center of man's being, attaching mind to body and to all other planes of existence as well, it is this that is all important. It passes from man's innermost being out to the body, which is the instrument whereby man is able to experience life on the surface. When he has knowledge of this a person begins to realize, "I am not as small as I had thought, not as weak as I had thought; I am much stronger on other planes. I can live much longer than I could on the physical plane. I can see myself on all the different planes by means of that inner knowledge of the breath."

Therefore to the mystic breath is like a lift, a lift in which he rises up to the first floor, and then to the second, and then to the third floor—in fact wherever he wishes to go.

The mystery of the Sphinx, and the mystery of *buraq*, which is mentioned in the life of the Prophet Muhammad, has to do with this. When the Prophet reached the court or gate of God, the *buraq* was sent. The *buraq* was an animal with wings, and the Prophet rode upon it in order to reach the gate of the highest heaven. He passed through gate after gate as he passed the seven heavens. In the end he arrived at the gate of the highest.

What does this allegory mean? The body of the *buraq* is this physical body. The wings represent the ability of the breath to reach far and yet retain its connection with the physical body. The Prophet mounting upon his back represents any soul who treads the spiritual path. Whoever has courage, whoever has faith, whoever has confidence, whoever has trust, whoever has patience and hope and perseverance, can tread this path and make use of the vehicle of the breath.

If we read the history of Buddha, who was a yogi, we shall find that without yoga and without spiritual meditation, which is accomplished by breath, no one in this world has ever attained spiritual perfection. The healing power of Christ, the magnetism of Muhammad, the miraculous power of Moses, the charm of Krishna, and the inspiration of Buddha—all these were attained by breath. How did they attain them if there were not a current passing between us on the earth and the source of energy, the source of power and magnetism?

Is it not plain that breath conveys even the words that go out from our lips to the ears of the hearer? The voice is breath. The word is breath. Without breath speech cannot be produced. Yet a person may easily accept this and acknowledge that it is true that it is breath that does this, but he will not willingly believe that thought also is breath. He can see the movement of the air that arises from speech, and he wonders if it is meant that thought also causes a movement of the air. This is because he does not understand that a life current runs through it all, and that is breath. It is easily seen when it manifests itself upon the physical plane, but on the higher planes it is not seen; yet it extends higher than the planes. If there is anything that connects the mortal with the immortal, it is this bridge which we call breath. It is a bridge whereby to pass from the world of mortality to the world of immortality; it is the bridge whereby immortality passes down to mortality. That life which seems mortal is really the ray of immortal life. What seems mortal is only the shell. It is not life that is mortal, it is the cover that makes it seem mortal.

From the time when man first perceived that there was a secret in breath, he has wanted to use his understanding of the secret in order to be able to perform wonders and reach the spirits, to master the elements, read thoughts, comvey thoughts, and to perform psychic or occult phenomena. But to seek to do these things is to give pearls to buy pebbles. How wasteful to spend life in gaining these powers when breath is the rope that takes us from this mortal plane to immortality, that saves us from the struggles and worries of this transitory life, and leads us to the happiness and joy and peace for which every soul longs! If breath can accomplish these pearls will it not also accomplish the small things, the

pebbles, the worldly needs? Yes, it will. After all, to have performed a few wonders is nothing.

One person is perhaps striving all day to earn his own bread
so that he may live in a comfortable manner; another is always
worrying about how to maintain himself and his children. Another is thinking, "What can I do to save my fellow man from
his trouble?" If we compare these people, in order to see
who is the greatest, we see that he is greatest whose ideal is
greatest.

When we consider the great heroes of the past and present,
those whom we admire and to whom we look with hope for right
guidance, we shall find that what has made them great has been
the greatness of their ideal. The lower the ideal, the less the efforts;
the higher the ideal, the greater the life. If we use all our intelligence and strength and wisdom to accomplish some little thing, it
is only a waste of life. To consider what great things one can
accomplish, to seek to do those things which will be most useful
and valuable to others, that is the ideal life. The person who has
earned money only to keep himself comfortable, what has he
accomplished with his life? If he has just gratified his wish to roam
about in a motorcar, to set up a comfortable home, to have people
waiting upon him, he cannot be happy, because he has not accomplished anything with his life. He may possess many houses, he
may possess much money in the bank, he may make a great name;
but it will amount to nothing in comparison with the person
whose power is greater than all wealth, position, or fame. Such a
one will be much happier with the small things of the world; he
has gained that peace with which the pleasures and transitory joys
of this earth offer no comparison.

The one life is like the lips touching a cup of delicious wine; the
other life is like drinking the whole cup full of heavenly wine.
What a difference between just touching the wine with the lips
and drinking it! The pleasures of life are like touching the wine.
The experience of these pleasures is only like a dream, a passing
joy; it comes and goes again. One longs for the joy of that little
pleasure to stay, but how can it stay? Even if one tried for thousands of years, one could not keep the happiness that is external.
The only way to obtain the eternal bliss is to do as the mystics do,

and to rise by the aid of the breath from plane to plane, finding the greater joy and the greater happiness.

It resembles the taking of a drug. A person may sit in meditation and dream and imagine he is very happy. A materially-minded person may easily say that a meditative person hypnotizes himself into thinking he is full of joy, but is it not hypnotism when a little word of flattery pleases one, when a little silver and gold produces such a change of expression in one's countenance? The materialist, not understanding this, will laugh at the mystic and call him a dreamer. But if the mystic is a dreamer, what is the worldly man? Is he not a dreamer too? What produces the joy in these things that are of no importance? If it is good to be hypnotized by silver and gold, is it not better when the mystic is hypnotized by his divine ideal of perfection? The silver and gold will certainly be snatched away; at least the mystic's ideal of God will last.

When we consider how this life and our environment can cramp and restrict us, we understand how it is that with all our hopes we still seek solitude, try to be by ourselves, and close our eyes to all the passing things. The life and activity that are directed to experiencing the pleasures of life, the transitory sources of joy and pleasure all fade away before that which we seek in solitude, where we strive to reach the inner and enduring things. Even if our bed is comfortable, if our house contains all the comforts that the heart can desire, the mind still goes through all manner of torments, and sleep will not come. We may take a little rest and sit still in order to obtain peace, but the real trouble never goes. It is to drown this trouble that people take drugs and intoxicants and lose themselves in the pursuit of common things, however undesirable. Everybody strives to obtain some remedy that will enable him to realize the joy and pleasure and peace that his inner life unconsciously seeks, but he cannot get it. If he tries to obtain it through drugs or intoxicants, he only becomes a slave to them. If, failing these, he seeks to gain his desire through other vices, he will never find the contentment he seeks.

Come to the mystic, then, and sit with him when you are tired of all these other remedies that you have employed in vain; come and take a glass of wine with him. The mystic wine is the inner absorption, which removes all the worries and anxieties and troubles and cares of the physical and mental plane. All these are now done away with forever. It is the mystic who is at rest; it is he who experiences that happiness which others do not experience; it is he who teaches the way to attain that peace and happiness which are the original heritage of man's soul.

Chapter 29

RHYTHMIC BREATHING

Rhythm is the principal thing to be considered in breath, as it is
on the rhythm of the breath that the working of the whole mechanism depends. The chief reason of irregularity of the beats of the
heart or head is lack of rhythm in the breath.

As man generally neglects to think of this breath, he overlooks
the fact that his health entirely depends on rhythmic breath.
Rhythm is the central theme of the whole creation. Therefore the
infant moves his hands and legs by turns, forming a rhythm. This
shows that nobody teaches anyone rhythm; it is natural to all
beings. It is rhythmic movement that enables the fish to swim and
the serpent to climb trees. If rhythm were not an instinct, the
animal would never have known how to walk, nor the bird how
to fly.

The life of man is so pulled from all sides, so divided, that he
often forgets things that are most essential to his life, which the
lower creatures seem to keep more correctly in their lives. Neat-
ness in man's work and balance in man's actions show rhythm in
him. When man shows lack of balance in his life and when his life
is disturbed and all things seem to go wrong, it is most often that
the rhythm of his breath has become wrong. Irregularity of activ-

ity and repose in the habits of life causes disorder of rhythm in the breath.

Very often the eastern mystical exercises are wrongly understood. When a teacher gives a breathing exercise to his pupil, often he does not mean the breathing itself but rhythm.

Thought given to the breath becomes a weight upon it and naturally holds it longer in its movement, altering it from what it would otherwise naturally be. It is the following of the rhythm of breath and the keeping of the rhythm regular that bring about the best results.

On breath depends the capability, thoroughness, and efficiency with which one does one's work. Shortness of breath causes impatience in man, and lack of endurance and irregularity of the rhythm of the breath causes confusion in man and inclines him to be easily upset. Breath being the life power, it is the same life power that gives one strength to endure all things. One will always find that those who easily get cross, who quickly get upset, and who become annoyed instantly have something wrong with their breath. People, not knowing their difficulty, are annoyed with them; they are put aside and are considered disagreeable people. What they need is training of the breathing. When their bodies and minds have been so repaired, one will find no more disagreeableness in their nature. Then the artist who gets tired of his work and feels a lack of enthusiasm to complete it, a lack of interest and absence of inspiration— often it is all caused by some disorder in the breath.

Regular and rhythmic breathing gives health to both body and mind. Inspiration comes from above, but it comes as light. It is the work of the mind to receive it; if the mind is not ready to receive it the inspiration will come, but it will not be realized. This is like the difference between the metal gong and the wooden gong: the former will resound, the latter will not resound. It is not the fault of the one who strikes the gong, it is the gong itself that does not resound. So it is with the mind that receives inspiration and the mind that cannot conceive it. Yet to every mind inspiration comes; the only difference is that one receives it, the other rejects it.

Right breathing makes the mind vibrate, and vibration is the sign of life. All that vibrates more is more living; what vibrates less is less living. So it is with trees and animals; they show their life in their vibration.

The horse one chooses as the best is that horse whose nostrils are fully open and whose breath is full, which it shows by the expression of the eyes. A good horse shows vibrations by the quivering of its skin when its back is patted. It is not like a stone-like horse, which takes one step after ten lashes have been laid on its back. In the human being, life can be seen in the same way. It is termed in Hindustani *pani,* which means water.

They say that a horse or a person has a watery nature, which means a fluid nature, living, pliable. And this life, breath gives to body and mind. The influence of the breath on the body is like the influence of the weather on the world. As body and mind act and react upon one another, so the influence of the breath takes the chief place in directing both mind and body. Every emotion is caused by the breath flowing in a certain direction; also by the degree of force of the breath.

There are three different rhythms of breath that have influence upon the mind. Slow breath gives tranquility to the mind, and to all the creative faculties of mind scope is given by this rhythm. Moderate breath helps the mind to continue its activities. If one wanted to make out a plan of work or wished to accomplish a certain work, the slow activity of breath spoken of above would not be helpful, although for poetry or music the slow activity of the breath is more helpful. But quickness in the rhythm of the breath produces confusion, though it gives force to physical activities. One can run well or swim well when the breath is in a fairly quick rhythm. When the rhythm of the breath is too quick it brings confusion to the mind and exhaustion to the body.

One who does not breathe fully, in other words freely and deeply, can neither be well physically nor make use of his mental faculties. Very often one finds most learned and intelligent people unable to work as they wish to and incapable of finishing a work which they have taken up. Sometimes a person thinks it is from bodily weakness or mental weakness or lack of enthusiasm or loss of memory, not knowing that it is very often a matter of regularizing the breath. Most often people think that it is the tired or exhausted condition of the external senses that prevents their thinking, but in reality it is the lack of right breathing, for right breathing can make the mental faculties clearer and the organs of the senses more capable of perceiving. This shows that the mind can live a fuller life by what I call full breath. For a Sufi, therefore, breath is a key to concentration. The Sufi, so to speak, puts his thought under the cover of the breath. This expression of Rumi's I would interpret as meaning that the Sufi lays his beloved ideal in the swing of the breath. I remember my murshid's saying that every breath one inhales conscious of the Divine Beloved is the only gain there is, and every breath inhaled without this consciousness, the only loss.

Thought is conveyed without speech through the breath. The true wireless telegraphy is the rightly established current of breath. It is difficult for anyone to try it without practice in concentration and lacking development of breath, though unconsciously thoughts are always exchanged through the agency of the breath. The scientist is ready to believe that contagious diseases are spread by means of the breath, but it is the province of psychology to realize that thoughts and mental states such as hilarity, depression, energy, or sloth are conveyed by means of the breath. In the presence of an angry person one feels excited and inclined to anger; the contact of a hilarious person spreads around an atmosphere of hilarity. In the presence of a cold person one becomes cold; the contact of a warm-hearted person warms one. All this is done through the breath as the medium. If an angry person were to close his breath while angry, much less of his feeling would affect another. If a person who is prone to hilarity would close his breath in the presence of an expert comedian, he could protect himself from being influenced by him.

Yogis who rise above the thoughts and feelings of those around them attain power by control of the breath. So the method of the inner cult of Sufis also depends upon the science of breath. Knowledge of another person's pleasure or displeasure, the message of affection, the warning of hostility—all are received by way of the breath. The one who is conscious of the rhythm of the breath and whose breath is pure from grossness begins to perceive a sense that in time becomes a language to him. Thought reading is not necessarily intuition, although many people confuse thought reading and intuition. There is not much difference between the action of these two faculties: the difference is like that between the telephone and the telegraph. Thought reading comes from without and intuition comes from within, yet for both, rhythmic breath and a clear mind are necessary. The rhythmic breath helps the mind to be clear. Breath breaks the congestion that in the head produces confusion and in the heart depression, which covers the thoughts of others from one's perception and even from one's own intuition. A thought is better conveyed to another through breath than by speech, for a feeling put into words becomes half dead. Feeling in its own sphere is fully living, and when conveyed from there through the breath it reaches the mind to which it is sent. When a person has not developed his mind by concentration and tries to send his thought by the breath, he is not always successful. He is like a person trying to hit the target without ever having practiced in his life. It is practice that makes man perfect.

It is by the power of breath that the animals search for their food. Through breath they perceive what they must eat, what they must not eat. Through breath the carnivorous animals search for their prey. It is through breath that certain animals receive warning of dangers, and again it is through the breath that some animals when ill find their remedy. If the lower creation can do so much by the power of breath, how much more can man do, if he only knows the right way of the development of breath! It is through the breath that birds receive warnings of the changes of the weather, and accordingly they migrate in flocks from one place to another. Through the breath the herds of deer perceive approaching storms, changes of weather, or the approach of a lion or a tiger. Man, who is more capable of perceiving by breath still deeper things—warnings and calls from the earth and from heaven, which places are meant for him to dwell in or to settle in, discriminating between friend and foe and discerning their pleasure and displeasure—owing to his interest in the superficial things of life, cannot fully benefit by the power of breath.

Therefore Sufis and all students of the inner cult believe that breath is the means of receiving all intuitive knowledge from every direction of life. Absorbed in a thousand things of daily life, man gives very little thought to breath. Therefore he keeps his heart closed to all the revelation that can be received by the help of breath. Man as a rule is never conscious of his breath, of its rhythm, of its development, except at the time when he is so tired that he is breathless, when he is so excited that he feels choked up, or when something keeps the breath from flowing. For a Sufi it is desirable to be conscious of every breath. In the schools of the Sufis in the East the members of certain associations take up as their duty to remind the whole assembly of the same. So one after another, in turn, takes it up as a duty. They call aloud *"Hush ba dam,"* meaning, "Keep conscious of the breath." *Nazar ba qadam* is added when the Sufis are walking, which means, "Look down and see whose feet are these that are walking."

Chapter 30

THE POWER OF BREATH
(BREATH LIFE)

Mind is creative and thought is living, but out of what does mind create a thought? Out of the atoms of the mental sphere? But the current that attracts the desired atoms to complete a thought is the breath—not that breath which is outwardly manifest, but that part of breath the action of which is not felt by everyone. The more length and breadth the breath has, the more scope it gives for the creation of thought. It is therefore that the thoughts of the sages and mystics who have gained mastery over breath are more substantial and complete in themselves. Besides this, they prove to be more expressive and impressive.

The breadth of the breath is in its volume. This comes by the facility one has of breathing through wide nostrils and open lungs. The secret of the power of voice is also to be found in this. The voice of the commander of an army, which carries through the army and impresses the soldiers, thus encouraging them to fight, has breath as its secret behind it. Ali by his invocation of the sacred word, which he sometimes used to cry aloud on the battlefield, caused his enemies to tremble.

The length of the breath shows the length of life; lengthy breath is the sign of long life. This comes not only by wide nostrils and open lungs, but also by the accommodation that the body has for the breath, not only the nose and the chest but also the head and the abdomen.

There are some whose breath has volume or breadth but not much length, and there are others who have length and no breadth. But it is the balance of the length and breadth of the breath that gives balance to the mind.

It is the vibrations caused by the breath that become thought-waves that carry thoughts from one mind to the other. Therefore thought reading much depends upon the position in which two people sit with regard to each other. A certain position makes it easier for the breath to reach than another, although it is not always necessary that a person be facing one in order to receive thoughtwaves through breath. If the thought power is strong and the breath is sound enough to carry the thoughtwaves, a person, whether facing one or having his back turned, must receive the thought.

The mystics not only project their own breath and see the condition of their being manifest before themselves, but also they can make themselves responsive to receive the thoughtwaves of another carried by his breath. This receptivity not only enables an adept to read other's thoughts, but also to a mystic the condition of another revealed by the projection of the other person's breath upon his heart.

Plainly speaking, souls are likened to mirrors, and two mirrors facing one another become projected on one another, one manifesting the reflection of the other. The mirror that has no reflection is capable of manifesting the reflection of the other mirror. In this way breath enables a Sufi not only to know and see his own condition of life, but also to know and understand the condition of those he comes in contact with.

The breath of one person may, so to speak, overpower the breath of another, as a little stream can be washed away by a large stream of water. In this is the secret of knowing the condition of another person. A Sufi whose breath is lively (which is called in Sufic terms *nafs-e garm*) has the influence of scattering the thoughts, feelings, the vibrations of the atmosphere of another. In this way he is able to convey his thought or feeling and create his

224 THE KNOWLEDGE OF VIBRATION

vibrations as the atmosphere for another who needs it for his own betterment. In this way a Sufi brings a life and health to another person and can have an influence on the character of another person.

There is a great difference between a developed breath and an undeveloped one. There is as vast a difference, or an even vaster one between the breath of two persons as between two voices. A specially produced singing voice is quite different from the uncultivated speaking voice. It is a psychological fact that the voice and word of a person whose voice is cultivated make a greater impression than the voice and word of an ordinary person. How much more then must the influence of breath work silently. It is in this that is the mystery of the mystic's magnetism, which is healing, harmonizing, exalting, and at the same time invigorating.

Breath penetrates, breath permeates, breath strikes, breath absorbs, breath invigorates, and breath heals. It is therefore that souls with great powers make their thoughts and feelings penetrate into the minds and the hearts of others. As breath creates an atmosphere it permeates the bodies of others and also the sphere, charging the whole atmosphere with its particular magnetism.

The hearts of people are likened to gongs in a temple. Every spoken word strikes them, but by the power of breath one strikes them without a word. It is by the breath that one contracts illnesses, but also one absorbs defects and the depression of others, as well as joy and happiness. The breath of personalities healthy in mind and body is vitalizing. The breath of spiritual beings, whose love and sympathy goes out to others, is naturally healing.

It is no exaggeration that the whole phenomenon of life has breath as its mystery, and once the knowledge of breath is attained and breath is mastered by practice, one beholds a most wonderful phenomenon within and without. There are many who remain skeptical till they have fathomed the mystery of breath. Once they know it, they call it, as Hindus have called it for ages, breath life.

THE POWER OF THE WORD

There is nothing that cannot be accomplished, there is nothing that cannot be known, by the power of the word. Therefore the principal and central theme of esotericism and mysticism is the word.

Chapter 31

THE WORD: THE SECRET OF LIFE

We find in the Bible the words, "In the beginning was the word, and the word was God." We also find that the word is light and that when that light dawned the whole creation manifested. These are not only religious verses; to the mystic or seer the deepest revelation is contained in them.

The first phrase conveys to us that if anything exists that we can express, we can express it only by what we term "*word*." The second phrase explains another aspect of this mystery, which is that to enable the soul, surrounded by the darkness of this world of illusion, to come to the light, first the word was necessary. This means that the original spirit was concealed in the mystery of the word, and that in the mystery of the word the mystery of the spirit was to be found.

Here is a thought that may be pondered for years, each time with fresh inspiration. It teaches that the first sign of life that manifested was the audible expression or sound; that is the word. When we compare this interpretation with the Vedanta philosophy, we find that the two are identical. All down the ages the yogis and seers of India have worshipped the word god, or sound god. Around that idea is centered all the mysticism of sound or of

227

utterance. Not alone among Hindus, but among the seers of the Semitic races too, the great importance of the word was recognized. The sacred name, the sacred word, were always esteemed in the Jewish religion. Also in Islam, one finds the doctrine of ism e-Azam, which can be interpreted as the doctrine of the mystical word. The Zoroastrians, who had their religion given to them long before the time of Buddha or Christ and who have lost many of their teachings through the changes of time and conditions, have yet always preserved their sacred words. Sanskrit is now a language long dead, but in the meditations of the Indian yogis, Sanskrit words are still used because of the power of sound and vibration they contain.

The deeper we dive into the mystery of life, the more we find that its whole secret is hidden in what we call words. All occult science, all mystical practices are based upon the science of the word or sound. Man is a mystery in all aspects of his being, not only in mind and soul but also in that organism which he calls his body. The human body, the Sufis say, is the temple of God. This is not a mere saying or belief, for if man studies his body from the mystical point of view, he will find it to be much more subtle and far-reaching, and much more capable of doing, understanding, and feeling, than he believes it to be.

There are faculties of the soul that express themselves through a certain center in the human body. As there are parts of lands that have never become fertile soil because water never reaches them, so it is with these centers when the breath never reaches them. They are intuitive, they are full of peace and balance, they are the centers of illumination, yet they have never been awakened, for the person has breathed only in those parts of his body by which he lives and eats and performs actions. He is only half alive if you compared his existence with the fullness of life that can be obtained by spiritual development.

It may be compared to living in a great town and not knowing that there are many beautiful things that one has never seen. As there are many people who travel to distant lands and do not know their own country, so it is with man. He is interested in all that brings beauty and joy, and yet does not know the source of all such things in himself.

Man breathes, but he does not breathe rightly. As the rain falls on the ground and matures little plants and makes the soil fertile, so the breath, the essence of all energy, falls as a rain on all parts of the body. This also happens in the case of the mind, but man can never perceive that part of the breath which quickens the mind; only that felt in the body is perceptible. To the average man it is not even perceptible in the body; he knows nothing of it except what appears in the form of inhalation and exhalation through the nostrils. It is this alone that is generally meant when one speaks of breath.

The first life that existed was the life of God, and from that all manifestation branched out. It is a manifold expression of that one life: one flower blooming as so many petals, one breath expressing itself as so many words. The sacred idea attached to the lotus flower is expressive of this same philosophy, symbolizing the many lives in the one God. As the Bible says, "In God we live and move and have our being." When man is separated from God in thought his belief is of no use to him and his worship is of but little use to him, for all forms of worship or belief should draw man closer to God, and that which separates man from God has no value.

What is it that makes a word sacred or important? Is not every word as sacred and important as every other? That is true, but to whom is it sacred? To the pure and exalted souls for whom every word breathes the name of God, but not to the average person. There are souls who are at the stage of evolution in which every word is the sacred name. But when a teacher gives a method it is not given to exalted souls but to beginners. Therefore words are selected and given to pupils by the teacher, the guru or murshid, as a physician would give a prescription, knowing for which complaint and for what purpose it is given. Hafiz says, "Accept every instruction thy teacher giveth, for he knoweth which is thy path and where is thy good."

Great importance is given by mystics to the number of repetitions, for numbers are a science, and every number of repetitions has a certain value. One repetition means one thing, and a few more may mean something quite different, as in medicine one grain of a drug may heal and ten may destroy life. When Christ commanded to abstain from vain repetitions he was not, as is often thought, referring to the sacred name as used in worship or religious practices. There was a custom among the Semitic peoples (and it still exists in the East) of the constant use of the name of God by people in the street or marketplace. They would bring it continually into commerce or business, into quarrels and disputes, and it was against this abuse of the most holy name that Christ was speaking. In repetition lies the secret power. Therefore it is a great mistake when people take the ways of spiritual culture lightly as an everyday interest, as a hobby, and learn from a book or from some slight instruction given to them. If they attempt to practice from such knowledge only, they are risking their lives. If a center that should be awakened at a certain time of a person's evolution were awakened before that time, it would be a disaster.

There are certain words that attract blessing in life: some attract power, some bring release from difficulties, some give courage and strength. There are words that can heal, others that give comfort and ease, and again others that have even greater effects. When a person in need of peace and rest uses words that bring courage and strength, he will become even more restless. It is just like giving someone a tonic to cure a high fever.

Then there is another question, namely, what makes a word powerful? Is it the meaning, the vibration, the way it is used, or the knowledge of the teacher who teaches the pupil to repeat it? The answer is that some words have power because of their meaning, others because of the vibrations they produce, again others for their influence upon the various centers. There are some words given by saints, sages, and prophets that have come inspirationally from God. In them is all blessing and the mystery of how to acquire all that the soul desires in life. If there exists any phenomenon or miracle it is in the power of words. But those who know of this power and who possess it never show it to others. Spiritual attainment is not a thing to be brought before people to prove that it is real, or as a show.

What is real is a proof in itself; what is beyond all price or value does not need to be made much of before people. What is real is real, and the precious is precious in itself; it needs no explanation nor pleading.

The greatest lesson of mysticism is to know all, gain all, attain all, and be silent. The more the disciple gains, the more humble he becomes. When any person makes this gain a means of proving himself in any way superior to others it is a proof that he does not really possess it. He may have a spark within himself, but the torch is not yet lighted. There is a saying among the Hindus that the tree that bears much fruit bows low.

Words have power to vibrate through different parts of the human body. There are words that echo in the heart, and there are others that do so in the head. Others again have power over the body. By certain words definite emotions can be quickened or calmed. There is also a science of syllables that has its own particular effect.

Wagner did but repeat the teaching of the mystics of the East when he said that he who knows the law of vibrations knows the whole secret of life.

Chapter 32

THE SOUND WITHIN

The mystic who knows the value of the word finds that word first in himself, for the secret of all the knowledge that one acquires in the world, whether worldly or spiritual, is the knowledge of the self. For instance, music is played externally, but where is it realized? It is realized within. A good word or a bad word is spoken outwardly, but where is it realized? It is realized within. Then where is the realization of this manifestation, of this creation that stands before us in all its aspects? Its realization is within.

At the same time the error of man always continues. Instead of finding realization within, he always wants to find it without. It is just like a person who wants to see the moon and yet looks for it on the ground. But if a person seeks for the moon for thousands of years by looking for it on the earth, he will never see it. He will have to lift up his eyes and look at the sky. So it is with the one who seeks the mystery of life outside: he will never find it, for the mystery of life is only to be found within. Both the source and the goal are within, and it is there that if he seeks he will find.

What is sound? Is it something outside, or is it something within? The outward sound only becomes audible because the sound within is going on, and when the sound within is shut off, then the body is not capable of hearing the outward sound. Today the human being has become so accustomed to external life that he hardly even thinks of sitting down alone, and when he is alone he occupies himself with a newspaper or something else. By always occupying himself with external life, a person loses his attachment to the life within. His life becomes superficial, and the result is nothing but disappointment. For in this world there is nothing in the form of sound, either visible or audible, that is as attractive as the sound within. This is because everything that the senses touch and that is intelligible to the mind of man is limited in time and effect, and thus makes no effect beyond its own limits.

The effect of a person's name has a great deal to do with his life, and very often one sees that a person's name has an effect upon his fate and career. This is because he hears that particular name called so often every day. Does it not happen that a person saying a humorous thing bursts out laughing, and a person saying a sad thing breaks into tears? If that is so, what an effect every word that one speaks in one's everyday life has upon oneself and upon one's surroundings!

One can see by this that the ancient superstition about not speaking an unlucky or an undesirable word has a meaning. In the East a child is always trained to think before it utters a word, for every word has psychological meaning and effect. Very often people reading a poem or singing a song of great love, a song of sorrow or tragedy, are affected by it; and very often their life takes a turn and is affected by it too.

A person who speaks of his illness certainly nourishes that illness. Very often I have heard people say that if a pain exists it must be a reality; how can one deny it? It is amusing to hear them say this, because reality is so far away, and our everyday life is such that from morning till night we do nothing but deny it. If one could only know where the truth lies, what the truth is. If one could only know it and see it, one would understand that in reality all else is nonexistent.

When one studies the secret behind this idea, one must admit the power of the word. This is a metaphysical science that should be studied. The depth of the word of each person is very different, and if a person has spoken a hundred words in one day, do you think that every word has the same power? No, the power and effect of any particular word depend upon the state in which that person was and from what depth the word rises, and upon that depend the power and light of that word. For instance, you will always find that the word of a person who has a habit of telling lies and who is insincere has no force, while the word of the one who speaks with conviction, who is sincere, and who tells the truth has strength. His word has light; his word penetrates. Sometimes a person's voice is full of sadness and heartbreak. His word is full of sincerity, and it has all the power to penetrate; such is its effect upon the listener. Then there is the person who is light-headed, who is not deep, who is not serious enough in life; everything he says and does is always on the surface. He inspires no one with confidence, for he himself has no confidence.

Besides this, the word will have power according to the illumination of the soul. Then that word does not come from the human mind, that word comes from the depth, from some mysterious part that is hidden from the human mind. It is in connection with such words that one reads in the scriptures phrases such as "swords of flame" or "tongues of flame." Whether it was a poet or whether it was a prophet, when that word came from his burning heart then it rose as a flame. In accordance with the divine spirit that is in the word, that word has life, power, and inspiration. Think of the living words of ancient times; think of the living words that one reads in the scriptures, the living words of the holy ones, the illuminated ones. They live and will live forever. It is a music that may be called magic and a magic for all times. Whenever such words are repeated they have the same magic and that power.

Those words that the illuminated souls of all ages have spoken have been preserved by their pupils. In whatever part of the world these sages were born or lived, what they let fall as words has been gathered up like real pearls and has been kept as scriptures. Therefore, wherever one goes in the East, one finds that the followers of the various religions use the words of the illuminated ones whenever they pray, and they do not need to put them into their own language. Words spoken by the great ones have been preserved for ages in order that they might be used for meditation.

There is a still more scientific and greater mystery of the word. It is not only what the word means, it is not only who has spoken the word, but the very word in itself has also a dynamic power. The mystics, sages, and seekers of all ages, knowing the mystery of the sacred word, have always been in pursuit of it. The whole meditative life of the Sufis is built upon the mystery of the word. For the word "Sufi," according to the explanation of the initiates, is connected with *sophia,* which means wisdom; but not wisdom in the outer sense of the word, because worldly cleverness cannot be wisdom. The intellect, which is very often confused with wisdom, is only an illusion of wisdom. Wisdom is that which is learned from within, and intellect is that which is acquired from without.

Wisdom is a form in which the souls that have come to realization have tried to perceive and interpret to themselves the word they found in life. Wisdom is the interpretation of life, made by someone whose point of view has become different by looking at life in the sunlight. One arrives at this point of view not by study alone, but by association with those who have that particular point of view. Besides, by diving deep into life one comes to the realization of truth, and for diving deep into life there is a way or process. It is possible that either with some difficulty or with ease one finds a place one is looking for in a town: one may look for it in different directions and at last find it, but by asking somebody who knows one can find it sooner.

The source of wisdom is above; the source of intellect is below. Therefore one does not adopt the same method or process to attain wisdom as that which one adopts to acquire intellect. In short, though the attainment of that wisdom is achieved in various ways by various people, yet the great mystery of attaining the divine wisdom lies in the mystery of the word.

The word is a body of the idea, and the idea is the soul of the word. As the body represents the soul, so the word represents the idea. The idea can only be expressed in the word, so the soul can only be seen in the body. And those who deny the existence of the soul must also deny the existence of the idea. They must say that only the word exists, without an idea, which in reality is impossible. Behind every word there is an idea veiled in one or a thousand veils, or clearly represented by the word. However, the word is a key to the idea, not the idea itself. It is not the word that is in itself an idea, but only an expression of it. The ears hear the word; the mind perceives the idea. If the idea were not there, the word would convey nothing to the listener. If one said to a child, "Sarcasm is an abuse of the intellect," what will the innocent child understand by it? The word "sarcasm" will be known by the one who is capable of being sarcastic. This opens up another idea, that those who accuse others with authority must necessarily know the fault themselves. A person, however evolved, will now and then show childishness in expressing his opinion about another, proving thereby guilty of the same fault in some proportion. No one can tell another, "You told a lie," who has not told a lie himself once at least in his life.

No doubt the idea is vaster than the word, as the soul is wider than the body. Every idea has its breadth, length, height, and depth. Therefore, as a world is hidden in a planet, so a world of ideas is hidden in a word. Think therefore how interesting life must become for the one who can see behind every word that is spoken to him its length, breadth, height, and depth. He is an engineer of the human mind. He then knows not only what is spoken to him, but he knows what is meant by it. By knowing words you do not know the language; what you know is the outside language. The inner language is known by knowing the language of ideas. So the language of ideas cannot be heard by the ears alone; the hearing of the heart must be open for it. The seer must understand from a word spoken to him what even the one who speaks does not know. For every human being sometimes thinks, speaks, and acts mechanically, subject to the condition of his body, mind, and situation in life. Therefore, as a physician finds out more about a complaint than the patient himself, so the mystic must comprehend the idea behind every word that is spoken to him. One might think with the continual growth of such perception the life of a Sufi must become very much troubled, for when the average person would be seeing a yard's distance a Sufi may be seeing the distance of a mile. Yes, [there is no doubt] it could be troublesome if the mystic did not develop all around. The elephant's strength is required to carry the load of an elephant. It is not enough to become a seer alone, but what is needed is to develop the strength that takes all things easily, the power that endures all things, and the might that enables one to surmount all difficulties in life.

Chapter 33

PSYCHOLOGICAL DEVELOPMENT BY THE WORD (MANTRAMS)

The idea of the power of the word is as old as the Vedas of the Hindus; the modern world is now awakening to it through what is called "psychology." Through psychology there is a possibility of exploring that ancient treasure which the seekers after truth developed for thousands of years in the East.

Man today looks at psychology as a side issue and as something that can help medical science, but there will come a day when mankind in this modern world will look upon the science of psychology in the same way that the people in the East have looked upon it: as the main thing in religion and spiritual development.

As to the power of the word, a new idea has been coming from various places under different names, and it is that the repetition of a certain word or phrase is of great help in curing oneself of certain illnesses. Psychology in the western world is discovering this today. But what about the Buddhists, who for so many centuries have repeated the different mantrams, sitting in their temples repeating them two thousand, three thousand times a day? What about the Hindus, who have preserved their age-old sacred mantrams and chants? Even though the language is extinct, they have preserved these ancient chants up till now. What about the Jewish people, who still preserve the sacred songs that they have inherited from the prophets of Beni Israel? What about the Muslims, who for ages have repeated the Qur'an every day for so many hours, and who still continue to repeat the verses of the same book today? And think of the secret there is behind the repetitions of the Catholic mystics!

The Zoroastrians, the Parsees, whose religion dates from perhaps eight thousand years ago, have still maintained their sacred words, and they chant their prayers several times a day, repeating the same words every day. But the modern person reads a newspaper today and throws it away, and tomorrow he will ask for another newspaper!

No doubt there is great value in the fact that millions of people have been clinging to these mantrams, repeating them day after day perhaps all their lives and never becoming tired of doing so. If it were, as it is sometimes called, a religious fanaticism, then nobody could continue those repetitions, as no intoxication can continue longer than its influence lasts; then it goes and a person is disillusioned.

This shows us that beneath the repetition of words a mystery is hidden. The day when man has fathomed it he will have discovered a great secret of life. One way of understanding this mystery is to keep in mind that as a reflector is needed behind the light in order to direct the light fully, so a reflector is needed for the voice, as every voice producer knows. The voice producer will always give exercises to the pupil to repeat and repeat in order to get this reflector into the right condition, so that all the possibilities of producing a full voice may be brought out.

That is the material side of the question, but then there is the psychological side of it. This is that not only the organs of the physical body have this quality of reflection, but also the mind, or what we call feeling, can be a reflector. We very rarely explore this question; we cut it short every time we are faced with it. For instance, when a person is telling a lie, naturally we feel it is wicked, and we cannot readily believe it. However loud his voice may be, however strongly he emphasizes his lie, since it is a lie we feel it is wicked, because psychologically the power of mind must act as a reflector. But in these circumstances it does not act as this person wishes, for his mind is not really behind it.

Take an ordinary phrase such as "thank you" or "I am very grateful to you." If during the day ten people say it to you, each one of them has a different power of conveying it, because if the reflector is not giving power from behind a person may say a thousand times, "I am so grateful to you," but it will have no effect.

There is another way of looking at the same question: suppose there is one person who tells you something, and you readily believe it; and there is another person who tells you the same thing perhaps fifty times over, and you do not feel inclined to believe it. What does this show? It shows that we must prepare ourselves before we say anything. It is not always what we say but how we feel it, how we express it, and what power is hidden behind our expression, what power brings it forth, that causes the word to pierce the heart of man.

Then there is the question as to how one can best prepare oneself to utter a certain word effectively. Symbolically speaking, a person may pronounce the same word a hundred times before people and it remains an iron word; he may say it fifty times, and it is a copper word; he may say it twenty times and it is a silver word; but another person may say it only once, and it is a golden word. For instance a certain person may talk and talk and talk, and in order to convince you he may dispute and discuss and argue and bring up a thousand arguments to make you believe him. But the more he wants you to believe him the less he convinces you. Yet there is another person who tells you something perhaps only once, and you cannot help saying, "Yes, I believe it, I understand it, I am convinced."

How does one prepare oneself? How does one prepare the reflectors in order to make an impression with word? Yogis and Sufis have discovered certain practices that produce psychological development. Through these a person becomes naturally more and more sincere and earnest, and everything he says carries that power. Perhaps these practices have no value from the point of view of voice production, but they have very great value from the

psychological point of view. The practices referred to are such as
concentration, meditation, contemplation, and realization.

Regarding ancient words, a student of languages will find that
these words can be traced back to one and the same source. The
closer you approach the ancient languages, the more you will find
a psychological significance in them, and the languages of today
will seem like corruptions of them. It is surprising how many
words in the languages spoken today come from the ancient languages, and many names of persons are derived from them.

In the ancient languages words were formed by intuition. Modern languages are based on the grammar one learns. Certainly
words that have come purely by intuition and that form a language which is an action and reaction of man's experience of life
are more powerful than the words of the languages we speak
today. Thus they have a greater power when repeated, and a great
phenomenon is produced when a person has mastered those words
under the guidance of someone who understands that path.

Every vowel has its psychological significance, and the composition of every word has a chemical and psychological significance.
The yogis use special words that they repeat in the morning or in
the evening, and by this they reach a certain illumination or come
to a certain state of exaltation. It is this very science that was called
by the Sufis of ancient times *dhikr.* This is the science of bringing
about desirable results by the repetition of the proper words or
phrases. A chemist may have all the medicines that exist, but if
everyone went and got whatever medicine he liked, though he
might cure himself, he might also kill himself.

Even more difficult and more reponsible is the use of the repetitions of certain psychological words and phrases. It is the physician's responsibility to give a certain person a proper medicine for
his condition. In the East one searches for a guru, or a murshid as
the Sufis call him, who has the experience of psychological prescription, and one takes what the murshid has prescribed as an
instruction. First the murshid makes a diagnosis of the person's
condition, and according to that evolution he prescribes a word or
a phrase by the repetition of which that person may arrive at the
desired goal. Those who have some experience of voice production
will know that in the beginning the teacher does not give any

songs; he gives certain words and notes, and a special way of practicing by which the voice is developed.

In Sufism there are certain words that are considered sacred, and a person of simple faith will only know them as such. But besides being sacred they have psychological significance, and by repeating them a certain effect is produced.

It is very interesting to observe that science seems to be awakening to the significance of vibrations and their phenomena. The modern systems are not yet very much developed, but the aim is the same: to find out the conditions of the vibrations in the physical body, in order to treat the body in a scientific way.

When we see that similar systems were developed by the ancient mystics and occultists, and tried for thousands of years by numberless people all their lives, it is clear that these systems must bring about satisfactory results and give to many a treasure that has been kept as sacred for centuries by the seekers after truth.

The Sufi movement has made it possible for the people of the West who wish to reach that treasure, that source, by serious study and practice to obtain glimpses of the truth that the ancient mystics possessed.

Chapter 34

THE ECHO OF THE WHOLE UNIVERSE

One might ask what it is in a word that helps and why it helps. In answer to this I would say that there is no expression of life more vital than words because the voice is an expressive manifestation of breath, and breath is life itself. Therefore the spoken word not only makes an effect upon another person but also upon oneself. Every word one says has its effect not only upon one's body but also upon one's mind and spirit. If one utters a tactless or foolish word it not only offends another, but can prove to be of great disadvantage to oneself.

Often a person in a pessimistic mood or in a disturbed condition may express the wish for death or failure or wish for anything to happen. If he only knew what effects such wishes have he would be frightened. Even in pain, if a person could only refrain from saying, "I am in pain," he would do a great deal of good to himself. If a person who has met with misfortune would avoid saying, "I am experiencing a misfortune," it would be a great thing. For when a person acknowledges the existence of something he does not want, he only gives it greater life. When a person says, "Oh, I have waited and waited and waited, but my ship never comes," he is keeping his ship back; his ship will never arrive in port. But the one who does not even see the ship but says, "It is coming, it is coming," is calling it, and it will come.

Now what I have said concerns the meaning of the ordinary word. But the mystical word has far greater value than the word one uses in everyday language. Mystical words have come from three distinct sources: intuitive, scientific, and astrological. Intuitive words have come as sudden expressions from God-realized souls. Whatever word or phrase comes from souls that are tuned to the whole universe is something that has a much greater power than the words in common use. But apart from spiritual people, there may perhaps be someone among our friends or acquaintances whose one word has weight and power; whereas another person may speak a thousand words that only go in at one ear and out at the other. This is because in one person his mouth speaks, in another person his heart speaks, and yet in another his soul speaks. There is a great difference.

One might ask if it would be possible for a spiritual person to bring forth intuitively a word that has power. The answer is that a soul may become so much in tune with the whole universe that he hears, as it were, the voice of the spheres. Therefore what he says is like the echo of the whole universe. The person who is in tune with the universe becomes like a radio receiver through which the voice of the universe is transmitted. This is the personal aspect.

As to the scientific aspect, a deep study of human anatomy will show that there are delicate nerve centers that can only be affected by certain vibrations, and upon which the equilibrium and health of mind and body depend. Very often people have been cured of illness by the use of resounding scientific words, because such words have given to a certain center the vibration that was needed to give life to it. If one goes deeper into the science of the word, one will find that every vowel and every consonant has its own specific effect upon one's mind and body. Very often you will find, before seeing a person, that on hearing his name you get a kind of impression of what that person is like. It shows that a person's name can have a great effect on his character.

The astrological aspect is a very vast subject, and it is connected with every art and science. Vowels and words have their connection with astrological science: by using a certain word one evokes a certain planet, either in order to diminish its influence if it is unfavorable or to increase its power if it is favorable. Therefore in India every name given to a person is given in accordance with Hindu astrological science.

Many holy scriptures give evidence of the power of the words; but where has the knowledge of that science gone, so well known to the prophets of all times? The science of the word has been lost to most of mankind. The reason for this is that people have occupied themselves with the things of the earth, and so lost the ancient art. By losing that great science, that mystical secret, what has the soul attained? The soul has attained an increasing deafness, and this deafness increases as the more material life prevails. Nevertheless, in every period there have been some thinkers, some servants of God, working knowingly or unknowingly, to whom it was always clear that the word was lost, which means that the secret of the whole life was lost.

This of course is an exaggeration. The word that exists cannot be lost, but man has lost his capability of knowing, of hearing that word. Man no longer heard the word from the sky; he heard it from the earth. The result was the great awakening and progress of material science. All the great inventions of this time, which are like miracles, have come to great minds that have so to speak communicated with matter. Matter has spoken with them face to face. All these great inventions are the answer from the earth to the communication of these great minds with matter. Thus the word was not lost, but the direction was lost.

Man learns continually from the objective world to make things he can touch and can make intelligible, but he is always disbelieving in matters that are not intelligible. In this way he has become far removed from the main part of life's mystery. Nevertheless, if at any time in the world's history man has probed the depths of life, he has found what he sought by communicating with the inner life, in artistic expression and by communicating with the heavens. And what is that communication? It is the word.

When the Prophet Muhammad felt the need to communicate, he went away from the town and remained in solitude on the top of a mountain, sometimes fasting or standing, and staying there night and day for two or three days. What did he find in the end? He found that a voice began to speak to him, a voice in answer to his soul's cry. His soul so to speak went forth, pierced through all the planes of existence, and touched the source of all things. But how did the answer come and in what form? The answer came from everything: from the wind, the water, the atmosphere, the air —everything was bringing the same answer.

This experience is not limited to a certain person or a certain time. In our everyday life there are times when sadness comes, and it seems as if everything in the world, even the voice of the beasts and birds, causes sadness. Then again comes the hour of profound joy: at that time the sun helps to give joy and the clouds covering the sun also give joy. The cold, the heat, the friend, the enemy— all help to give joy.

This world to a mystic is like a dome, a dome that re-echoes all that is spoken beneath it. What is spoken from the lips reaches only as far as the ears, but what is spoken from the heart reaches the heart. The word reaches as far as it can, and that depends from what source it has come and from what depth it has risen. The Sufis of all ages have therefore given the greatest importance to the word, knowing that the word is the key to the mystery of the whole life, the mystery of all planes of existence. There is nothing that cannot be accomplished, there is nothing that cannot be known, by the power of the word. Therefore the principal and central theme of esotericism or mysticism is the word.

What is the word? Is the word just what we speak? Is that the word? No, that is only the surface of the word. Our thought is a word, our feeling is a word, our voice, our atmosphere is a word. There is a saying, "What you are speaks louder than what you say." This shows that even when a person does not speak, his soul speaks. How do fortunetellers read the future? They hear it. They say that they read it from the lines of the hand, by astrology, or from the actions of people. But what is all this? It is all a word, because word means expression: expression in voice, in word, in form, in color, in line, in movement. It is in this that we see that everything is united in the esoteric side of mysticism. Of course, many people in the West have said that for them it is very difficult to lead a meditative life in the activity of their world; they have so many responsibilities and occupations. My answer to this is that for that very reason they need more meditation.

I have heard many persons say that they have the greatest desire to give their time and thought to spiritual things, but that because they have not attained to a way of living that would free their mind to attend to these things, they believe they cannot take up anything spiritual. I see the reasonableness of their argument, because it is quite true that in this world, as life is today, it is difficult to move without money. Material things apart, even in spiritual things one cannot do without money. If I were to give a lecture and I had no room to give it in, it could not be done. If there were no advertisements in the newspapers no one would know about it and perhaps only two or three persons would be kind enough to come and listen to me. It is therefore natural that a person thinks like this, and he is not to be blamed.

At the same time, when we look at it from a different point of view, we still see that every moment lost in waiting for spiritual attainment is the greatest loss conceivable. Besides, one may go on thinking, "The day will come when I will change my life and yield to something higher, spiritual," and that day will never come. One has to do it today, just now, instead of saying, "Tomorrow I will do it." Otherwise one repents. Life is assimilating, time passes. Hours, months, years slip by before one realizes that they have done so. To the one who understands the value of time, spiritual attainment comes first. As Christ has said, "Seek ye first the kingdom of God, and all these things shall be added unto you."

I do not say, "Let everything go in order to pursue spiritual things." Spiritual attainment does not deprive one of material gains. One has only to keep in mind that spiritual things come first. In order to become spiritual it is not necessary to give up worldly things or all that is good and beautiful and valuable from the point of view of the material world. Solomon with all his wealth was not less wise. One need not give up all one has in order to become spiritual. If one should think that, it is a great pity. But to wait, saying, "I shall wait till my ship comes home, then I shall become spiritual"—who knows when the ship will come? It is never too late to start on the spiritual path, but at the same time it is never too early. The best thing therefore is that the moment one thinks, "It is already late, I must begin," one should start and go through all the tests and trials of this path, confident that there is nothing that cannot be accomplished once the spiritual path is taken.

A person may say that he would have to overcome many weaknesses, but the way of getting above weaknesses is by meditation. When there are many responsibilities in life, one's very reason tells one that it is better to meditate and make the responsibilities lighter. It is not getting worried over one's responsibilities that helps one, it is being responsible, but at the same time being strong enough to shoulder one's responsibilities. There are words that are known to the mystics which do not belong to any language, yet the words of many languages seem to have sprung from these mystical words. It is by the help of these words that one develops two faculties: seeing and hearing. By seeing I do not mean seeing with the eyes, but penetrating. It is the penetrating quality of seeing that makes a person a seer, and it is the real meaning of the word clairvoyance. Nowadays people have misused this word so much that one does not like to use it anymore, but then, there is no word left in the world that has not been misused. If one were so sensitive about words one would have to reject all language.

By hearing I do not mean listening. I mean responding; responding to heaven or to earth; responding to every influence that helps to unfold the soul. Through the response and the penetration that one gains by the power of the word in the end one attains the goal, the goal that is the yearning of every soul.

Chapter 35

SOUND: THE MAIN PRINCIPLE
IN MAN'S LIFE

In all the different languages spoken in the world today one central language can be traced as the mother language. No doubt it is difficult to establish the exact relation between languages, yet the relation between one language and another shows that the human race had one common language to begin with. Some linguists have held that it was the Sanskrit language; there are others who say that before Sanskrit there was another language.

Historians have different opinions, but metaphysics teach us that in the beginning there was only one language of the human race, and that from it all the other languages were derived. A historian cannot be a historian if he does not give a name to a language that is supposed to have been the first language, but for a metaphysician this does not matter. It is he alone who really understands and knows for certain that there was only one language. He does not mind if he does not know the name of that language.

This first language was more natural than the languages we know today, which are more complicated. Take for instance the language of birds and animals. These languages are not grammati-

248

cal; they are natural expressions of their real sentiments, of their real needs. It is by this natural expression that other animals of the same kind understand the warning they give to protect themselves, to leave the place where they are, the warning of death or danger, of a change of climate, of storm or rain coming. They have a certain way of expressing the affection, passion, wrath, anger they feel at that moment. Yet it is not a mechanical language, it is a natural expression, a natural language.

The primitive language of mankind was also a language of feeling, of natural expression, just like primitive figures. If we go back thousands of years we find that the name of every object was written as a sort of picture that suggested that object. Now that thousands of years have passed those symbols and forms have changed and the words of the primitive language have been changed. Yet the one who can see into life can trace back at least some forms, sounds, and words that came from the original human race. The effect of the original language of humanity was that every word and sound that was expressed not only conveyed a meaning to the mind of the person who said it, but also conveyed a sensation of particular feeling or sentiment to the one who heard it. As the ancient people cultivated this science they began to understand that sound in the form of voice is the main principle in human life.

It is the voice that shows whether a person is hard or tender, willful or weak-willed; a person's every characteristic can be recognized by his voice. The grade of evolution, his tendency, and his condition at that moment can be realized by his voice. This shows that far more than a face or expression or movement, the word can express a feeling or a condition, the real being of man. The central point of his life is to be found in his breath, for voice is only an expression of breath. When this voice is expressed outwardly, it is in the form of a word. It also has a kind of inward reaction, which again has an effect upon a person's mind, upon his body, upon his soul.

There are certain parts of the human body that may be considered as the factors of the intuitive senses. When by voice, by word, by breath those parts are brought into action and are awakened, a person begins to experience a fuller life. If that person is an artist, a musician, a writer, or a scientific genius, whatever he is, by cultivating all the natural faculties that are within him he can express his art or his science more fully.

It was with this secret in mind that the ancient people developed the science of yoga. By the repetition of certain vowels and certain words and by a particular way of breathing, they touched within themselves those centers which are connected with the intuitive faculties. This was not so only in the past. The school of the Sufis, whose origin was the ancient school of Egypt where Abraham was initiated, still exists; and there are words still used which maintain their ancient power. At the same time these schools have not treated this sacred idea as something ordinary. They have not spread it among people who would abuse it, because if you put a sharp sword into the hands of a child, the consequences will be fatal. If a person who has not yet risen above greed and pride and conceit is given all the power there is, how will he use it? What will he do with it? Therefore in the schools people were first taught moral culture and the attitude they should have towards their fellow men. For they believed, and they still believe, that any power that is ever attained must be used for one purpose only, and that is drawing nearer to God. If it is not used for that purpose but for selfish aims, then it is just as well that man remains without powers. It is for this reason that in the ancient schools, which have a long tradition behind them and which are meant to help humanity in drawing nearer to God, initiations are given.

What does initiation mean? Initiation means confidence on the part of the teacher and trust on the part of the pupil. Initiation is not given to the one who is curious, who comes to examine the teacher, or who comes to find out if in a particular method, in a certain cult, there is truth or not. If by any chance such a person received an initiation, he would go through it all and then without finding anything leave by the same door by which he had entered. For this treasure house is a magic house, a house wherein is every treasure—and yet a thief cannot find it. He will go through the house, he will go all around it, but he will not see anything, and he will go out with his hands empty. For truth is only for the one who is sincere. It is the one who is hungry who must be given food; it is the one who is thirsty who must be given water. He who is not hungry, to him food will do no good; and he who is not thirsty, water will not satisfy his need.

If a person wants to know these things in order to develop magnetic power, to accomplish his ambition, to gain power or influence, or to obtain more than he can get in his daily life, then it is useless. For the word, and especially the sacred word, is the key. As it is said in the Bible that first was the word, so the last key is also the word. It was the word that was the beginning of creation, and it is the word that opens the mystery of creation. The different centers of intuition, of inspiration, of evolution, are touched by the sacred word.

Scientists have discovered how radio messages can reach through space without any intermediary means, but one day they will discover the truth that has been known to the mystics for thousands of years: that man himself is the instrument, the receiver and the sender of that radio which is above all other kinds of radio. Radio can explain to us many of the possibilities that otherwise are difficult to comprehend; it explains to us that no word once spoken is lost. It is there and it can be caught. This supports what is said above: that the sacred word has such power that nothing, whether distance, space, air, or sea, can prevent it from entering and reaching the hearts that can catch it. Only, the difference is that the radio is used by those who communicate between themselves from one country to another, but the mystery of the word is known to those for whom communication between different parts of this world is nothing. Their aim is communication between this world and the other world.

But although the word was first, there was not at the beginning any specific word; there was only one life and one existence. When we speak of this world and that world, it is for our convenience. It is our speculation; it is our way of distinguishing between the different dimensions. But what in reality is a dimension? A dimension is a conception, and if anything it is a form of existence.

It is the same with time. In reality there is no such thing as time; it is we who have made a certain conception of it. There is only existence; there is an eternal continuity of life. In the same way, what we call this world and that world is really only our conception of all that hides the outer world from our material, physical eyes with which we have been accustomed to look at life. But there is only one existence, one life, eternal, everlasting. In short, words can be transmitted by radio from one place to another. This proves to us that if there is only one existence, one life, then in this world or in that world, here or in the hereafter, communication is possible for us, but possible in only one way: through man tuning himself, winding himself as it were to that condition where he lives fully.

Since the world contains so much falsehood, every good thing is imitated and every writing falsified. As there is such a great desire in people's minds to know something about reality, it seems that many institutions, societies, and groups try to speak about things that they themselves do not understand. We could count hundreds of groups today that are trying to bring belief in God by teaching what they call "spirit communications." But by doing this they spoil that sacred science, that very great phenomenon which one can only truly realize by attaining to the kingdom of God.

Chapter 36

NAME

The variety of things and beings and the peculiarities that make them differ cause the necessity of name. Name produces the picture of a form, figure, color, size, quality, quantity, feeling, and sense of things and beings, not only perceptible and comprehensible, but even of those beyond perception and comprehension. Therefore its importance is greater than all things. There is a great secret hidden in a name, be it the name of a person or a thing, and it is formed in relation to the past, present, and future conditions of its object. The right horoscope tells you therefore about the conditions of a person.

All mystery is hidden in name. The knowledge of everything rests on first knowing its name, and knowledge is not complete that is devoid of name. Mastery depends upon knowledge; one cannot master a thing of which one has no knowledge. All blessings and benefits derived from earth or heaven are gained by mastery, which depends upon knowledge, knowledge depending upon name. A person without the knowledge of the name of a thing is ignorant, and the one who is ignorant is powerless, for man has no hold over anything of which he has no knowledge.

The reason of man's greatness is the scope of the knowledge with which he is gifted, all the mystery of which lies in his recognition of the differences between things and beings. This not only gives man superiority over all creatures of the earth, but it even makes him excel the angels, the hosts of heaven. The Qur'an explains it in the following words, "When thy Lord said unto the angels, 'We are going to place a substitute on earth,' they said, 'Wilt Thou place there one who will do evil therein and shed blood, while we celebrate Thy praise and sancitify Thee?' God answered, 'Verily We know that which ye know not.' He taught Adam the names of all things, and then presented them to the angels, and said, 'Declare unto Me the names of these things if ye say truth.' They answered, 'Praise be unto Thee, we have no knowledge but what Thou teachest us, for Thou art all-knowing and wise.' God said, 'O Adam, tell them their names.' And when Adam came he told their names."

Every name reveals to the seer the past, present, and the future of that which it covers. Name is not only significant of form, but of character as well. The meaning of name plays an important part in a person's life, and the sound, the vowels in the name, the rhythm, number, and nature of the letters that compose it, the mystical numbers, symbol, and planet, as well as the root from which it is derived and the effect that it produces, all disclose their secret to the seer.

The meaning of a name has a great influence upon its possessor as well as upon others. From the sound of the letters and the word they compose the mystic can understand much about the character and fate of a person. An intelligent person generally gets the idea from the sound of letters that compose a name whether it is beautiful or ugly, soft or hard, consonant or dissonant, but he does not know what makes it so. The one who understands knows why it is so.

Letters singly or together are pronounced either smoothly or with difficulty, and have their effect accordingly upon oneself and upon another. Names that are smooth and soft-sounding make a soft effect upon the speaker and listener, whereas hard-sounding names have a contrary effect. Man naturally calls soft things by smooth names and hard things by hard-sounding names, as for instance flower and rock, wool and flint, etc. Language, and especially name, shows the class of people and character of families, communities, and races. Vowels play a great part in the name and its influence. *E* and *i* denote *jemal,* the feminine quality of grace, wisdom, beauty, and receptivity. *O* and *u* denote *jelal,* the masculine quality of power and expression. *A* denotes *kemal,* which is significant of the perfection in which both these qualities are centered. The above-named vowels in the composition of the name have an effect according to their place in the name, whether in the beginning, center, or end.

Fate in Sanskrit is called *karma,* meaning the rhythm of past actions. The influence of rhythm suggested by a name has an effect upon the entity whose name it is, as well as upon those who call him by that name. Evenness of rhythm gives balance, while unevenness causes a lack of balance. The beauty of rhythm beautifies the human character.

By rhythm is meant the way in which the name begins and how it ends, whether evenly or unevenly, on the accent or before the accent. The accent falling on the beginning, middle, or end varies the effect, which plays a part in a person's character and fate. The rhythm of the name suggests the main thing in life, balance or its lack. Lack of balance is a deficiency in character and causes adversity in life. The number of letters plays a great part in the name of a person. An even number shows beauty and wisdom, and an odd number shows love and power.

Number plays a great part in life, and especially in name. Each letter of a name has its numerical value; in oriental science this is called *jafr.* By this system not only are names given to buildings, objects and people, conveying their period of commencement and completion, but the combination of these numbers conveys to the seer its mystical effect.

Names have a psychic effect upon their owners and even upon surroundings. The names of elementals and djinns, the sacred names of God, and the holy names of the prophets and saints, written according to the law of their numerical value, act as a magical charm for the accomplishment of different objects in life. And by the combination of such names written or repeated in their numerical form, wonders are performed.

Every letter, either singly or when grouped in a word, produces a picture that tells its secret to the seer. For instance *x* makes a cross and *o,* zero, both of which have a meaning. The alphabet used in modern times is a corruption of the original ones, though the old Arabic and Persian writings which are found on arches, walls, hems of garments, brass vessels, and carpets are of most perfect and beautiful design. A great symbolic significance may be seen in the Chinese, Japanese, Sanskrit, and other ancient scripts. Every line, dot, and curve has a meaning. The ancients used to write every name not with different letters but as a picture signifying what they wished to express. The picture was divided into different parts and each part was used to represent a certain sound, and in this way the alphabets were made. By this breaking the true picture was lost, but a certain likeness may still be traced. Even in the present day, although we have a most corrupted form of writing, still from the appearance of a certain name a person's life, fate, or character may be read, in whatever language it may be written. For instance, a name beginning with *I* shows a steadfast and righteous ego, uniqueness, and love of God and the pursuit of truth. *E* shows a shy and backward nature and an interest in three directions.

As one letter makes a picture, in the same way a whole word makes a picture. The idea of Allah has come from man, and one can read in the form of the hand the word "Allah."

The Christian name has a greater influence than the surname. Sometimes a nickname has a still greater effect. The effect of the name is according to its use: the more it is used, the greater the effect. Shortened names such as May for Mary or Bill or Willie for William lessen the effect of the name. The names given by the holy ones have a double effect, that of the name itself and that of the will of the one who gave it. Moula Bakhsh, the greatest musician in India of his day, was given his name by a faqir who was charmed on hearing his music. It means "God bless." After taking this name he had success wherever he went and was blessed with merit and reward, both of which are the rare gifts of God.

There are many instances to be found where a change of name has brought change in a person's entire life. We read in the Bible that the blessing of Jacob was the name Israel given to him by the angel.

In the Qur'an, Muhammad is constantly addressed by a special name, each name having its effect not only on the life of the Prophet but on his followers who adopted and worked mystically with any of these names. Sufis have for ages experienced the mystical value of these names. Among Sufis the murshid gives to his pupils the name *talib* or *mureed,* the purpose of which is to give him in time the identity of the name.

PART IV

THE ANALYSIS OF ATOMS
(HEALING)

Illness has many causes, but if there is a general cause, it is the lack of the music that we call order. Does this not show that man is music, that life is music? In order to play our part best the only thing we can do is to keep our tone and rhythm in proper condition: in this is the fulfillment of our life's purpose.

Chapter 37

HEALTH

Illness is inharmony—either physical inharmony or mental inharmony; the one acts upon the other. What causes inharmony? The lack of tone and rhythm. How can it be interpreted in physical terminology? *Prana* or life or energy is the tone; circulation or regularity is the rhythm, regularity in the beating of the pulse and in the circulation of the blood through the veins. In physical terms the lack of circulation means congestion; and the lack of *prana* or life or energy means weakness. These two conditions attract illness and are the cause of illness. In mental terms the rhythm is the action of the mind, whether the mind is active in harmonious thoughts or in inharmonious thoughts, whether the mind is strong, firm, and steady or weak.

If one continues to think harmonious thoughts it is just like regular beating of the pulse and proper circulation of the blood; if the harmony of thought is broken, then the mind becomes congested. Then a person loses memory; depression comes as the result, and what one sees is nothing but darkness. Doubt, suspicion, distrust, and all manner of distress and despair come when the mind is congested in this way. The *prana* of the mind is maintained when the mind can be steady in thoughts of harmony. Then the mind can balance its thoughts, then it cannot be easily shaken, then doubt and confusion cannot easily overpower it. Whether it is nervous illness, mental disorder, or physical illness, at the root of all these different aspects of illness there is one cause, and that cause is inharmony.

The body that has once become inharmonious turns into a receptacle of inharmonious influences, of inharmonious atoms; it partakes of them without knowing it; and so it is with the mind. The body that is already lacking in health is more susceptible to illness than the body that is perfectly healthy; and so the mind that already has a disorder in it is more susceptible to every suggestion of disorder, and in this way goes from bad to worse. Scientists of all ages have found that each element attracts the same element, and so it is natural that illness should attract illness. Thus in plain words inharmony attracts inharmony, whereas harmony attracts harmony. We see in everyday life that a person who has nothing the matter with him and is only weak physically, or whose life is not regular, is always susceptible to illness. Then we see that a person who ponders often upon inharmonious thoughts is very easily offended. It does not take long for him to get offended; a little thing here and there makes him feel irritated, because irritation is already there and it wants just a little touch to make it a deeper irritation.

Besides, this harmony of the body and the mind depends upon one's external life, the food one eats, the way one lives, the people one meets, the work one does, the climate in which one lives. There is no doubt that under the same conditions one person may be ill and another may be well. The reason is that one is in harmony with the food he eats, with the weather he lives in, with the people whom he meets, with the conditions around him. Another person revolts against the food he eats, against the people he meets, against the conditions that surround him, against the weather he must live in. This is because he is not in harmony, and he perceives and experiences similar results in all things in his life. Disorder and illness are the result.

This idea can be very well demonstrated by the method that present-day physicians have adopted of inoculating a person with the same element that makes him ill. There is no better demonstration of this idea than the practice of inoculation. This puts a person in harmony with the thing that is opposed to his nature. If one understands this principle one can inoculate oneself with all that does not agree with one and with that to which one is continually exposed and from which there is no means of getting away. Woodcutters do not as a rule get sunstroke; seamen do not catch cold easily. The reason is that the former have made themselves sunproof, while the latter have made themselves waterproof. In short, the first lesson in health is the understanding of this principle, that illness is nothing but inharmony and that the secret of health lies in harmony.

Disorder of tone and irregularity in rhythm are the principal causes of every illness. The explanation of this disorder of tone is that there is a certain tone that the breath vibrates throughout the body, through every channel of the body. This tone is a particular tone, continually vibrating in every person. When the mystics say that every person has his note, it is not necessarily the note of the piano, it is the note that is going on as a tone, as a breath. If a person does not take care of himself and allows himself to be influenced by every wind that blows, like the water in the sea disturbed by the air, he goes up and down. The normal condition is to be able to stand firm through fear, joy, and anxiety, not to let every wind blow one hither and thither like a scrap a paper but to endure it all and to stand firm and steady through all such influences.

One might say that even water is subject to influences, if not the rock. The human being is made to be neither rock nor water; he has all in him. He is the fruit of the whole creation, and he ought to be able to show his evolution in his balance. A person who is likely to rejoice in a moment and to become depressed in a moment, who changes his moods cannot keep that tone which gives him equilibrium and which is the secret of health. How few know that it is not pleasure and merrymaking that give one good health! On the contrary, social life as it is known today is merrymaking for one day, and afterwards one may be ill for ten days, for that kind of life does not take care of equilibrium. When a person becomes sensitive to every little thing that he comes across, it changes the note of the tone. It becomes a different note, to which his body is not accustomed, and that causes an illness. Too much despair or too much joy—everything that is too much should be avoided. However there are natures that always seek extremes: they must have so much joy and amusement that they get tired of it, and then they collapse with sorrow and despair. Among these people you will find continual illness. If an instrument is not kept in proper tune, if it is knocked about by everyone who comes and handled by everyone, then it gets out of order. The body is an instrument, the most sacred instrument, an instrument that God Himself has made for His divine purpose. If it is kept in tune and the strings are not allowed to become loose, then this instrument becomes the means of that harmony for which God created man.

How must this instrument be kept in tune? In the first place, strings of gut and wires of steel both require cleaning. The lungs and veins in the body also require cleaning; it is that which keeps them ready for their work. How should we clean them? By carefulness in diet, by sobriety, and by breathing properly and correctly. For it is not only water and earth that are used for cleansing, the best means of cleansing is the air and the property that is in the air, the property that we breathe in. If we knew how by the help of breathing to keep these channels clean, then we should know how to secure health. It is this that maintains the tone, the proper note of each person, without being disturbed. When a person is vibrating his own note, which is according to his particular evolution, then he is himself, then he is tuned to the pitch for which he is made, the pitch in which he ought to be and in which he naturally feels comfortable.

Now we come to rhythm. There is a rhythm of pulsation, the beating of the pulse in the head and in the heart, and whenever the rhythm of this beating is disturbed it causes illness because it disturbs the whole mechanism that is going on, the order of which depends upon the regularity of rhythm. If a person suddenly hears of something causing fear, the rhythm is broken; the pulsation changes. Every shock given to a person breaks his rhythm. We very often notice that, however successful an operation, it leaves a mark, even for the rest of one's life. Once the rhythm is broken, it is most difficult to get it right.

If the rhythm has been lost, it must be brought back with great wisdom, because a sudden effort to regain the rhythm may make one lose it still more. If the rhythm has become too slow or too fast, by trying to bring it to its regular speed one may break the rhythm, and by breaking the rhythm one may break oneself. This should be a gradual process; it must be wisely done. If the rhythm has gotten too fast, it must be brought gradually to its proper condition; if it is too slow, it must be gradually made quicker. It requires patience and strength to do this. For instance, someone who tunes a violin wisely does not at once move the peg and bring it to the proper tone, because in the first place it is impossible, and then he always risks breaking the string. However minute may be the difference in the tone, one can bring it to its proper place by gradual tuning; in this way effort is spared and the thing is accomplished.

Gentleness that is taught morally is a different thing, but even gentleness in action and movement is also necessary. In every movement one makes, in every step one takes there must be rhythm. For instance, you will find many examples, if you look for them, of the awkward movements people make. They can never keep well because their rhythm is not right, and that is why illness continues. It may be that no illness can be traced in these people, and yet the very fact of their movements not being in rhythm will keep them out of order. Regularity in habits, in action, in repose, in eating, in drinking, in sitting, in walking, in everything, gives one that rhythm which is necessary and which completes the music of life.

When a child's rhythm and tone are disordered, the healing that the mother can give often unconsciously physicians cannot give in a thousand years. The song she sings, however insignificant, comes from the profound depths of her being and brings with it the healing power. It cures the child in a moment. The caressing, the patting of the mother does more good to the child than any medicine when its rhythm is disturbed and its tone is not good. The mother, even without knowing it distinctly, feels like patting the child when it is out of rhythm, singing to the child when it is out of tune.

When we come to the mental part of our being, that mechanism is still more delicate than our body. There is a tone also, and every being has a different tone according to his particular evolution.

Everyone feels in good health when his own tone is vibrating, but if that tone does not come to its proper pitch, then a person feels lack of comfort, and any illness can arise from it. Every expression of passion, joy, anger, fear that breaks the continuity of this tone interferes with one's health. Behind the thought there is feeling, and it is the feeling that sustains that tone; the thought is on the surface. In order to keep the continuity of that tone, the mystics have special practices.

The secret of the continual ringing of the bell practiced by the churches at all times, even now, is that it is not only a bell to call people, it is to tune them up to their tone. It was to suggest, "There is a tone going on in you, get yourself tuned to it!" If that tuning is not done, even if a person has recovered from his illness weakness still remains. An external cure is no cure if a person is not cured mentally. If his spirit is not cured the mark of illness remains there, and the rhythm of mind is broken.

When a person's mind is going at a speed that is faster or at a speed that is slower than it ought to be, or if a person jumps from one thought to another and so goes on thinking of a thousand things in five minutes, however intellectual he may be he cannot be normal. Or if a person holds one thought and broods on it instead of making progress, he will also cling to his depression, his fears, his disappointments, and that makes him ill. It is irregularity of the rhythm of mind that causes mental disorder.

I do not mean that the rhythm of the mind of one person must be like that of another person. No, each person's rhythm is peculiar to himself. Once a pupil who accompanied me on my walk, in spite of all his kindness and pleasure in accompanying me, felt a great discomfort at times because he could not walk as slowly as I did. Being simple and frank, he expressed this to me. In answer I said, "It is a majestic walk."

The reason was that his rhythm was different. He could not feel comfortable in some other rhythm; he had to be galloping along in order to feel comfortable. And so one can feel what gives one comfort and what gives one discomfort in everything one does. If one does not feel it, that shows that one does not give attention to one's being. Wisdom is to understand oneself. If one can sustain the proper rhythm of one's mind, that is sufficient to keep one healthy.

Mental illnesses are subtler than physical illnesses, though up to now mental illnesses have not been thoroughly explored. But when this has been done we shall find that all physical illnesses have some connection with them. The mind and the body stand face to face. The body reflects its order and disorder upon the mind, the mind reflecting at the same time its harmony and disharmony on the body. It is for this reason that you will find that many who are ill outwardly also have some illness of the mind, and very seldom will one find a case where a person is mentally ill and physically perfectly well.

Once I happened to go to the asylum for the insane in New York, and the physicians very kindly laid before me a number of skulls showing the different cavities in the brain and the spots of decay that had caused insanity in the life of the patients. There is always a sign of it in the physical body. It may be apparent suffering or it may be some decay at the back of it, yet it is not known. I asked them, "I would like to know whether the cavity brought about the insanity or the insanity brought about the cavity?" Their argument was that the cavity brought about the insanity. But it is not always so. The mental disorder is not always caused by a cavity in the brain, for the inner being has a greater influence on the physical being than the physical body has on the mental existence. Yet is is not always the mind that brings about the physical illness; very often it is so, but not always. Sometimes from the physical plane illness travels to the mental plane, and sometimes illness goes from the mental plane to the physical plane. There are many causes, but in short, if there is a general cause, it is the lack of that music which we call order. Does this not show that man is music, that life is music? In order to play our part best, the only thing we can do is to keep our tone and rhythm in proper condition: in this is the fulfillment of our life's purpose.

Chapter 38

HEALING WITH SOUND

Modern science has discovered recently that on certain plates the impression of sound can be made clearly visible. In reality the impression of sound falls clearly on all objects, only it is not always visible. It remains for a certain time on an object and then it disappears. Those who have scientifically studied the different impressions that are made by sound have found the clear forms of leaves and flowers and other things of nature, which is proof of the belief held by the ancient people that the creative source in its first step towards manifestation was audible and in its next step visible. It also shows that all we see in this objective world, every form, has been constructed by sound and is the phenomenon of sound.

When we look further into this subject from a mystical point of view, we see that every syllable has a certain effect. As the form of every sound is different, so every syllable has a special effect. Therefore every sound made or word spoken before an object charges that object with certain magnetism. This explains to us the method of the healers, teachers, and mystics who by the power of sound charged an object with their healing power, with their power of thought. When this object was given as a drink or as food, it brought about the desired result. Besides that, many masters of occult sciences who have communicated with the unseen beings by the power of sound have done still greater things. By the power of sound they created beings; in other words by the power of sound they gave a body to a soul, to a spirit, making it into a kind of being that is not yet a physical being but a being of a higher kind. They called such beings *muwakkals,* and they worked through these beings, using them in any direction of life for a certain purpose.

The physical effect of sound has also a great influence upon the human body. The whole mechanism, the muscles, the blood circulation, the nerves are all moved by the power of vibration. As there is resonance for every sound, so the human body is a living resonator for sound. Although by sound one can easily produce a resonance in all such substances as brass and copper, yet there is no greater and more living resonator of sound than the human body. Sound has an effect on each atom of the body, for each atom resounds. On all glands, on the circulation of the blood, and on pulsation sound has an effect.

In India a feast is celebrated every year where the people commemorate the great heroes of the past and mourn over their life's tragedy. Certain instruments are played, certain drums, sometimes very badly and sometimes better. There are some who on hearing those drums instantly fall into ecstasy because the sound of the drum goes directly into their whole system, bringing it to a certain pitch where they feel ecstasy. When they are in ecstasy they can jump into the fire and come out without being burned; they can cut themselves with a sword and they are instantly healed; they can eat fire and they are not burned. One can see this every year at that particular time.

They call such a condition *hal. Hal* means the same as "condition"; it is an appropriate term for it, because by hearing the drum they think of that condition and then they enter into it. They need not be very educated to go into that trance, nor very evolved. Sometimes they are very ordinary people, but sound can have such effect upon them that they are moved to a higher ecstasy.

The question was raised by a physician in San Francisco, Dr. Abrams, of how the sudden healing of a sword cut in ecstasy is brought about. Although all doctors disagreed with him, he intuitively thought that by the help of vibrations illnesses could be cured. But instead of looking for the power of vibrations in the word, he wanted to find it in electricity. Yet the principle is the same: he took the rate of vibrations of the body, and by the same rate of electrical vibrations he treated the elements of the body. He began to get some good results, but it is a subject that will need at least a century to develop fully. It is a vast subject and this is just the beginning; therefore there is still no end to the errors. But at the same time, if people could bear with it, after many years something might come out of it that could be of great use to the medical world.

This example shows that when a person can cut himself and be healed at the same time, he has created such a condition in his body that its vibrations are able to heal any wound immediately. But when that same person is not in that condition, then if there is a cut he cannot be healed. He must be in that particular condition; the vibrations must be working at that particular rate.

There is a school of Sufis in the East which is called the Rifai school. Their main object is to increase the power of spirit over matter. Experiments such as eating fire, jumping into fire, or cutting the body are made in order to get power and control over matter. The secret of the whole phenomenon is that by the power of words they try to tune their bodies to that pitch of vibration where no fire, no cut, nothing can touch it. Because the vibrations of their bodies are equal to fire, the fire has no effect.

Now coming to the question of music, why has music an effect upon a person; why does someone naturally like music? It is not because he is trained in it or because it is a habit but because attraction is a natural effect of sound. One may ask why it is that some people have no feeling for music. It is because that feeling has not yet been created in them. The day when they begin to feel life, they will begin to enjoy music also.

It is on this account that the wise considered the science of sound to be the most important science in every condition of life: in healing, in teaching, in evolving, and in accomplishing all things in life. It is on this foundation that the science of *dhikr* was developed by the Sufis and that the yogis made *mantra shastra.* By *dhikr* is not meant here one particular phrase, but a science of words. In the spoken word finer vibrations act. The vibrations of the air are nothing, but because every word has a breath behind it and breath has a spiritual vibration, the action of breath works physically, while at the same time breath itself is an electric current. The breath is not only the air but an electric current; therefore it is an inner vibration.

Apart from the meaning a word has, even the sound of the syllables can bring about a good result or a disastrous result. Those who know about this can recall several instances in history when, through the mistake of a poet who did not use the proper words in the praise of a king, his kingdom was destroyed. Yet how little one thinks about this! In saying, "Well, I may have said it, but I did not mean it," people believe that by saying something they have done nothing as long as they did not mean it. But even saying something without meaning has a great effect upon life.

Chapter 39

THE EFFECT OF SOUND ON
THE PHYSICAL BODY

Wind instruments, instruments with gut or steel strings, and instruments of percussion such as drums and cymbals have each a distinct, different, and particular effect on the physical body. There was a time when thinkers knew this and used sound for healing and for spiritual purposes. It was on that principle that the music of India was based. The different ragas and the notes that these ragas contain were supposed to produce a certain healing or elevating effect.

Sound first touches the physical plane. When we consider what effect single notes or sounds can have upon the physical body, this will lead us to think deeply on the subject. Even today there are snake charmers, mostly to be found in India, who by playing their *pungi,* a simple wind instrument, attract cobras and other snakes from the vicinity. Often and often this experiment has been made, and one always sees that snakes of any kind are attracted on hearing the sound of the *pungi*. First they come out of the hole in which they live, and then there is a certain effect on their nervous system that draws them closer and closer to the sound of the *pungi.* They forget that instinct that is seen in every creature of protecting itself from the attack of man or of other creatures. At that time they absolutely forget; they do not see anyone or anything. They are then aroused to ecstasy: the cobra begins to raise its head and move it right and left, and as long as this instrument is played the cobra continues to move in ecstasy. This shows us that, as well as the psychical effect and the spiritual effect that sound has on man, there is also a physical effect.

From the metaphysical point of view the breath is the life current or *prana*, and this life current exists also in such things as the gut string or the skin of drums. There is a part of life in these things too, and to the extent that their life current becomes audible it touches the life current of the living creatures and gives it an added life. It is for this reason that primitive tribes, who have only a drum or a simple instrument to blow, get into such a condition by the continual playing of these instruments that they enjoy the state of ecstasy.

How does the great success of jazz come about? It comes from the same principle. It does not make the brain think much about the technicality of music; it does not trouble the soul to think of spiritual things; it does not trouble the heart to feel deeply— without affecting the heart or the soul it touches the physical body. It gives it a renewed strength by the continuation of a particular rhythm and a particular sound, and that gives people— I mean the generality—a greater strength and vigor and interest than music which strains the mind. Those who do not wish to be spiritually elevated, who do not believe in spiritual things and who do not wish to trouble, it leaves alone. Yet at the same time it affects everyone who hears it.

When you compare the voice with the instrument, there is no real comparison, because the voice itself is alive. The movement, the glance, the touch, even the breath that comes from the nostrils do not reach as far as the voice reaches.

There are three degrees of breath current. One degree is the simple breath that is inhaled and exhaled by the nostrils. This current reaches outside and has a certain effect. A greater degree of breath current is blowing. When a person blows from his lips, that breath current is directed more intensely. Therefore healers who have understood this principle make use of it. The third degree, in which the breath is most intense, is sound because in that degree the breath coming in the form of sound is vitalized.

Among Orthodox Christians and Armenians there is a custom that they do not use an organ in church; they use a chord or sound made by ten or twelve persons sitting with closed lips. Anyone who has heard it will say that they are right; the sound of the organ is most artificial in comparison with the sound produced by the voices of ten or twelve persons with closed lips. It has such a wonderfully magical effect, it reaches so far and so deeply into the heart of man, and it produces such a religious atmosphere that one feels that there is no necessity for an organ; it is a natural organ that God has made.

Brahmans when they study the Vedas even now do not study only what is written there or the meaning of it; they study also the pronunciation of each syllable, of each word, of each sound, and they study it for years and years and years. The Brahman does not hear the sound once with the ears and think, "I have learned it." No; he believes that a thousand repetitions of the word will one day produce that magnetism, that electricity, that life current which is necessary and which only comes by repetition.

What action does this life current take which comes through the breath and manifests as a voice and touches another person? It touches the five senses, the sense of sight, the sense of hearing, the sense of smell, the sense of taste, and the sense of touch, although it comes directly through the sense of hearing. But a person does not hear sound only through his ears; he hears sound through every pore of his body. It permeates the entire being, and according to its particular influence either slows the rhythm or quickens the rhythm of the blood circulation; it either wakens the nervous system or soothes it. It arouses a person to greater passions or it calms him by bringing him peace. According to the sound and its influence a certain effect is produced.

Therefore the knowledge of sound can give a person a magical instrument by which to wind and tune and control and use the life of another person to the best advantage. The ancient singers used to experience the effect of their spiritual practices upon themselves first. They used to sing one note for about half an hour and study the effect of that same note upon all the different centers of their bodies: what life current it produced, how it opened the intuitive faculties, how it created enthusiasm, how it gave added energy, how it soothed, and how it healed. For them it was not a theory, it was an experience.

Sound becomes visible in the form of radiance. This shows that the same energy that goes into the form of sound before being visible is absorbed by the physical body. In that way the physical body recuperates and becomes charged with new magnetism.

By a keen study of psychology you will find that singers have a greater magnetism than the average person. Because of their own practicing their voice makes an effect upon themselves, and they produce electricity in themselves. In that way they are charged with new magnetism every time they practice. This is the secret of the singer's magnetism.

Coming to the question which is the right and which is the wrong use of sound, it all depends upon the particular case. In one case a certain sound may be rightly used and in another case the same sound may be wrongly used. Whether it was right or wrong can be seen by the harmonious or disharmonious effects it produces. Every pitch that is a natural pitch of the voice will be a source of a person's own healing as well as of that of others when he sings a note of that pitch. But the person who has found the keynote of his own voice has found the key of his own life. That person, by the keynote of his own voice, can then wind his own being, and he can help others. There are, however, many occasions when this knowledge is not enough, as it only concerns oneself, the knowledge of what is one's own note, and the natural pitch of one's own voice.

The great pity in the world of sound today is that people are going away from what is called the natural voice. This is brought about by commercialism. First a hall was made for one hundred persons, then for five hundred, and then for five thousand. A person must shout to make five thousand people hear him in order to have a success, and that success is one of the ticket office. But the magical charm lies in the natural voice. Every person is gifted; God has given him a certain pitch, a natural note. If he develops that note it is magic; he can perform a miracle. But today he must think about the hall where he has to sing and of how loud he must shout.

There was a man from India visiting Paris, and for the first time in his life he went to the opera to hear the music there. He tried hard to enjoy it. The first thing he heard was a soprano doing her best, and then came the tenor or baritone and he had to sing with her. That made this man very annoyed and he said, "Now look, he has come to spoil it!"

When we come to the essence and inner principle of sound, the closer to nature one keeps it, the more powerful, the more magical it becomes. Every man and woman has a certain pitch of voice, but then the voice producer says, "No, this is alto," "soprano," "tenor," "baritone," or "bass," He limits what cannot be limited. Are there then so many voices? There are as many voices as there are souls; they cannot be classified. As soon as a singer is classified he has to sing in that pitch; if his pitch is different, he does not know it. Because the voice producer has said, "This is a soprano," then that person cannot be anything else. Besides this, the composer has probably never heard the voice of that particular singer and has written only for a certain pitch, either this one or that one. When a person has to depend upon what the composer has written and has to sing in a pitch that is thus prescribed, then he has lost the natural pitch he had. But singing apart, even in speaking you will find among one hundred persons one who speaks in his natural voice and ninety-nine who imitate. They imitate someone else, although they may not know it.

The same thing that you find in grown-up people you will find in little children. The tendency in a child is to change its ways and to imitate. Every five or ten days, every month a child changes its way of speaking, its voice, its words; it changes many things. Where does the child learn these? It learns them from the children in school. It sees a child walking in some way or making gestures or frowning or speaking in a certain way. The child does not realize it, but it has heard or seen it and then it does the same thing, and so it goes on changing.

In the same way every person, also without realizing it, changes his voice, and by that the natural voice is lost. To retain one's natural voice is a great power in itself, but one cannot retain it always. In order to obtain a powerful or good effect of one's voice and sound, one need not be a singer. What one has to do is to practice the science of breath in different ways. One must first know how to breathe, then one must know how to blow, and then one must learn how to make a sound, how to say a word. If one practices in these three ways, one will attain to that power which is latent in every soul. One need not be a singer, but for every person it is necessary that he should give some part of his day, even the shortest time he can give, five or ten or fifteen minutes, to his voice, to the development of his voice.

Chapter 40

THE HEALING POWER OF MUSIC

The idea of healing through music really belongs to the initial stage of developing through the art of music. The end of this is attaining through music, or as it is called in the Vedanta, *samadhi.*

In the first place, if we saw what is at the back of all the medicines that are used for healing purposes, if we ask what it is in them that heals, we shall find that it is the different elements that constitute our physical being. The same elements are present in these medicines, and that which is lacking in us is taken from them, or the effect that should be produced in our body is produced by them. The vibration that is necessary for our health is created in the body by their power and the rhythm that is necessary for our cure is brought about by bringing the circulation of the blood into a certain rhythm and speed.

By this we learn that health is a condition of perfect rhythm and tone. And what is music? Music is rhythm and tone. When the health is out of order, it means the music is out of order. Therefore, when the music is not right in us, the help of harmony and rhythm is very necessary to bring us into a state of harmony and rhythm. This way of healing can be studied and understood by studying the music of one's own life, by studying the rhythm of the pulse, the rhythm of the beating of the heart and of the head. Physicians who are sensitive to rhythm determine the condition of the patient by examining the rhythm of the pulse, the beating of the heart, the rhythm of the circulation of the blood. To find the real complaint a physician, with all his material knowledge, must depend upon his intuition and upon the use of his musical qualities.

In ancient times, and even now in the East, we find two principal schools of medicine. One came from the ancient Greek school through Persia; the other came from the Vedanta and is founded on mysticism. And what is mysticism? It is the law of vibration.

Good health is induced by understanding the nature of a complaint through the rhythm and tone that can be perceived in the human body and by regulating the body through rhythm and tone according to one's understanding of their proportions.

Besides this there is another way of looking at it. Every illness apparently has its special reason, but in reality all illnesses come from one reason, from one cause, from one condition, and that is the absence of life, the lack of life. Life is health. Its absence is illness, which culminates in what we call death.

Life in its physical form, as perceived in the physical spheres, is called *prana* in Sanskrit. This life is given by food or medicine, or the body is prepared by a certain food or medicine to be able to breathe in this life itself in order that it may be in better health or may experience perfect health. But this *prana*, which also means the central breath, attracts from space all the different elements that are there, as the herbs and plants and flowers and fruits all attract from space the element they represent. All these elements are attracted by the breath. Therefore the mystics, whether from Greece, Persia, or India, have always taken as their basis of spiritual evolution the culture of breath, the science of breath. Even now you will see in the East healers who magnetize water or food or the atmosphere. What is the secret of this magnetism? It is their breath. It is the influence of their breath upon the water or food.

The religious people of India have a ceremony where something like a sacrament is given by a holy person to someone who is suffering, and it is very helpful. Their power of breath is so balanced, so purified and developed, that it attracts all elements, all that one can get from an herb, a flower, or a fruit, and even more.

Therefore their breath can achieve a thousand times more than medicine can. There are healers in the east who whisper some spiritual words; but what is whispering? It is breath again; breath with words directed through it.

What is music? According to the ancient Indian thinkers there are three aspects of music: singing, playing, and dancing. All three represent rhythm, and all three represent tone in some form or other. What is the effect of music? The effect of music is to regulate the rhythm of another person and to tune a person to the music that is being performed.

What secret is there in music that attracts all those who listen to it? It is the tone of that music that tunes a soul and raises it above the depression and despair of everyday life in this world. If one knew what rhythm was needed for a particular individual in his trouble and despair, what tone was needed, and to what pitch that person's soul should be raised, one would then be able to heal him with music.

One might ask why it is, if music is rhythm, that so often musicians are temperamental and easily disturbed. But is it not beautiful to have a little temperament? Life is unmusical when there is no temperament. A person who does not get angry once in a while does not live. It is human to have all kinds of minor faults; the joy is in overcoming these faults. Music is not all sadness: there are higher octaves and lower octaves. Music is all, music takes in all. That is why music is even greater than heaven.

There was a time in India when music was much used for healing. It was used as healing for the mind, for the character, and for the soul, because it is health of the soul that brings health to the physical body. But the healing of the physical body does not always help the soul. That is why the material medical science, though it can do good for some time, does not entirely suffice the need of the patient. I do not mean by this that outward treatment is useless. There is nothing in this world that is useless, if we only knew how to make use of it. All things in this world are needed, all things have their benefit and use, if we only know how to use them properly. But if a cure is brought about outwardly while inwardly the illness remains, sooner or later the illness that is buried in the body will come out and show itself.

Once I met a lady who said she had been to many physicians for the complaint of neuritis. She was temporarily cured, but it always came back, and she asked me for something that would help her. I said to her, "Is there any person in the world whom you dislike, whom you hate, or whose action is troubling your mind?" She said, "Yes, there are many people whom I dislike, and especially there is one person whom I cannot forgive." "Well," I said, "that is the neuritis; that is the root of the disease. Outwardly it is a pain of the body, but inwardly it is rooted in the heart."

Often the cause of illness is within, though no doubt many things are caused outwardly. No single rule will cover everything. Undoubtedly as things have changed in the world and materialism has spread throughout the world this has influenced things, not only in the West but in the East also. The use of music for spiritual attainment and healing of the soul, which was prevalent in ancient times, is not found to the same extent now. Music has been made a pastime, the means of forgetting God instead of realizing God. And it is the use one makes of things that constitutes their fault or their virtue.

Still, the memory of the ancient use of music remains among the poor in India. There are healers there who have a particular instrument of healing on which they play, and the people go to them for healing. By playing that instrument they arouse some special feeling that had become cold, and that deep feeling which was buried begins to come out. It is really the old way of psychoanalysis. Music helps that patient to express in full the hidden influence that was there, and in this way many people are helped without going to a physician. But it is no doubt a crude way of healing.

Once the maharajah of Baroda, on hearing that healing could be accomplished through music, introduced concerts into certain hospitals. The amusing result was that all those who were suffering began to cry out, "For God's sake, keep quiet! Go away!" That was not the music to soothe them. It only made them suffer more; it was like giving a stone for bread.

In order to give healing through music one must study what is needed, what is wanted. In the first place one must study the complaint: what elements are lacking, what is its symbolical meaning, what mental attitude is behind the illness. Then, after a close study, one can do a great deal of good to the patient with the help of music.

Even if music were not used as a prescription particularly intended for a certain illness, the power of illness that has its abode in a person's heart can still be reduced by lifting up his heart, by changing his thought. What brings illness is the thought of illness rather than illness itself. The existence of illness in the body may be called a shadow of the true illness, which is held in the mind. By the power of music the mind may become exalted so that it rises above the thought of illness; then the illness is forgotten. You will ask, "What kind of music can heal people? Is it singing or playing or music for dancing?" Singing is the most powerful, for singing is living. It is *prana.* The voice is life itself. No doubt it is also life that is working through an instrument by the touch, but in singing it is the direct life, the breath touching the heart of the listener. However, behind this voice there must be a heart, charged like a battery with what is needed. With what is it charged? With what we call love and sympathy, the greatest power there is.

A person who is material, who is struggling for himself from morning till evening, who is seeking his own benefit, who is in trouble or bitter or in the midst of conflict cannot heal. The healer must be free: free to sympathize, free to love his fellowman even more than himself.

What teaches this love? Where can one learn it? Where can one get it? The key to this love element is God. When we look at life today, with all its progress, what is lacking? It is God. God is the key to that unlimited store of love which is in the heart of man.

Once a very godly and good-natured housemaid was not able to answer a knock at the door as quickly as it should have been answered, and the lady visitor who was waiting at the door became very impatient and spoke crossly to her. When asked what had happened, the maid was not upset at all; she smiled and said, "Yes, that lady was very cross with me.' When she was asked if she knew what was the matter with the lady and what had made her cross, the maid with perfect innocence replied, "The reason? There was no God!" A beautiful answer. Where God is lacking there is no love. Wherever there is love, there is God. If we interpret rightly, what causes pain and suffering is the lack of life.

What is life? It is love. And what is love? It is God. What every individual needs, what the world needs is God. All we need to attain, all we need to gain, to bless our lives by music, by harmony, by love, by the science of right tuning, by a life of good is God. This is the central theme of all good.

PART V

THE HARMONIOUS GROUPING OF ATOMS
(ART)

Now we come to that we call in everyday language music. To me architecture is music, gardening is music, farming is music, painting is music, poetry is music. In all the occupations of life, where beauty has inspired, where the divine wine has been outpoured, there is music.

THE CREATIVE PROCESS

Chapter 41

THE DIVINITY OF ART

People belonging to different faiths very often make the mistake of considering art as something outside of religion. The fact is that the whole creation is the art of the Creator, and one sees the perfection of His art in divine man. This shows that the source of the whole creation has the spirit of art at the back of it.

In all ages man has developed his artistic faculty, and he has tried to progress in art. But in the end where does he arrive? He remains far from touching either the beauty of nature or the art of creation. Man's art always fails to equal the art of God.

This shows that the source of every soul is the spirit of art and art is spirit; that everything that has come out from that spirit has manifested in the form of art. The more man looked at nature—at the heavens, at the beauty of the stars and planets, of the clouds and the sun, the sun's rising and setting, its zenith, the waxing and waning of the moon, the different shades of color that we can see in the sky—the more man would always marvel at the art at work behind it all.

When one is alone with nature—near the sea, on the river bank, among the mountains, in the forest, in the wilderness—a feeling comes over one that is never felt among a crowd, not even if one were in the crowd for years. In one moment a feeling is born, as soon as one is face to face with the true art of God. It then seems as if the soul had seen something that it has always admired and worshipped. The soul now begins to recognize One whom it has always silently worshipped, and now the presence of that mighty Creator, that Artist, is realized through seeing His art. Many experience this, but few will express it. None can come back from such an experience without a deep impression, without something having been awakened to consciousness through having seen the divine art.

This shows that this creation, this manifestation that is before us, has not been made mechanically, has not been created blindly or unconsciously. As the great poet of Persia Sa'adi says, "The more one looks at nature, the more one begins to feel that there is a perfection of wisdom, a perfect skill behind it, which has made it. And it will take numberless years for mankind to imitate that art. In fact mankind will never be able to attain it perfectly."

Whoever studies the kingdoms of flowers, of vegetables, of minerals, the birds, the insects, the germs, the worms, the animals and their forms and colors, and the beauty that each form suggests will surely recognize, as did the prophets of old, that the world is created by the Spirit, the divine Spirit who created it with eyes wide open. The world shows perfect wisdom behind it, perfect skill in it, and a sense of beauty so perfect that man must always be incapable of achieving it.

But now the question comes, "What is man?" Man is the miniature of God, and man has inherited as his divine inheritance the tendency to art. Therefore anyone with intelligence and with tender feeling—which goes to make a person normal—must admit the beauty of art. He is born with that tendency. A child is born with the love of art, as is proved by the infant being attracted to toys and beautiful colors. Lines attract him, and the first thing that he begins to like or desire is color and movement. This is the time of his life during which he is impressed by artistic things. When a person loses his sense of art, it is just as when the heart has become blind. It cannot see the art anymore because of the clouds of all manner of ugliness and undesirableness, and all that one does not like to look upon. All such things and impressions cover his heart and his soul and make him, so to speak, blind to beauty, blind to art. But this is not the normal condition. The normal state of a sound mind in a sound body with tender feeling is love of beauty, is to admire art.

No doubt very often a person does not live a natural life. That is, his business or profession or responsibility holds him. Some work or some thought for the needs of the body, for bread and butter or any other everyday need, holds him and absorbs the whole of his thoughts, so that he becomes useless for the discovery of the beauty, joy, and happiness of life. Hence, as we see around us today, life is becoming so difficult and so full of anxiety, trouble, and responsibility. From morning till evening man is just loaded with his responsibilities, toiling day and night. He has never a moment to think of the beauty of art. Since art is the first step that leads man to the cause of art, how can a person who has never admired or understood the beauty of art hope to admire or understand the Artist? So God remains unrecognized, and not through the fault of God, but through the fault of humanity.

The Creator in the role of an artist has created His beautiful art, which is not far from human eyes, but people are so engrossed in thoughts and occupations that have nothing to do with that art. All a person's time and thought and effort are devoted to occupations that never allow him one moment to think of art, to admire, understand, and appreciate it. Naturally, then, he remains as if his eyes were covered over from the vision of the Artist. The real purpose of human life was not that man be born to toil for bread and butter; the real purpose of human life was not that man should be avaricious, competing with his fellow man, hating him, viewing another with prejudice, and using the whole of his time in a kind of spirit of rivalry and competition in which there can be no harmony or joy or peace. With the necessarily ever-increasing avariciousness there is an absence of that beauty for which the soul so constantly longs.

It would be no exaggeration to say that all the disagreeable things that go on in this world—wars, diseases and the like—come from the lack of artistic attitude in life, the lack of a sense of beauty and the lack of that vision which unites the whole humanity in one center, the center which is God. When man closes his eyes to beauty, he will never think of looking for the beautiful, although beauty is constantly beside him. Behind the beauty, as the Qur'an says, God is. "God is beautiful and He loves beauty." The natural tendency to love and admire beauty is a divine inheritance; it is the spiritual thing which leads to spirituality. Through this tendency one accomplishes one's spiritual duty in life. When this tendency has gone and religion is left without art, then religion may perhaps be useful for an inartistic society, but it turns into a sort of formality. One does one thing, one does another. As one does weekday work, so one also does Sunday duty.

If God is not to be connected with beauty, in what form shall humanity idealize HIm? In what form could humanity think of Him? In what form should it see Him? It would be kept away from Him. So when religion is covered in its form and when man keeps art aloof instead of promoting it, man's life becomes empty, for his occupation necessarily keeps art out of his life to a great extent. If then when he goes to a religious place he also finds no art there, his visit comes to be exactly like a visit to any other place to which habit may take him in daily life. There is nothing to pierce through him; there is nothing to awaken that impulse which arises from the earth to Heaven; there is nothing to make him think even for that one moment that God is beautiful and that by beauty we reach out to God.

Man very often separates nature from art. He considers nature different from art, the one superior and the other inferior. But in reality art is that which, by divinely inherited tendency, plays its role through man. God working in nature with His hidden hands has created nature, and He shows His art in that nature. In the other aspect of art, which we call art, God produces beauty through the human hand and the human mind, and so finishes that which has been left over to be finished and has not been finished in nature. Therefore in one respect art is a step forward to nature, although compared with nature art is so limited. Nature is unlimited, but at the same time art is an improvement of nature.

Seen metaphysically, the artistic spirit of God is satisfied by fulfilling its artistic tendency through the art of the human being. Therefore those who consider art from a higher point of view recognize the artistic impulse not only as a human impulse, not only as brain work, but as a true artistic impulse, as an inspiration in itself.

In order to prepare the mind for the artisitic impulse, what is necessary? Does one need some kind of learning or study? Is there some preliminary study to be made first? No. It requires a tuning, a bringing of ourselves to an object to whose beauty the human heart can respond, a beauty that the heart can appreciate. When the heart can concentrate upon beauty, then it works itself up to a certain pitch, for inspiration is not a thing that one can pull upon to obtain as by pulling a rope. Inspiration is a thing that comes only when the heart is tuned to that object, when it is in a position to receive it. Therefore inspired artists have been divinely gifted, and the spirit of art is one, though the arts are so many. When the heart is tuned to the proper pitch, it is capable not only of producing or appreciating one kind of art and beauty but all kinds.

Thus there can be an art in architecture: a gifted architect can produce a great deal of beauty in his work. So too with drawing, with embroidery, with the work of dyeing, of sewing. In fact there is nothing that man does that cannot have art in it if he knows how to attune himself to that pitch which enables the art to be expressed. Poetry is an art in the same way. Unless a person is tuned to the proper pitch, he may write poetry all his life, and yet it will not please either him or anyone else. So with a painter or a musician (violin, piano, any instrument) he will not please himself or anyone else during his whole life unless he has become tuned to that pitch.

This shows that the question as to what grade of evolution a person has attained comes in every walk in life. Whether a person be a painter, sculptor, architect, designer, singer, or dancer, whatever path he may follow, there is no better source from which to draw inspiration from above in nature than by means of art. The more cultivated the sense of art is in man, the more able he is to respond to the beauty of art and to produce or create something beautiful in himself. The more he comes into touch with that Spirit who is constantly helping every soul toward beauty, the more man can produce. Everything that helps man to approach the beauty of God is sacred. Therefore art can become religion. It would not be an exaggeration to say that there is no better religion than art itself.

When one has reached that degree of understanding, when one has reached that knowledge of art by which he can become profited, when the heart is once tuned to that pitch by which one can understand and appreciate art and when one has changed one's outlook upon life so as to see in the beauty of art the beauty of the Divine Being, then one can progress in the true art.

From this we learn that consciously or unconsciously that which our soul is really seeking is art. Yet at the same time a person very frequently avoids this very thing that he is really seeking. The right way and the wrong way are so near to one another. The only difference is that a person is journeying along the right way when at every step he can say, "I see the signs that support and help me to go on further and promise that the goal is before me." When he is journeying along the wrong way every step tells him, "I am not in the right way, I must go back. I am not on the road on which I ought to be." Consciously or unconsciously every soul seeks for beauty, and if at each step of our lives we think that beauty is receiving us as we go, that beauty meets us at every step on our path, then our soul is satisfied, is full of hope, knowing that the road we are on is our proper road, and that some day or other we will arrive at our goal. The person who thinks at every step of his journey, "I am not on a right road, I do not like this; I am not pleased with that," is making no progress. The beauty he is looking for he is ever leaving behind. He is traveling in quite another way from that which he is expecting.

So we see that whether our road is right or wrong depends on our appreciation of the artistic side of life or on our lack of it. But by saying this, one does not wish it to be understood that everyone must necessarily practice to become an artist or learn some branch of art. It is only to say that there is a spark of artistic faculty in every soul. There is not a single soul who does not have this spark. Some have more, some have less, yet that spark does not have to be used by everybody to that extent which causes a person to be called artist. No, but we must exhibit and utilize that faculty in our everyday life. A person with the artistic faculty is sure to show it in everything he does, even in dusting a room, keeping it tidy, or in keeping a machine in order. In all these directions can a person show art. One does not require a palace before one can begin to manifest art. If one really has the love for beauty, one can show the artistic faculty in quite small things.

Besides this there is the fact that the soul manifests outwardly that which it holds inwardly, so that it is the beauty that man has within himself that he expresses without. Man shows his artistic faculty in his manner towards his friend and towards his surroundings. A person who has no sense of art is called rude, inconsiderate, thoughtless, foolish, simple-minded, crude, course.

A person does not need to have much money in order to be able to express his art. He can express it in various circumstances. He may be the poorest person in the world, and yet he can express the beauty of his soul in whatever state he may be placed. Beauty will not be hidden. One shows one's art in one's words. When one is in business, in one's family, or among friends, one does not know how many times during the day one hurts the feeling of others; one does not even notice them. Even though one were very learned or experienced, the lack of art would still manifest. Even a loving, kind, and good person will never be able to express the goodness that is hidden in his heart if art is lacking.

Jesus Christ taught in the Sermon on the Mount, "Blessed are they who are gentle, who are meek, humble, poor in spirit." What lesson does this teach us? It is this lesson of art. The lesson is, "Produce art in your personality." Even so-called artists, musicians, poets, painters, if they have not fostered art, if art is not impressed on the soul, and if the soul has not expressed the beauty of art, do not know art; they are profane; they claim to be something they are not.

Having thought much upon this subject, and being specially interested in art, I have come in contact with artists of different countries both in the East and West. It has always proved that those who have really attained some greatness in their art were those who showed glimpses of art in their personality. It showed in the words they spoke, in the way they received me, and in the manner in which they spoke with me: their tenderness of heart, their friendliness, their interest in my affairs. Every sign of art could be seen in such personalities. Even if one is not literally an artist, a painter, a singer, a poet, whatever one's real occupation, it does not matter as long as one has realized beauty in that occupation, has perceived beauty around one, and has collected around one all that one finds beautiful. All this must be expressed in return, and it is that which is true art.

In the Hindu language there are two attitudes mentioned by the philosophers, *hansadi suhradi*. The former attitude is that of a bird of paradise, a mythical bird of the Hindus called *hansa*. If you put milk mixed with water before the *hansa,* it will drink the milk and leave the water behind. The *suhradi* attitude is that of the people. It is the tendency of-looking to find a dirty spot and then wanting to sit in it. Such is the tendency of man. One person is always looking for what may be wrong in people, is delighted to hear something wrong about them, and is very interested in discussing their faults and hearing of their being disgraced or insulted in some way. Such persons are always wanting to see the evil around them, in whatever form it may be. This pleasure grows until the whole life becomes a burden, for the presence of evil produces its bad impression and had thoughts collect around him, for they are reproduced just as a gramophone record produces sounds. Such a person becomes a gramophone record for the evil be collects. He utters it, he retains the bad feelings within and he spreads these feelings abroad wherever he goes. Nobody likes him, nor does he like anyone. The time will come when he cannot even like himself.

Another kind of character is he who overlooks all that does not seem to be harmonious; he looks only for good in every person, and finds some good even in the worst person in the world. This person seeks for good, wishes to see it wherever he can find it, and in this way constantly gathers good impressions.

What is good? Good is beauty. What is beauty? Beauty is God. What is virtue? Virtue is beauty. What is beauty is also virtue. One does not have to learn in a book or a scripture or from some other person what is good and what is bad. We can learn from our own sense of art. The greater one's sense of art, the more it will show one what is right and what is wrong, what is good and what is bad.

As soon as the senses begin to develop and understand what it is that takes away beauty and what it is that imparts beauty, then one gathers beauty as one gathers flowers. Such persons welcome others with beauty, they express beauty, they impart it to others. Others love them. They love others. They live and move and have their being in love, just as it is said in the Bible, "They live and move and have their being in God." So a person who lives and moves and has his being in love will certainly also live and move and have his being in God.

This may be called the divine art, for which a person may study and strive. But besides this there is the art which every person must look for and develop in his own nature. The message of Sufism to the western world has this as its chief object, to awaken the spirit of the world from this thought of antagonism and mutual hatred and to bring about the feeling of human brotherhood so that all humanity may meet with one another—whatever be their nation, race, or religion—in one place, in one center, namely, in the thought of God. In order to rise to this ideal and in order to tune our soul to this pitch, so necessary from beginning to end, it is necessary to seek the path of beauty, and to recognize in beauty the being of God.

Chapter 42

INSPIRATION

The question where inspiration comes from may be answered, "It comes from within." There are some who are inspired by unseen entities, and some who receive from living personalities, but only that which comes directly from within can be called inspiration.

The question is, does inspiration come to a poet in words, to a musician in notes, to a painter in lines and colors? No, although it seems so. The language of inspiration is one, and inspiration comes to a poet, a painter, and a musician in the same language. Yet very often even the inspired ones do not know the mystery and truth of it unless they have reached to the point of revelation. For the one to whom revelation comes hears the voice, and the inspired one hears the re-echo.

Inspiration is not only the act of the spirit within. It is a mutual action that results in inspiration, an action performed by the inspiring spirit from within and the soul of the inspired one from without. It is hunger, desire for inspiration, and concentration on the part of the inspired one that work. Pouring out all knowledge concerning the subject from the divine store and directing it with a lighted torch is the work of the inspiring spirit within. If the three factors mentioned above are not active in the soul desiring inspiration, the inspiring spirit from within becomes helpless, for the inspiring spirit is more willing to inspire than the soul that desires inspiration is to receive.

As sound needs capacity to manifest and become audible, so the inspiring spirit needs capacity to manifest itself. The light comes from the divine spirit, and the knowledge comes from the subconscious mind of the universe. These two things together function in the accommodation that the one desiring inspiration offers them. It is thus that inspiration becomes clear and complete.

Inspiration is a higher form of intuition, for it comes as an idea, as a complete theme with its improvisation, as a phrase creative of a poem. Inspiration is a stream of wonder and bewilderment. The really inspired person, whether a writer, a poet, a composer —whatever be his work—when once he has received an inspiration, has found satisfaction, not with himself but with what has come to him. It gives his soul such relief. For the soul was drawing from something, and that object from which it was drawing has yielded to the soul, has given it what it was asking for. Therefore inspiration may be called the soul's reward.

It is not being anxious to receive something that enables one to receive it. It is not by straining the brain that one can write poetry; it is not by worrying for days together than one can compose a piece of music. One who does so cannot receive an inspiration. The one who receives an inspiration is quite tranquil and unconcerned about what is coming. Certainly he is desirous of receiving something; he is passionately longing to conceive it. But it is only by focusing his mind upon the divine mind that, consciously or unconsciously, a person receives inspiration.

The phenomenon is so great and so wonderful that its joy is unlike any other joy in the world. It is in this joy that the inspirational genius experiences ecstasy. It is a joy that is almost indescribable; it is the upliftment of feeling that one is raised from the earth when one's mind is focused on the divine mind. For the inspiration comes from the divine mind. What the great musicians, poets, thinkers, philosophers, writers, and prophets have left in the world is always uplifting, although it is not every soul who comprehends their work fully and therefore can enjoy it fully. But if you can imagine their own enjoyment of what has come to them, there are no words to express it. It is in inspiration that one begins to see the sign of God, and the most materialistic genius begins to wonder about the divine spirit when once inspiration has begun.

Does it come as a finished picture? Does it come as a written letter? No, it comes to an artist as if his hand was taken by someone else, as if his eyes were closed and his heart open. He has drawn something, he has painted something and he does not know who painted it, who has drawn it. It comes to a musician as if someone were playing, singing, and he were only taking it down, a complete melody, a perfect air. After he has written it down, then it enchants his soul. To a poet it comes as if someone were dictating and he were only writing. There is no strain on his brain, there is no anxiety in receiving inspiration.

Because of this many confuse it with spirit communication. Many inspirational people are glad to attribute the inspiration to a spirit, knowing that it does not come from them. But it is not always spirit communication. It is natural that it comes from a living being just now on earth or from someone who has passed. Yet the most perfect inspiration is always from the divine mind, and to God alone the credit is due. Even if an inspiration comes through the mind of a living person on earth or through a soul that has passed on to the other side, still it has come from God, for all knowledge and wisdom belong to God.

There are three forms in which inspiration comes by the mediumship of a living being: when you are in the presence of someone who is inspiring; when you are in the thoughts of someone who is inspiring; and when your heart is in a state of perfect tranquility and inspiration flowing through the heart of an inspirational person is coming into your heart. It is just like the radio: sometimes you connect it with a certain station from which you are to receive the music and sometimes you do not connect it, but it remains a radio. If anything passing through is not received, it is not heard, but the sound is there just the same. In the same way one receives inspiration from the above-named three different sources.

There are different processes in inspiration. It all depends upon how the heart of the person is focused upon the divine spirit. There may be someone whose heart is focused upon the divine spirit directly; there is another to whom the divine spirit is too remote. His heart is focused on a center, the center that is focused on the divine spirit; therefore he receives his message. But it all comes from the divine spirit just the same. It is a fault on the part of mankind to attribute it to some limited being who is nothing but a shadow concealing God. Besides, when a person believes that an old Egyptian comes from the other side to inspire him or an American Indian comes to lead him on his way, he is building a wall between himself and God. Instead of receiving directly from the source that is perfect and all-sufficient, he is picturing his limited idea, making it a screen between himself and God.

The easiest way for the genius is to make himself an empty cup, free from pride of learning or conceit of knowledge, to become as innocent as a child who is ready to learn whatever may be taught to him. It is the soul who becomes as a child before God, longing and yearning at the same time to express music through his soul, who becomes a fountain of God. From that fountain divine inspiration rises and brings beauty to all those who see the fountain.

There is one step further, and that is when the person no longer remains simply a poet or a musician or a philosopher, but has become God's instrument only. Then God begins to speak to him through everything, not only in a melody or in verse or in color or light. He begins to communicate with God in all forms. Everything he sees above and below, right or left, before or behind, either heavenly or earthly is communicative. He then begins to speak with God, and it is this step that is called revelation.

In the story of Moses it is said that he was looking for fire to bake bread when he happened to see a light on top of a mountain. In order to take this fire he climbed to the top of the mountain, but the fire became lightning. Moses could no longer withstand that great flashing and he fell to the ground. When he awoke he began to communicate with God.

This is allegorical. The idea is that Moses was looking for light to make it his life's sustenance, but he had to climb on to the higher planes. It was not possible to get it on the earth where he stood; it was necessary that he should climb to the top. Then it was not only a light but it was lightning; it was a light that it was beyond the power of Moses to withstand, and he fell down. What is this falling down? To become nothing, to become empty. When he reached that state of emptiness, then his heart became sonorous, and he found communication with God through everything in the world. In the rock, tree, or plant, in the star, sun, or moon, in whatever he saw he found communication with his soul.

And so everything revealed its nature and its secret to Moses. It is in connection with this revelation that Sa'adi says that every leaf of the tree becomes a page of the sacred scripture once the soul has learned to read.

Chapter 43

THE ACTION OF GOD, THE REACTION OF MAN

Nature is the perfection of whatever choice man can make, and this itself is the proof that it is a creation of a Creator who has not created blindly but with intention and choice, proving thereby His perfect wisdom and skill. Nature therefore is the art of an artist who has made it to come up to His choice. Mineral, vegetable, animal, even human creation are from Him, but in the human creation He changes His choice by experiencing life through a human mind and body.

As the perfect spirit, God creates in nature all He wishes to come into being, and He does not find anything lacking, for He has the capability of creating what is not there. But when the ray of the same spirit works through the human garb, in the first place it is incapable of seeing nature as a whole and enjoying the perfection of its beauty. And yet, being the ray of the perfect spirit, and as by nature it seeks perfection, it wants to create what it does not find there. It is this that brings about the necessity for action. Nature therefore is an action of God, and art the reaction of man.

Art is divided into two classes: imitation (copying) and production (improving and improvising).

The first wave of the artistic impulse is to imitate what he admires, and in this there are two tendencies that the artist shows, to copy and to improve. One artist is more capable of copying, another of improvising. The skill in both aspects is equally great. To copy nature fully is beyond human capacity, and the greater an artist is in his art, the better he can copy nature. To copy nature not only a keen observation but a deeper insight into the object before him is necessary.

The improvising faculty may in certain ways be greater, for the artist tries to make the copy of nature better than it is. In reality nature cannot be bettered, considering it as a whole, but when nature is observed in its parts it most often requires to be made better. The ray of the Creator's spirit, which is the soul of the artist, tries to perfect that piece of nature which is imperfect when taken as apart from nature, proving thereby the action of God and the reaction of man.

In copying nature there are two essential things: single-mindedness and fixed observation. Single-mindedness comes from concentration. The artist must realize that it is the hand that can keep still that is capable of holding the brush, and so it is only the mind that can stand still that has the power to copy.

By fixed observation is meant the capability of holding in focus the gaze, the penetrating glance. It depends a great deal upon the object that the artist paints. If its beauty is catching the eyes and the mind of the artist, and if it can hold his interest, it helps the artist to paint. There is always one thing that works against the artist: that is his ever-changing temperament. It may work so actively that it may take away his fixed glance towards something more glaring, and thereby he may not have the patience to persevere in observing the one object before him.

Though the changeableness of the artist in a way shows the liquidity of his mind, which is natural to him, still his control over that changeableness brings his efforts in his art to a successful issue. Concentration therefore helps the artist most in his work. Keen insight into beauty not only helps in art, but it leads the artist to spiritual perfection. There is a very thin veil between the artist and God, and it is his insight into beauty, with constant practice, that can sometimes lift the veil so that all the beauty of nature will become to the artist one single vision of the sublime immanence of God.

Copying is the pupil's tendency, and the great master is he who is a great pupil. The one who copies must by nature be a respondent lover of nature and a follower of nature. There is a verse of a Hindustani poet, "I will undo your curls, O blowing wind, if you disturb the curls of my beloved." The copier is the lover of the beauty he sees, and he does not wish to alter it. His whole effort is to keep its originality; that is the nature of the lover of God.

The copier in his constant effort draws closer and closer to beauty, thereby producing in his own nature beauty. Holding the beauty in himself, he develops harmony in his nature and arrives at oneness with nature. The copier develops the faculty of thinking deeply. Patience is naturally developed by copying. Also the copier will always keep balance, since nature, when seen as a whole, is nothing but balance. Balance is life, and the lack of it is death. The copier develops moderation in his nature, for he gently follows nature. So he is always protected by nature, which has every support and protection of the Almighty Being, itself the very manifestation of God.

The tendency to improve upon nature is a wave of activity of the mind that rises higher than the tendency of copying nature, the former being productive, the latter more impressive. However, the virtue of both tendencies is peculiar in every case. The former tends towards the Creator, whereas the latter tends toward creation. Success in the first aspect of art is slow but sure. But in the second aspect, that of improving, it may turn the right or the worng way. The rhythm of the former is smooth, slow, and mobile; that of the latter active, emphatic, and balancing.

The art of copying is less intelligible to many than the art of improving. To appreciate the art of the one who copies, a deep insight is needed, even so deep an insight as that of the artist who dived deep into the ocean of beauty and from the bottom brought forth pearls in form and color.

There is a tendency that often seems to increase in an imaginative artist, whereby the interest in his own art may go far from nature. Very often even this may prove successful, but at the end of a close examination it must prove to have turned fatal, for the safety of art rests only in staying hand in hand with nature.

The improver has two tendencies. One tendency is to respect the form he improves by refraining from demolishing the originality of the form. He walks gently after nature as a follower of nature, which no doubt assures the success of his art. He improves but does not go very far from nature. He touches the original form and yet does not touch it; he gently works out his destiny of perfecting the original nature. This he does by patience and by thoughtfulness. He is, so to speak, diffident before the Creator.

The other tendency is the tendency of exaggeration. In this there are two kinds. One is to give one's own form to the color of nature or one's choice of color to the form of nature. Another is a slightly pronounced tendency of exaggeration, which is to improve a form even to the extent of deforming it, so that the artist may make a leaf which originally is the length of a palm the size of an elephant's ear, make round what is oval, make an oval into a round form, make even into uneven, and turn a natural into an odd form. Undoubtedly in doing so the artist, if really gifted, will produce what very few artists will be able to do, and surely he will get successful results as a prize for his courageous ventures. But since this tendency of an artist is adventure, it has every chance of failure. Very few artists are able to succeed in exaggeration in their artistic executions, and those who are incapable of doing this when attempting to exaggerate their art prove themselves to be nothing but premature. In the art of improvement no doubt the creative faculty of the artist has as vast a scope as he may require, but no artist has ever been able to produce, nor will any artist ever be able to produce, the form that does not exist. There is no form nor color that does not exist in nature, and there are many forms and colors that remain and will remain unknown and unexplored by science or art. This shows that man, however great an artist, is but a copier of nature. By this one comes to the realization that, after all, man is man and God is God

The artist who improves indeed develops the creative faculty, and this is rooted in that spirit which is the spirit of the Creator.

To improve upon nature is to add to it that which human nature has produced by a certain angle of vision. Improving is the perfecting of nature. The path of the improver is risky: he sometimes has to produce what the human eye has never seen. Therefore his art, instead of appealing to the sense of beauty, often appeals to the sense of curiosity, and instead of bringing satisfaction, which must come through beauty, it may create a feeling of marvel. The artist must have a wonderful grace of form in order to improve to satisfaction.

There are many artists who develop an art that produces confusion in the spectator, and these are called illusionists. They sometimes answer to the symbolical fancies of humankind; sometimes they appeal to the spiritualistic point of view; sometimes they produce a vision in their art, a feeling of something in a mist.

This kind of art becomes of course a means of expressing the mystical ideas, but in the hands of the incompetent it is nothing but a meaningless art, and in the hands of the pretentious, who wish to mystify people with their skill, it is nothing but a means of entertainment. The best way of improving upon nature is by keeping close to nature and yet amplifying the beauty of nature in painting, which is no doubt the true art.

Illusion is produced in art by two kinds of artists: the one who has great intelligence with the fine sense of art, and the one whose mind is not clear and who expresses in his art his own confusion. Therefore the former is the real illusionist; the latter may be taken for what he is not.

One kind of illusion is art is to show at first sight something quite different from what a second sight would suggest. This no doubt requires great skill besides a gifted talent in that side of art. In this particular side of art one can see many forms in one form. By looking from different sides, and sometimes from each side, quite a different picture is seen, each proving the skill of the artist. In this form of art no doubt skill is more pronounced than beauty. An example of this may be seen in the Lion Gate of Mycenae. This represents "seek all power at the feet of God." The column represents the foot of God; the lions represent power. It also represents that God is all power, that all the powerful of the world receive their power from God. This means that God is all powerful, God is the source of all power, in God is centered all power. The four round marks at the head of the column signify the four directions, which means that the reign of God is everywhere. The two altars show that the power manifests in two aspects, although they are one and the same God, one aspect being might and the other being beauty. The whole figure also shows a human head, the column being the nose, the altar the mouth, and the two heads (now missing) being the eyes. This represents that the all-powerful God is found in man, the true temple and altar of God.

There is another kind of illusion, which is to produce before the concentrated gaze a picture that appears as real. This is a proof of the best gift in art. The third kind of illusion is a suggestive art in which a suggestion is made of a certain idea or action so that only the mind developed enough to comprehend it may know it, although to all others it stands as a picture. This no doubt requires an awakening mind with creative power, and in this the artist has an opportunity in the realm of art to convey his thought to others. The artists of ancient times were generally mystics, and they always expressed their thoughts concerning the law of life and nature and their imagination of heaven in art.

There is a fourth kind of illusion which is more mystical than a simple suggestive illusion. It is to picture thought or feeling, a character or a quality that is of the abstract. It is like putting into form and color what is much beyond it. However, this art cannot be a common language. It is a language that no one understands better than its inventor, and yet it is beyond the capacity of the ordinary mind to picture the abstract. In this way there are many who try to picture music or thought forms or emotions. No doubt this kind of art may easily lead an artist to mystify people with meaningless forms and colors of his fantasy, though in every case it must prove to be an advanced adventure on the part of the artist.

The most important aspect of illusion in art is symbology. Symbology is a language of art. It does not mean something to the artist only, but is known to all who are supposed to know its meaning. Symbology means recognized illusion. The origin of symbology is in the inspiration of the artist, for to the artist wisdom is revealed in dreams of art. Although an inspired artist certainly gives a message in the form of art, it is not necessary that every artist should be equipped in symbology, for talent in this direction is inborn in certain artists. An artist in the mystical path may develop this, but there must already be a spark of it in the heart.

Symbolic art lies in between the art of copying and the art of improving. In symbolic art the art of copying and improvising unite, and therefore in symbolism both principal aspects of art become perfected. A person inspired by the symbolic expression of nature sees in all things of nature symbols representing something to him and at the same time revealing to him some mystery of life and nature. This knowledge is a key to the whole creation. To a person possessing this knowledge, everything in the world seems a closed box, the key to which he possesses. As soon as he gives his attention to anything he sees, he immediately finds at hand a symbolic expression which, used as a key, opens the door to every hidden treasure.

There are two aspects of symbolic knowledge. One aspect is *nazul,* when everything in nature begins to give its key to the artist in the form of a symbol. By using the key, the artist becomes able to find out the mystery that every form represents.

The other aspect is *uruj,* in which a wave arises from the heart of the artist, bringing before his view a design by which he can best express his thought symbolically. The artist produces this wave that rises in his heart by his pain, satisfying thereby the demand of the spirit for perfection. In *nazul,* therefore, the artist receives the message, and in *uruj* he gives it to the world, thereby fulfilling the spiritual act to which the inspired artist is destined. According to the temperament of the artist, he is more inclined either to *nazul* or to *uruj.* The one who is inclined to *nazul* has the *jemal* temperament, and the one who is inclined to *uruj* has the *jelal* temperament. However, *uruj* and *nazul* both act and react upon each other. Without *uruj, nazul* is impossible; without *nazul, uruj* cannot be. Perfection lies in receiving both, at times *nazul* and at times *uruj,* as one divides the time of his life during day and night into action and repose.

POETRY

Chapter 44

THE DANCING SOUL

There is a saying that a poet is a prophet, and this saying has a great significance and a hidden meaning. There is no doubt that though poetry is not necessarily prophecy, prophecy is born in poetry. If one were to say that poetry is a body that is adopted by the spirit of prophecy, it would not be wrong. Wagner has said that noise is not necessarily music, and the same thing can be said in connection with poetry: that a verse written in rhyme and meter is not necessarily true poetry. Poetry is an art, a music expressed in the beauty and harmony of words. No doubt much of the poetry one reads is meant either as a pastime or for amusement, but real poetry comes from the dancing of the soul. No one can make the soul dance unless the soul itself is inclined to dance. Also, no soul can dance that is not alive.

In the Bible it is said that no one will enter the kingdom of God whose soul is not born again, and being born means being alive. It is not only a gay disposition or an external inclination to merriment and pleasure that is the sign of a living soul, for external joy and amusement may come simply through a person's external being, although even in this outer joy and happiness there is a glimpse of the inner joy and happiness which is the sign of the soul's having been born again. What makes it alive? It makes itself alive when it strikes its depths instead of reaching outward. The soul, after coming up against the iron wall of this life of falsehood, turns back within itself, it encounters itself, and this is how it becomes living.

In order to make this idea more clear I should like to take as an example a person who goes out into the world; a person with thought, with feeling, with energy, with desire, with ambition, with enthusiasm to live and work in life. Because of the actual nature of life, his experience will make him feel constantly up against an iron wall in whatever direction he strikes out. And the nature of the human being is such that when he meets with an obstacle then he struggles; he lives in the outer life, and he goes on struggling. He does not know any other part of life, for he lives only on the surface. Then there is another person who is sensitive because he has a sympathetic and tender heart, and every blow coming from the outer world, instead of making him want to hit back outwardly, makes him want to strike at himself inwardly. The consequence of this is that his soul, which after being born on this earth seems to be living but in reality is in a grave, becomes awakened by that action. When once the soul is awakened in this way it expresses itself outwardly, whether in music, in art, in poetry, in action, or in whatever way it wishes to express itself.

In this way a poet is born. There are two signs that reveal the poet: one sign is imagination and the other is feeling, and both are essential on the spiritual path. A person however learned and good who lacks these two qualities can never arrive at a satisfactory result, especially on the spiritual path.

The sacred scriptures of all ages, whether those of the Hindus, the Parsees, the race of Beni Israel, or others, were all given in poetry or in poetic prose. No spiritual person, however great, however pious and spiritually advanced, has ever been able to give a scripture to the world unless he was blessed with the gift of poetry. One may ask if this would still be possible nowadays, when sentiment takes second place in life's affairs and people wish everything to be expressed plainly, "cut and dried" as the saying is, and when one has become so accustomed to having everything, especially in science, explained in clear words. But it must be understood that although facts about the names and forms of this

world may be scientifically explained in plain words, when one
wishes to interpret the sensation one gets when looking at life it
cannot be explained except in the way that the prophets did in
poetry. No one has ever explained, nor can anyone ever explain,
the truth in words. Language exists only for the convenience of
everyday affairs; the deepest sentiments cannot be explained in
words. The message that the prophets have given to the world at
different times is an interpretation in their own words of the idea
of life that they have received.

Inspiration begins in poetry and culminates in prophecy. One
can picture the poet as a soul that has so to speak risen from its
grave and is beginning to make graceful movements. When the
same soul begins to move and to dance in all directions and to
touch heaven and earth in its dance, expressing all the beauty it
sees, that is prophecy. The poet when he is developed reads the
mind of the universe, although it very often happens that the poet
himself does not know the real meaning of what he has said. Very
often one finds that a poet has said something, and after many
years there comes a moment when he realizes the true meaning of
what he said. This shows that behind all these different activities
the divine spirit is hidden, and the divine spirit often manifests
through an individual without his realizing that it is divine.

In the East the prophet is called *paghambar,* which means the
messenger, the one who carries somebody's word to someone else.
In reality every individual in this world is the medium of an
impulse that is hidden behind him, and that impulse he gives out,
mostly without knowing it. This is not only so with living beings,
but one can see it even in objects, for every object has its purpose,
and by fulfilling its purpose that object is fulfilling the scheme of
nature. Therefore whatever be the line or activity of a person,
whether it is business or science or music or art or poetry, he is a
medium in some way or other. There are mediums of living beings,
there are mediums of those who have passed to the other side, and
there are mediums who represent their country, their nation, their
race. Every individual is acting in his own way as a medium.

When the prophet or the poet dives deep into himself he
touches that perfection which is the source and goal of all beings.
And as an electric wire connected with a battery receives the force

or energy of the battery, so the poet who has touched the inner-most depths of his being has touched the perfect God, and from there he derives that wisdom, that beauty, and that power which belong to the perfect self of God. There is no doubt that in all things there is the real and the false, the raw and the ripe. Poetry comes from the tendency to contemplation. A person with imagi-nation cannot retain the imagination, cannot mold it, cannot build it up unless he has this contemplative tendency within him. The more one contemplates, the more one is able to conceive of what one receives. Not only this, but after contemplation a person is able to realize a certain idea more clearly than if that idea had only passed through his mind.

The process of contemplation is like the work of the camera: when the camera is put before a certain object and properly fo-cused, then only that object is received by the camera. Therefore when an object before one is limited one can see that object more clearly. What constitutes the appeal of the poet is that he tells his readers of something he has seen behind these generally recog-nized ideas. The prophet goes still further. He not only contem-plates one idea, but he can contemplate any idea. There comes a time in the life of the prophet or of anyone who contemplates when whatever object he casts his glance upon opens up and reveals to him what it has in its heart. In the history of the world we see that besides their great imagination, their great dreams, their ectasy, and their joy in the divine life, the prophets have often been great reformers, scientists, medical men or even states-men.

This in itself shows their balance; it shows that theirs is not a one-sided development. They do not merely become dreamers or go into trances, but both sides of their personality are equally developed. It is an example of God in man that the prophets manifest. We can see this in the life of Joseph: we are told that he was so innocent, so simple that he went with his brothers yielding to them, and that this led to his betrayal. In his relationship with Zuleikha we see the human being, the tendency to beauty. At the same time there is the question he continually asks, "What am I doing? What shall I do?" Later in his life we see him as one who knows the secret of dreams, as the mystic who interprets the dream of the king. And still later in his life we see that he became a minister, with the administration of the country in his hands, able to carry out the work of the state.

Spirituality has become far removed from material life, and so God is far removed from humanity. Therefore one cannot any more conceive of God speaking through a person, someone like oneself. Even a religious person who reads the Bible every day will have great difficulty in understanding the verse, "Be ye perfect, even as your Father in heaven is perfect." The Sufi message and its mission are to bring this truth to the consciousness of the world: that man can dive so deep within himself that he can touch the depths where he is united with the whole of life, with all souls, and that he can derive from that source harmony, beauty, peace, and power.

Chapter 45

THE POETIC SPIRIT

In poetry the rhythm of the poet's soul is expressed. There are moments in the life of every human being when the soul feels itself rhythmic, and at such moments children, who are beyond the conventionalities of life, begin to dance, to speak in words that rhyme, or to repeat phrases that resemble each other and harmonize together. It is a moment of the soul's awakening. One person's soul may awaken more often than another's, but in the life of everyone there are such times of awakening, and the soul that is gifted with the means of expressing thoughts and ideas often shows its gift in poetry.

Among all the valuable things of this world the word is the most precious. For in the word one can find a light that gems and jewels do not possess; a word may contain so much life that it can heal the wounds of the heart. Therefore poetry in which the soul is expressed is as living as a human being. The greatest reward that God bestows on man is eloquence and poetry. This is not an exaggeration, for it is the gift of the poet that culminates in the gift of prophecy.

There is a Hindu idea that explains this very well, and it is that the vehicle of the goddess of learning is eloquence. Many live and few think, and among the few who think there are fewer still who can express themselves. Then their soul's impulse is repressed, for in the expression of the soul the divine purpose is fulfilled, and poetry is the fulfillment of the divine impulse to express something.

No doubt there is true poetry and there is false poetry, just as there is true music and false music. A person who knows many words and phrases may fit them together and arrange something mechanically, but this is not poetry. Whether it be poetry, art, or music, it must suggest life. It can only suggest life if it comes from the deepest impulse of the soul; if it does not do that, then it is dead. There are verses of the great masters of various periods that have resisted the sweeping wind of destruction; they remain ageless. The endurance of their words was in the life that was put into them. The trees that live long have the deepest roots, and so have the living verses. We only read them in the same way in which we look at the trees, but if we could see where the roots of those verses are we would find them in the soul, in the spirit.

What is it that awakens the soul to this rhythm that brings about poetry? It is something that touches in the poet that predisposition which is called love. For with love there come harmony, beauty, rhythm, and life. It seems that all that is good and beautiful and worth attaining is centered in that one spark that is hidden in the heart of man. When the heart speaks of its joy, of its sorrow, all of it is interesting and appealing. The heart does not lie; it always tells the truth. By love it becomes sincere, and it is through the sincere heart that true love manifests. One may live in a community where there is always amusement, pastimes, merriment, and beauty; one may live that life for twenty years, but that moment one realizes the movement in the depths of one's heart, one feels that those whole twenty years were nothing. One moment of life with a living heart is worth more than a hundred years of life with a heart that is dead.

We see many people in this world who have every comfort and good fortune and everthing they need, and yet they lead an empty life. Their life may be more unhappy than that of someone who is starving. He whose soul is starving is more to be pitied than he whose body is starving; for the one whose body is starving is still alive, but the one whose soul is starving is dead. Those who have shown the greatest inspiration and have given precious words of wisdom to the world were the farmers who were plowing the soil of their hearts. This is the reason why there are so few real poets in this world, for the path of the poet is contrary to the path of the worldy man. The real poet, although he exists on this earth, dreams of different worlds from which he gets his ideas. The true poet is at the same time a seer, otherwise he could not bring forth the subtle ideas that touch the heart of his listeners. The true poet is a lover and admirer of beauty. If his soul were not impressed by beauty he could not bring it out in his poetry.

What stimulates the gift in the one who is born with the gift of poetry? Is it pleasure or is it pain? Not pleasure; pleasure freezes the gift. The sensitive poet's soul has to go through pain in his life. One may ask whether it would then be a wise thing to seek pain if one wants to be a good poet, but this would be just like thinking that crying was a virture if one hurt oneself and cried a little. Who, with a living heart, can live in this world as it is and not suffer and not experience pain? Who with any tendency to feel, to sympathize, to love does not go through pain? Who with any sincerity in his nature could experience daily the insincerity, falsehood, and crudity of human nature and yet avoid suffering? At every step he takes the poet will meet with suffering. A poet begins with the admiration of beauty, and because of his talent he naturally tends to shed tears over the disappointments that he meets with in life. When he has passed that phase, then comes another phase, and he begins to smile and even laugh at the world.

The further one advances in life, the more does life offer things that can give one a good reason for enjoying and amusing oneself. The first thing that can make one smile is seeing how everybody is running after his own interests: how a person finds his way along devious routes, how he knocks another person down in order to go forward himself, how he pushes another from behind, and how he silences the next one. Is there anything that we cannot find in human nature? Biting, kicking, and fighting—it is all there. There is nothing of the animal nature that is not in the human being; man even excels the animal. All this, however, only makes one smile; the laughter comes afterwards, when one can see where it all ends. If one is capable of seeing all the various endings, in the end there will be laughter.

It is in this period of a poet's advancement that in some way pity, sentiment, and the sympathy that he already had turn into smiles and laughter. It is like something that is turned inside out. The pity and the shedding of tears which were at first outside are now inside, and outside is the smile and the laughter. Thus both exist at the same time: laughter or a smile on the lips, and pity in the heart. When the poet is laughing his heart is crying at the same time; this is his nature.

The poet rises above tears when he has shed enough. This does not mean that he becomes critical or that he sneers at life, but that he sees the funny side of things and that the whole of life, which he once saw as a tragedy, now appears to him in the form of a comedy. This stage is a consolation for him from above after his moments of great pain and suffering. But then there comes yet another stage where he rises higher still, where he sees the divine element working in all forms, in all names, where he begins to recognize his Beloved in all forms and names.

This experience in the life of a poet is like the joy in the life of a young lover. It inaugurates another period in his life. Whatever be his condition, rich or poor, in comfort or in need, he is never without his Beloved. His divine Beloved is always in his presence. When he arrives at this stage he pities the lover who has only a limited beloved to admire and to love, for now he has arrived at a stage where, whether alone or in a crowd, whether in the north or the south, the west or the east, on earth or in heaven, he is always in the presence of his Beloved.

When he goes one step further still, then it becomes difficult for him to express his emotion, his impulse, in poetry. For then he himself becomes Poetry. What he feels, what he thinks, what he says, what he does, all is poetry. At this stage he touches that ideal of unity which unites all things in one. But in order to reach this stage the soul must become so mature that it is able to enjoy it, for an infant soul would not be able to enjoy this particular con-sciousness of all-oneness. From this time on one will find in the poetry of that poet glimpses of prophetic expression. Then it is not only the beauty of the words and their meaning, but his words become illuminating and his verses become life-giving. There are souls in this world who are pious, who are wise, who are spiritual; but among them the one who is capable of expressing his realization of life, of truth, is not only a poet but a prophet.

Chapter 46

THE MISSION OF POETRY

The poet was born first and poetry came afterwards; poetry was born in the spirit of the poet. It is said in the East that as one can already see in the cradle what features the child will have later, so one can recognize a poet before he learns to speak. Poetry came before language, for it was the poetic spirit in man that made language. Thus the poet is not the son of language but its father: instead of only taking words, he makes them. If it had not been for the poet, the languages of all races would only have been shouting and howling. In all the different aspects of life we can recognize the signs of inspiration most fully in the poet.

Poetry is the best art there is, for besides everything else it is also drawing or painting with words. The mission of poetry is the same as the mission of the other forms of art. Poetry is a living picture that says more than a picture on canvas, and its mission is to inspire. Poetry comes to a poet through the suffering caused by disappointment. But any pain or suffering is a preparation, and just as in order to be able to play on a violin one must first tune it, so the heart must be tuned in order to express wisdom. The heart is tuned by suffering, and when the heart has suffered enough pain, then poetry comes. The natural birth of poetry takes place on the day when the doors of the heart are opened.

There is an example in the Sanskrit language of what has been said above, that poetry comes before learning, for in Sanskrit many everday words rhyme. Mother and father rhyme: *matr* and *patr*. Also brother and friend rhyme: *britra* and *mitra*. If one goes through the *Kosh*, which is the Sanskrit dictionary, one will find that all the words that are related to one another in some way rhyme. This shows that for the ancient people poetry was the everyday language; in other words, their everyday language was poetry.

There is a Sanskrit saying that is perhaps an exaggeration, but it is significant: that a person without any interest in music and poetry is like an animal without a tail. If we wish to compare music with poetry, we can only say that poetry is the surface and music is the depth of one and the same thing. As with mind and heart the surface is the mind and the depth is the heart, so it is with poetry and music. The ancient poets were also singers, they composed poetry and they sang. The perfection of the soul could be seen in these two faculties, the faculty of poetry and at the same time its expression in the form of music. Those who separate music from poetry are the same as those who separate religion from life; they are interested in separating everything.

When we study the earliest Sanskrit poetry, we see that it was composed of words that had a fixed measure, each word containing three consonant root-letters to which different vowels were attached. This divided them into two kinds: words of one syllable and words of two syllables. For instance, to the consonant root *mtr* could be attached one vowel *a*, giving *matr*, mother; or two vowels *i* and *a*, giving *mitra*, friend. The arrangement of the words thus composed formed a meter, and there were a great number of these meters in use.

The rhythms in which ancient people composed their poems were taken from the rhythm of nature: the rhythm of the air, the rhythm of running water, the rhythm of a flying bird, the rhythm of waving branches. They tried to keep near to nature so that nature could teach them. To each of these ancient rhythms or meters they gave a name that was related to something in nature. For instance there is a rhythm called *hansa*, after the sound of the bird of that name. Poets used the rhythm of the *hansa's* call in the composition of their poetry.

Thus the Sanskrit poets were very particular about the psychology of rhythm, words, letters, and syllables. They found that poetry had a *mantric* effect, which means that poetic inspiration creates a certain effect in the same way as *mantrams*, sacred words, and that thereby a person might unwittingly bring about bad or good luck for himself or for others, or be the cause of harm or success.

There are superstitions that when a certain bird makes a sound it is a warning of coming death. This superstition exists in many different countries. It means that the sound this bird makes creates a destructive rhythm, and whenever that sound is heard it causes a destructive vibration. It is the same with poetry: the arrangement of words, syllables, and letters—all has an effect. When the wind blows from the north, from the south, from the east, or from the west, when it blows straight, slanting, zigzag, upward, or downward, it causes different conditions in the atmosphere. It may bring germs of a plague, it may culminate in a storm, it may create heat or cold, it may change the season, or it may cause destruction, good health, cheerfulness, or depression among people. When by his breath, which can be likened to the wind that blows in the world, the voice of a singer pronounces a certain letter, then that breath has to take a certain direction. Either it goes upward or downward, to the right or to the left, staight or zigzag; and in accordance with this direction it has an influence upon a person's life.

One might think that if breath has such an influence on a person's life, it is only for himself, whereas the influence of the wind is for the whole country, perhaps for the whole world. But man is more powerful than the world, though he may not realize it. The ancient people used to say that one person can save the world and the thought of one person can cause a ship to sink. If one wicked thought can cause a ship to sink, what a great power man has! The reason is that the wind is not so directly connected with the divine spirit as is the human breath, and therefore that breath is more powerful than the wind. When we consider words and their meaning, modern psychology supports the idea that the meaning of every word acts upon our life and has an influence on the lives of other people. Poetry can thus be considered to be a psychological creation, something with psychological power, either for good or for ill.

What was most remarkable about the poets of the Sanskrit age was that all their life they practiced diction, the right pronunciation of every syllable and sound. Everything had to be in rhythm; it also had to be of the right tone and it had to create the right vibrations. The most learned people, not only among poets but among doctors and others, spent half an hour or longer every day in practicing and pronouncing different syllables and words so that they could speak with greater fluency. Just as a singer today practices pronouncing every word clearly, so did the poets of that time, because they believed in the influence of sound: how it is produced and what effect it has.

The Vedas, which are supposed to have come from the divine source, are all in verse, as are the Puranas and other sacred scriptures of ancient times. This shows that when the divine mind wished to express itself, it did not do so crudely; it always expressed itself in a fully poetic, rhythmic, and lyrical form. So often we meet people who proudly and boldly say, "I speak the truth. I do not care whether anybody likes it or not. I have the courage to tell the truth no matter if it hurts or kills". But they do not know what truth means; they do not know that truth comes in the form of poetry, of music, of delicacy and fineness.

After the Sanskrit age came the Prakrit age. Poetry became more human, not as philosophical and scientific as in the Sanskrit age. At this time the poet began to conceive in his mind different pictures of human nature and character. This was called *rasa shastra,* the science of human nature. In writing lyrics they distinguished between three aspects of love and they classified the female and male natures in four different aspects.

It has always been the poet's natural inclination to set the feminine aspect of life and of nature on a high pedestal; it is this that inspires the poet to give a beautiful form to all that he creates. Thus poets of great repute in all ages have always been attracted by the moon. They have not written so many lyrics about the sun since they had more appreciation for the feminine aspect of creation. For the same reason the crescent was the sign of the Prophet, for if a prophet were not responsive to God as the crescent moon is to the sun, illumination would not come to him. It is through his response to the voice of God that a prophet receives or conceives in his spirit the message that he then gives to humanity.

Kings at all times have been very much interested in knowledge and learning, and their associations with poets softened their characters and balanced their warlike tendencies, their roughness and crudeness. Poets helped kings to look at life in a different way. It was the poetic inspiration of the emperor Shah Jihan that made the Taj Mahal. If it had not been for poetry he would not have become such a great lover.

The one who reads poetry, the one who enjoys poetry, and the one who writes poetry must know that poetry is something that does not belong to this earth: it belongs to heaven, in whatever form one shows one's appreciation and love for poetry, one really shows one's appreciation and love for the spirit of beauty.

Chapter 47

THE PERSIAN POETS

At all times Persia has had great poets. It has been called the land of poetry, in the first place because the Persian language is so well adapted to poetry, but also because all Persian poetry contains a mystical touch. The literary value of the poetry only makes it poetry, but when a mystical value is added this makes the poetry prophecy. The climate and atmosphere of Persia have also been most helpful to poetry, and the very imaginative nature of the people has made their poetry rich. At all times and in all countries, when the imagination has no scope for expansion, poetry dies and materialism increases.

There is no poet in the world who is not a mystic. A poet is a mystic wbether consciously or unconsciously, for no one can write poetry without inspiration, and when a poet touches the profound depths of the spirit, struck by some aspect of life, he brings forth a poem as a diver brings forth a pearl.

In this age of materialism and ever-growing commercialism humanity seems to have lost the way of inspiration. During my travels I was asked by a well-known writer whether it is really true that there is such a thing as inspiration. This gave me an idea of how far nowadays some writers and poets are removed from inspiration. It is the materialism of the age that is responsible for this;

if a person has a tendency towards poetry or music, as soon as he begins to write something his first thought is, "Will it catch on or not? What will be its practical value?" Generally what catches on is that which appeals to the average person. In this way culture is going downward instead of upward.

When the soul of the poet is intoxicated by the beauty of nature and tbe harmony of life, it is moved to dance, and the expression of the dance is poetry. The difference between inspired poetry and mechanical writing is as great as the difference between true and false. For long ages the poets of Persia have left a wonderful treasure of thought for humanity. Jelaluddin Rumi has revealed in his *Masnavi* the mystery of profound revelation. In the East his works are considered as sacred as holy scriptures. They have illuminated numberless souls, and the study of his work can be considered to belong to the highest standard of culture.

The poet is a creator, and he creates in spite of all that confronts him. He creates a world of his own, and by doing so he rises naturally above that plane where only what is visible and touchable is regarded as real. When he sings to the sun, when he smiles to the moon, when he prays to the sea, and when he looks at the plants, at the forests, and at life in the desert, he communicates with nature. In the eyes of the ordinary person he is imaginative, dreamy, visionary; his thoughts seem to be in the air. But if one asked the poet what he thinks of these others, he would say that it is those who cannot fly who remain on the ground. It is natural that creatures who walk on the earth are not always able to fly; those who fly in the air must have wings. Among human beings one will find that same difference, for in human beings there are all things. There are souls like germs and worms, there are souls like animals and birds, and again there are souls like djinns and angels. Among human beings all can be found: those who belong to the earth, those who dwell in heaven, and those who dwell in the very depths.

Those who were able to soar upward by the power of their imagination have been living poets. What they said was not only a statement, it was music itself; it had not only a rhythm, but it had also a tone in it. It made their souls dance and it would make anyone dance who heard their poetry. Thus Hafiz of Shiraz gives a challenge to the dignified, pious people of his country when he says, "Pious friends, you would forget your dignity if you would hear the song that came from my glowing heart." It is such souls who have touched the highest summits of life, so that they have been able to contribute some truth, giving an interpretation of human nature and the inner law of life.

It is another thing with poets who have made poetry for the sake of fame or name or popularity, or so that it might be appreciated by others, for that is business and not poetry. Poetry is an art, an art of the highest degree. The poet's communication with nature brings him in the end to communicate with himself, and by that communication he delves deeper and deeper, within and without, communicating with life everywhere. This communication brings him into a state of ecstasy, and in his ecstasy his whole being is filled with joy. He forgets the worries and anxieties of life, he rises above the praise and blame of this earth, and the things of this world become of less importance to him. He stands on the earth but gazes into the heavens; his outlook on life becomes broadened and his sight keen. He sees things that no one else is interested in, that no one else sees.

This teaches us that what may be called heaven or paradise is not very far from man. It is always near him, if only he would look at it. Our life is what we look at. If we look at the right thing then it is right; if we look at the wrong thing then it is wrong. Our life is made according to our own attitude, and that is why the poet proves to be self-sufficient and also indifferent and independent. These qualities become as wings for him to fly upward. The poet is in the same position as anyone else in regard to the fears and worries that life brings, the troubles and difficulties that everyone feels in the midst of the world, and yet he rises above these things so that they do not touch him.

No doubt the poet is much more sensitive to the troubles and difficulties of life than an ordinary person. If he took to heart everything that came to him, all the jarring influences that disturbed his peace of mind, all the rough edges of life that everyone has to rub against, he would not be able to go on. On the other hand, if he hardened his heart and made it less sensitive, then he would also close his heart to the inspiration that comes as poetry.

Therefore in order to open the doors of his heart, to keep its sensitiveness, the one who communicates with life within and without is open to all influences, whether agreeable or disagreeable, and is without any protection. His only escape from all the disturbances of life is through rising above them.

The prophetic message that was given by Zarathushtra to the people of Persia was poetic from beginning to end. It is most interesting to see that Zarathushtra showed in his scriptures and all through his life how a poet rises from earth to heaven. It suggests to us how Zarathushtra communicated with nature and its beauty, and how at every step he took he touched deeper and deeper the depths of life. Zarathushtra formed his religion by praising the beauty in nature and by finding the source of his art, which is creation itself, in the Artist who is behind it all.

What form of worship did he teach? He taught the same worship with which he began his poetry and with which he finished it. He said to his pupils, "Stand before the sea, look at the vastness of it, and bow before it, before its source and goal." People then thought that it was sun worship, but it was not; it was the worship of light, which is the source and goal of all. That communication within and without sometimes extended the range of a poet's vision so much that it was beyond the comprehension of the average person.

When the Shah of Persia said that he would like to have the history of his country written (for one did not exist at that time), Firdawsi, a poet who was inspired and intuitive said, "I will write it and bring it to you." He began to meditate, throwing his searchlight as far back into the past as possible, and before the appointed time he was able to prepare the book and bring it to the court. It is said tbat the spiritual power of that poet was so great that when someone at the court sneered at the idea of a person being able to look so far back into the past, he went up to him and put his hand on his forehead and said, "Now see!" And the man saw with his own eyes that which was written in the book.

This is human. It is not superhuman, although examples of it are rarely to be found, for in the life of every human being, especially of one who is pure-hearted, loving, sympathetic, and good, the past, present, and future are manifested to a certain extent. If one's inner light were thrown back as a searchlight it could go much further than one can comprehend. Some have to develop this gift, but others are born with it, and among them we find some who perhaps know ten or twelve years beforehand what is going to happen. Therefore a poet is someone who can focus his soul on the past and also throw his light on the future and make that clear which has not yet happened but which already exists in the abstract.

Such poetry becomes inspirational poetry. It is through such poetry that the intricate aspects of metaphysics can be taught. All the Upanishads and the Vedas are written in poetry; the suras of the Qu'ran and Zarathushtra's scriptures are all in poetry. All these prophets, whenever they came, brought the message in poetry.

The development of poetry in Persia occurred at a time when there was a great conflict between the orthodox and the freethinkers. At that time the law of the nation was a religious law, and no one was at liberty to express his free thoughts, that might be in conflict with the religious ideas. There were great thinkers such as Firdawsi, Fariduddin Attar, Jelaluddin Rumi, Sa'adi, Hafiz, Jami, and Omar Khayyam, who were not only poets but who were poetry itself. They were living in another world, although they appeared to be on earth. Their oulook on life, their keen sight were different from those of everyone else. The words that arose from their hearts were not brought forth with effort; they were natural flames rising up out of the heart. These words remain as flames enlightening souls of all times, whatever soul they have touched.

Sufism has been the wisdom of these poets. There has never been a poet of note in Persia who was not a Sufi, and every one of them has added a certain aspect to the Sufi ideas. But they took great care not to affront the minds of orthodox people. Therefore a new terminology had to be invented in Persian poetry; the poets had to use words such as "wine," "bowl," "beloved," and "rose," words that would not offend the orthodox mind and would yet at the same time serve as symbolical expressions to explain the divine law.

It belongs to the work of the Sufi movement to interpret the ideas of tbese poets, to express their ideas in words that can be understood by modern people, for the value of those ideas is as great today as it ever was.

MUSIC

Chapter 48

THE CELESTIAL ART

In all ages the thoughtful have called music "the celestial art."
Artists have pictured the angels playing on harps, and this teaches
us that the soul comes on earth with the love of music. It is not
after being born on earth that man learns to love music; the soul
was already enthralled by music before it came to earth. If one asks
why then every soul does not love music, the answer is that there
are many souls who are buried. They are alive, yet they are buried
in the denseness of the earth, and therefore they cannot appreciate
music. But in that case they are not able to appreciate anything
else, for music is the first and the last thing to appeal to every soul.

The heaven of the Hindus, *Indra-loka,* is filled with singers. The
male singers are called *gandharvas* and the female singers *upsaras.*
In Hindu symbology music seemed the best symbol to express
paradise.

Why does music appeal so much to humanity? The whole of
manifestation has its origin in vibration, in sound. This sound,
which is called *nada* in the Vedanta, was the first manifestation of
the universe. Consequently the human body was made of tone
and rhythm. The most important thing in the physical body is
breath, and the breath is audible; it is most audible in the form of
voice. This shows that the principal signs of life in the physical

body are tone and rhythm, which together make music. Rhythm appeals to man because there is a rhythm going on in his body. The beating of the pulse and the movement of the heart both indicate this rhythm.

The rhythm of the mind has an effect upon this rhythm that is going on continually in the body, and in accordance with its influence it affects the physical body. The notes appeal to a person because of the breath. Breath is sound and its vibrations reach every part of the body, keeping it alive. Therefore, in having an effect on the vibrations and on the atoms of the body, sound gives us a sensation.

It is said that Shiva, or Mahadeva, invented tbe first musical instrument. Wben he was wandering about in the forest, engrossed in spiritual attainment, he wanted to have some source of amusement, a change in his meditative life. So he took a piece of bamboo and two gourds, which he attached to the bamboo, and the strings be made out of animal guts. When he had fixed these on the instrument he had invented tbe vina. That is why the Hindus call the vina a sacred instrument, and for many years they did not allow any strings except gut strings to be used. Afterwards this instrument was improved and made more refined, and now steel strings are mostly used, but the reason why gut string is appealing to the human soul is that it comes from a living body. Even after being separated from the body it still cries out , "I am alive!" Thus the violin gives out a more living sound than the piano. Tbe piano may drown the violin, but the life that comes from the gut string manifests as a voice.

There is a Chinese legend that says that the first music was played on little pieces of reed. The great musician of ancient times who introduced music in China made holes in a piece of reed at a certain distance from each other, the distance between two fingers, and so the flute of reed came into being. From this came the scale of five notes: one note was the original note produced by the reed, and tbe four otber notes were made by placing the fingers on the holes. Afterwards many other scales were developed. Hindu philosophy distinguishes four different cycles of the human race: *krita yuga*, the golden age; *treta yuga*, the silver age; *dvapar yuga*, the copper age; and *kali yuga*, the iron age. This cycle in which we are living now is the iron age. In the golden age there was the music of the soul, a music that appealed to the soul itself and that raised it to cosmic consiousness, the music of the angels, the music that was healing and soothing. The music of the silver age was the music of the heart, that appealed to the depths of the heart, creating sympathy and love of nature, inspiring people and helping the heart quality to develop. The music of the copper age appealed to the mind, to the intellect, so that one could understand the intricacies of musical science, the differences between the many scales, the quality of the rhythm. Finally, the music that belongs to the iron age has an influence on the physical body; it helps soldiers to march and moves people to dance.

A story told in India illustrates this idea. At the court of the last emperor, Muhammad Shah, a singer came who had invented a new way of composing. When this man sang his new compositions, he won the admiration and praise of everyone at the court. The singers and musicians were simply amazed to think that there could be a new development in music. But one of the old musicians who was present said, "If Your Majesty will pardon me, I would like to say a word. There is no doubt that this is most beautiful music, and it has won the admiration of all those present, and also my own. But I must tell you that from this day the music of the country, instead of going upward, will go downward. The music that was handed down to us has weight, it has substance; but now it seems that this has been lost and that the music has become lighter. Therefore from now on it will go downward." And so it happened; step by step after that, music was brought down.

Chapter 49

MUSIC EAST AND WEST

Ancient Greek music seems to have been largely the same as the music of the East. The Greeks had certain scales like the ragas in India, which also resembled the Persian scales. In this way there was a similarity in the music of the human race. But there came a division between the music of the East and that of the West when western music, especially the German, progressed in another direction. In the traditions and the history of the world, as far as one can trace, one finds that melody was considered the principal thing in the East as well as in the West, and composers, according to their stage of evolution, enriched this melody as much as they could. At first the melodies were chiefly folksongs, but sometimes also more elaborate compositions, and as such they were the expression of the soul. They were not compositions in the sense of modern, more technical, compositions; they were in reality imaginations. An artist made a melody, that melody became known after he had sung or played it, and then it was taken up by others. In this way one melody was sung by perhaps ten different musicians in various ways, each retaining his liberty in singing it. No doubt it was difficult even to recognize the same melody after four or five persons had sung or played it, yet each of these had his freedom of expression, right or wrong.

Music in the East was based on ragas, which are certain arrangements of notes, themes that were recognized and distinguished. These ragas were composed by four different classes of people: those who studied and practiced folksongs and out of these folksongs arranged certain themes or ragas; poets and dramatists who composed ragas and their "wives," *raginis,* as well as "sons," "daughters," and "daughters-" and "sons-in-law," creating in this way families of ragas in their imagination; and finally musicians who out of the three above-mentioned kinds of ragas composed new ones with their musical gift. On these ragas the music of India was based.

The credit for every song a musician sang and for every theme he played went to him, because while the theme might consist of only four or eight bars, he improvised extensively on it and made it more interesting. Therefore a performer in India had at the same time to be a composer, although in these improvisations due consideration was given to the original theme and rhythm of the raga so that the audience might be able to recognize it. Even today, if a musician sings a raga that is not exactly as it ought to be, there may be someone among the audience who, while not knowing precisely what is wrong, will yet feel immediately that it does not sound right, just as in Italy when an opera singer makes one little mistake, someone from the audience will immediately show his disapproval. This is because the music of the opera has become engraved upon the spirit of the lovers of opera, and as soon as it seems slightly different from what they are accustomed to hear they know there is something wrong.

What is most remarkable is that the mystics played such an important part in the development of Indian music. Music is the most wonderful way to spiritual realization; there is no quicker and no surer way of attaining spiritual perfection than through music. The great Indian mystics such as Narada and Tumbara were singers, and Krishna played the flute. Thus music in its tradition and practice has always been connected with mysticism. Musicians have always held to the principle that modern scientists have rediscovered, that the ear is incapable of fully enjoying two sounds played or sung together. That is why they enriched the melody to such an extent for the purpose of their meditation.

When Persian music with its artistry and beauty was brought to India, it was wedded to Indian music, and there resulted a most wonderful art. The desire of the people of all classes and ages has always been and still is that music, no matter whether it is technical or non-technical, theoretical or non-theoretical, should touch the soul deeply. If it does not do so, the technical, theoretical, and scientific side of it does not appeal to them. Therefore it has often been very difficult even for the great masters of music who have developed the technique and science of music, and who are masters of rhythm and tone, to please the audience. For the audience, from the king to the man in the street, everyone wants only one thing, and that is a great appeal to the soul from the voice, from the word, from melody. Everything expressed in music should appeal to the soul. This is true even to the extent that when a beggar in the street does not sing a song that appeals to the passers-by, he will not get as many pennies as another who is more appealing.

No doubt the music of India has changed much during the last century. That which the Indians call classical music, or music with weight and substance, is not patronized anymore because of the ignorance of most of the princes and potentates of the country, and therefore the best music is no longer understood. Then people have taken to smoking and talking while listening to music, and music was not made for that. It seems that the spirit of the great musicians is dead; for a great vina player, who considered his instrument sacred and who worshipped it before taking it in his hand, practicing and playing it for perhaps ten hours a day, regarded music as his religion. But if he had to play before people who were moving about, smoking, and talking with other people, as at a social gathering, then all his music would go to the winds. It was the sacredness with which the people of ancient times invested music that kept it on a higher level.

When Tansen, the great singer, left the court hurt by a remark of the Emperor Akbar, he went to Rewa, a state in central India. When the maharajah of Rewa heard that Tansen was coming he was perplexed, wondering in what way he should honor him. A chair was sent for Tansen, to bring him to the palace, and when he arrived Tansen expected the maharajah at least to receive him at the door. As soon as he got out of the chair he said, "Where is the maharajah?" The man who he asked replied, "Here is the maharajah!" pointing to the one who had been carrying the chair all through the city. Tansen was most touched, and he said, "You could not have given me a greater reward." From that day Tansen saluted him with his right hand, saying, "This hand will never salute anyone else all my life." And so it was. Tansen would not even salute the emperor with his right hand. Such was the appreciation, the acknowledgment of talent in ancient India.

Now a new music has come to India that is called theatrical music. It is neither eastern nor western; it is a very peculiar music. The themes of march and galop and polka and airs that no one wants to hear anymore in the western world are imitated and an Indian twist is given to them. Thus they are spoiled for the ears of the western listener and also for good eastern ears.

Pope Gregory I, after whom the Gregorian scales are named, coordinated those beautiful melodies that had come from ancient Greece via Byzantium to form the religious music of the church. This is all that remains as a relic of the music of those times, though one finds traces of this Gregorian music in the compositions of the seventeenth and early eighteenth centuries, for instance in Handel's Messiah. Later composers, however, created a type of music that was quite different. No doubt in this way they laid the foundation for western music and helped it to evolve, but evolve in what way? Mechanically. They were able to make use of large bands, either brass bands or string bands, and also of an orchestra in which hundreds of instruments could be played at the same time. This naturally made a great impression, and it gave the world of music much opportunity and scope for the development and evolution of music. Nevertheless, there was one thing that was lost and is being lost more and more every day: the appeal to the soul, which is the main purpose of music.

Debussy was looking all his life for something new to introduce into modern music, and Scriabin once told me, "Something is missing in our music; it has become so mechanical. The whole process of composition nowadays is mechanical. How can we introduce a spirit into it?" I have often thought that if Scriabin, with his fine character and beautiful personality, had lived longer, he could have introduced a new strain of music into the modern world.

Will someone else try to do what Scriabin wanted? When there is a need, if there is a real desire for its fulfillment, that fulfillment must come. It only seems that we do not need it enough; that is the difficulty. We become so easily contented with what we have. If the world feels a greater need for a better kind of music, then it will come, but if people mostly enjoy jazz and that is sufficient for them, then naturally it will only come slowly, because so few want anything better.

The music of the future will be different from the music of the past in this way: the ancient music developed only in one direction, that every instrument was played alone and every song was sung alone; there was no other instrument or voice. The modern development is that there is a variety of voices and there are many instruments playing together. The development of music in this direction has its origin in what is recognized as classical music. It certainly has its value, but on the other hand something has also been lost. In order to make music perfect, its ancient aspect should be developed more.

There is music that makes one feel like jumping and dancing; there is music that makes one feel like laughing and smiling; and then there is music that makes one feel like shedding tears. If one were to ask a thoughtful person which he preferred, no doubt he would say, "The last; the music that brings tears." Why does the soul want sad music? Because that is the only time when the soul is touched. The music that reaches no further than the surface of one's being remains only on the surface. It is the music that reaches to the depths of one's being that touches the soul. The deeper the music reaches, the more contented is the soul. No doubt a person who is very cheerful and has had dinner and a glass of wine could be quite happy with some dance music. But then he need not have serious music; for him jazz will be quite sufficient.

The modern revival of folk music is an effort in the right direction, but it should be carried out without spoiling the folk music. For the tendency of most composers is to take this music and then put too much of their own touch into it. If, however, they can preserve the folk music without spoiling it, it will be something worthwhile. Composers sometimes take folk music and attach modern harmony to it, and this spoils it too, for generally folk music is the expression of the soul of that particular time when there was no harmonization such as there is now. The modern method of harmonization, when it is applied to folk music, takes away its original atmosphere.

We can observe two principal tendencies in modern music. One is the tendency to make the music of our time more natural, and in that way to improve it. This can surely be developed more and more, as there will be a greater appreciation of solo music, for instance of the cello or the violin. Musicians will again go back to the ancient idea of one instrument playing or one voice singing at a time. When they again come to the full appreciation of this idea, they will reach the spiritual stage of musical perfection. People today like music that has more than one voice because they do not listen enough to solo music, but the more they hear it and the closer they come to it the more they will forget the other kind. There are big symphony concerts given in the concert halls of London, New York, Paris, and all the large cities, but if one notices carefully what the audience likes best, it will be a solo on the cello, on the flute, or on the violin.

People are accustomed to hearing music of many sounds, and after the solo concert is over they will enjoy the other kind of music. But in the depths of their being they will surely still prefer the solo music, for the human soul is the same now as in ancient times, and the same in the East as in the West. The ringing of one bell has a greater appeal than the ringing of many bells. One sound always goes deeper than many sounds. The reason why two sounds are in conflict with each other is that however much they are tuned to one another, yet they are two, and that in itself is a conflict.

There is another tendency that is working hand in hand with this one and is dragging music downward. Composers are not content with the chords that the great masters such as Mozart, Beethoven, or Wagner have used in their music, but they are inventing new chords, chords that tend to confuse thousands of listeners. What will be the outcome of this? It will have an unconscious effect upon the nervous system of humanity; it will make people more and more nervous. As we often see that those who attend good concerts only go there out of vanity, they will accept any kind of music. But, as Wagner has said, noise is not necessarily music. It is not the newness of the music that will give satisfaction in the end; it will not do any good to the souls who have gone to the concert hall only to satisfy their vanity. Music should be healing; music should uplift the soul; music should inspire. There is no better way of getting closer to God, of rising higher towards the spirit, of attaining spiritual perfection than music, if only it is rightly understood.

Chapter 50

INDIAN MUSIC

A characteristic of Indian music is that it depends upon the creative talent of the musician in improvisation. An outline is given by the composer, and the musician fills it in as he pleases. Very little is given by the composer, and the rest is the expression by the singer of his feeling at the time of singing. Music in India has always been used not as an amusement but as a means of mystical development. Therefore the sound of the instruments is faint, and even when several instruments are played together the effect is not produced by the chord or by harmony but by melody. Each instrument has the melody.

There is very little written music in the East. There are many reasons for this. There is a system in the Sanskrit manuscripts, but very few read it. The system must needs be a very complicated one, yet that is not the hindrance. Notation would hamper the musician and not leave him free to sing and play what his soul speaks.

In India a singer, when he begins to sing, sings first the keynote. He repeats it over and over again so as to put himself so much in union with his instrument that his voice and the tone of the instrument may be one. Next he goes a little further and returns to the keynote. Then he goes a little further still, but always returns to the keynote. The musician may take one raga and play that for hours, or he may go from one raga to another. But the more he plays one raga, the more he indulges in that, the more he impresses his soul with it and the more he will find in that.

The ragas have sometimes been understood as scales. They are not scales but patterns of notes within the octave. Different ragas have always been played at different times of day. The inner reason for this is that every time of day has its atmosphere and its influence on us. The material reason is that as evening dress is wanted at a banquet because for so long the eyes have been accustomed to see it, so our ears have been accustomed for very long to hear these ragas at night, in the evening, or at midday. Several ragas are usually sung before dawn. In India before dawn, everyone goes to his work or to his devotions, and there he finds himself very much helped by the stillness of the hour, by the finer vibrations. At midday the noise from all around is much greater and stronger notes are needed. The ragas for midday are made all with natural notes. The ragas of the night are with odd notes. The ragas of the early morning are made with flat notes.

I have seen myself when I played the vina and sang the raga *jogia* in the early morning when people were going to the temple and to the mosque, sometimes they would stop to listen and be enraptured with the music. At other times, with the same raga, I did not even impress myself, according to the prevailing mood.

In the old legends we find that in ancient times music had an effect not upon people or upon animals only, but upon things, upon objects, upon the elements. The flames of fire burst out or the waters stopped running when music was sung or played. A person may ask, "Is this an exaggeration, is music different now from then, or have we lost this art?" I will say that such singers as I have heard sing in India when I was a boy I never heard again in the next generation. The singers of the ancient times sang the same raga, the same song, hundreds of times, thousands of times, a million times. It is by repetition of one thing, by association that we can produce in ourselves the creative power. To have acquired a great store of knowledge, so many songs or ragas, is nothing. It is the power of producing from within oneself, of creating, that is great.

Indian music gained very much by its contact with Persian music. It learned the grace and the expression of Persian music. It also gained much from the beauty of the Arabic rhythm. After the rise of the Moghul empire it was much more beautiful then it had been before. That it is very highly developed is shown by its rhythm also. There are rhythms of five and rhythms of seven, which are very difficult to keep, and there are songs in which no rhythm is apparent for some bars, but the musician keeps it in his mind and after several bars he comes in upon the right beat. There are rhythms that do not begin upon the beat, which always mislead the hearer.

There are four different kinds of songs: the *dhrupad*, the *qawwal,* the *tumri*, and the *ghazal*. The *dhrupad* requires a special training of the voice, just as it is not everyone's work to sing opera music. The *qawwal* means imagination, the song of imagination.

The science of Indian music is founded on a most natural basis. Sound is graduated into tones, semitones, and microtones. Time is divided into six finer divisions besides the usual six. Each note has its color, planet, and element, according to the mysticism of sound. Our music is based upon the principle of ragas. Mystically they are subject to time and season, and each raga has an effect upon the spheres. Poetically ragas have their images. Mathematically they have increased from one to innumerable ragas; artistically they are taken from the natural music of diverse people, and scientifically they have five divisions: ragas of seven notes, six notes, five notes, even notes, and odd notes.

The art of Indian music is remarkable for its vocal culture, and it requires years of study to attain proficiency in it. Our instrumental music is considered next to the vocal in importance. The vina is the oldest instrument in the world's history, and it is also the only instrument for the correct production of Indian music.

Indian dancing follows on the same principles as vocal and instrumental music. The Indian musician is recognized chiefly for the inspirational beauty he expresses by his improvisation. Therefore our composers are much less known, because their compositions are performed differently by each artist; only the foundation

and poetry remain the same. The artist is supposed to be a composer himself before he can become an artist. Even if he sings one
song it will be different each time. Therefore notation did not
become universal in India until of late, when Moula Bakhsh, the
great composer, invented a system of notation for beginners and
founded a school on modern principles in the state of Maharajah
Gaekwar of Baroda.

The Vina

You wish to hear from me the praise of the vina. Therefore I
shall quote the words of a great Indian poet in Sanskrit, who says
in the praise of the vina (be not surprised to hear the interpretation
of this), "That instrument of gut strings! By looking at it, by
touching it, by hearing it, you can be made free, even if you kill
a Brahman." (To kill a Brahman is considered to be the greatest
sin.)

This instrument was invented by the lord of yogis Shiva, who
gave to the world his lifelong experiences in the practice of yoga
and who is worshipped in India as a godhead. His literature is
considered as holy scriptures. He was a great master of breathing
and an ascetic. He lived in the mountains, where he sat and
breathed the free air of the wide horizons of the East and practiced
mantras, words and phrases that change the whole being of man.
He practiced the vina in solitude, and it is said that when the deer
in the forest heard him play, they used to say, "Make the gut
strings of my own entrails and put them on your vina, but as long
as I live, continue to play."

Mahadeva made his instrument by the help of the human body
and mind, considering its condition in the morning, in the midst
of the day, in the afternoon, in the night, and at dawn when
wakening. He found that at every time of the day and night a
particular effect was made upon the human body and spirit and
that a rhythm akin to that particular time must be prescribed

psychologically and mystically in order to elevate the soul. Therefore a psychological science of music was made by Mahadeva, a
science called raga, which means "emotion," emotion controlled
and utilized to the best purpose. When his consort Parvati saw this
instrument, she said, "I must invent my vina." So she took half the
part of the pumpkins and produced another kind of vina, the
Sarasvati vina. So there are two vinas; one is played by men, the
other by women. On this instrument not only sharp and flat notes
are produced, but also semitones. In this way the music becomes
rich, but to develop to the science of semitones is so difficult that
it takes a lifetime.

The musicians of India devote twelve hours of the day or more
to the practice of the different rhythms, improvising on them. In
the end they produce a psychological effect that is not music but
magic, a magic that can thrill a person and penetrate his heart. It
is a dream, a meditation, it is paradise. By hearing it one feels in
a different world. Yet the music is hardly audible. Instead of playing before thousands of people, only one or two or three persons
of the same quality and nature must be together to enjoy that
music thoroughly. If a foreign element is present, the musician
does not feel inspired.

You will be amused to know that once a musician was invited
to a house to play vina. The musician came and was welcomed. He
opened his vina. Then he looked here and there and found some
discord. He covered his vina, saluted, and left. Those present felt
disappointed and begged him to play, but his answer was, "No
matter what you give me, I do not feel like playing." This is quite
a different thing from making a program for months ahead. The
musician in the West is bound six months before to play a certain
program; he is helpless. In this way it is not music, it is labor; it
is mechanically done. Would you believe that a singer in the East
never knows what he is going to sing before he starts singing? He
feels the atmosphere of the place and the time, and whatever
comes to his mind, he begins to sing or to play. It is quite a
different thing.

I do not mean to say that music of this kind can be universal
music. It belongs to some rare person in a remote place. In India

musicians are dying now for the reason of lack of appreciation. Those potentates, those gurus, those teachers of high inspiration who lived in the past appreciated this music. Even in India people are becoming industrialized and civilized and music is dying away. There are no more now those musicians who before would make all those who listened spellbound; they do not exist any longer. Among millions there are perhaps three or four, and they will have vanished in a few years. It may be that one day the western world will waken to India's music as now the West is wakening to the poetry of the East, as it is beginning to appreciate such works as those written by Rabindranath Tagore. There will come a time when they will ask for music of that kind, but it will not be found; it will be too late. But there is no doubt when that music that is magic, is built on a psychological basis, when that music is introduced in the West, it will root out all such things as jazz bands. People seem to spoil their senses; this music is destroying people's delicacy of sense. Thousands every day are dancing to jazz music, and they forget the effect it has upon their spirit, upon their mind, upon their delicate senses. I know of a prince of Rampur who wanted to study music from a great teacher. The teacher said, "I can only teach you on one condition." He knew the character of the prince, who was fond of music, and he understood that many musicians would want to show their talent before him. He said, "I do not want you to hear any musician who is not an accomplished artist, because your sense of music must not be destroyed. It must be preserved for delicate music; it must be able to appreciate its fine intricacies." When the education of the public destroys the delicacy of its musical appreciation, it cannot help that it does not like to hear that which really is music, but prefers jazz. Instead of going forward, people are going backward. If music, which is the central theme of the whole human culture, is not helping people to go forward, it is a great pity.

Vina music has a likeness to the human voice. If you hear the vina played, you will never think that it is an instrument; you cannot imagine that it is an instrument. Vina music is not as magnetic as the music of the human voice, but it is more attractive,

more impressive. All the delicacies of the human voice and its silky
structure are finished in the sound of the vina.

The Connection of Dance with Music

The word "dance" has been much debased, because the dance
has been taken up only by entertainers who have made of it an
amusement, and we see that when a thing is made an amusement
it always degenerates.

When we come to Indian music we find that it has three parts:
singing, playing, and dancing.

The voice that comes from the lungs and abdomen cannot express itself fully without the bones of the head, the lips, the teeth,
the tongue, the palate. So we see that this body is the instrument
of sound. When the tree swings in the wind, each leaf gives out
a sound. The breeze alone cannot produce the full sound. The
leaves of the trees rustle and become the instrument for the air.
This shows us that the whole framework of this world is the
instrument of sound.

If while speaking to you I remained as still as a statue, my words
would have had much less effect than they can have when accompanied by the gesture. If a person says, "Go away from here,"
and does not move, his words will not have much expression. If he moves his arms, they will have more expression. In
India, the pupil is taught to sing with gestures. These take the
place of notation and guide him. A person might think, "notation would be a much clearer method," but Indian music is so
complicated that no notation can render it exactly. Then, too,
the intervals are all filled up, and the movements of the hand
and arm can express and guide more easily than any written
signs.

The third part of music, dancing, is not made-up dance but
expression by movement.

Mahadeva, the greatest avatar, danced himself. If you sing or
play before a dervish, he may begin to move his head and his
hands.

A great Indian poet, when speaking of what the singer must be, says:

> He must have a good voice,
> He must know the ragas
> And be able to sing them.
> He must be a master of graceful movements;
> He must be calm, unaffected by the audience.
> He must impress the audience.

Our life is so full of occupations that we have little time to observe the animals. If we did, we should see that most of their language is movement. They speak little with one another; mostly they express things by their motions. If you call a dog, the dog will at once begin to wag its tail; it will move its whole body to show its joy and affection. If you speak roughly to the dog, its whole body shows its feeling at once by its movements. We waste much energy in useless speech. In the old races we see that a motion of the hands, an inclination of the head for many things takes the place of words.

As soon as a person comes into the room, we see by his movements, by his manner of walking what he is, how much refinement he has. If we compare the horse whose price is five thousand guineas with the horse whose price is fifty guineas, we see what a difference there is in the movements. The horse worth five thousand guineas has not been taught to move as he moves, but in every movement he is graceful. We see that the beauty given to the peacock has inspired in him graceful movements.

Dance is a very wonderful thing, and in itself a great proof of mysticism. We have in each of us the nature of the bird and the nature of the animal. The nature of the bird is to fly; the nature of the animal is to jump. The tiger will jump from here to the top of the wall. If we cannot do this, it is because by eating, drinking, and sleeping we have lost the power. If a person sits in an armchair and to get up he pulls himself up by the arm, then by eating, drinking, and sleeping he has become so heavy that he is not what he should be. That government is proper which knows what each of the governed is doing. Our mind governs the body. Our mind must have every muscle, each atom of the body under its command. When we move up, all must come up; when we turn to the right, all must turn to the right; when we turn to the left, all must turn to the left. In India there is a dance, the tiger dance, that is kept for religious festivals. The dancers paint themselves as tigers and show the tiger dance. This dance has come to us from Egypt as a sacred dance.

I gave up my music because I had received from it all I had to receive. To serve God, one must sacrifice the dearest thing, and I sacrificed my music, the dearest thing to me. I composed songs; I sang and played the vina. Practicing this music, I arrived at a stage where I touched the music of the spheres. Then every soul became for me a musical note, and all life became music. Inspired by it, I spoke to people, and those who were attracted by my words listened to them instead of listening to my songs. Now if I do anything, it is to tune souls instead of instruments; to harmonize people instead of notes. If there is anything in my philosophy, it is the law of harmony: that one must put oneself in harmony with oneself and with others. I have found in every word a certain musical value, a melody in every thought, harmony in every feeling; and I have tried to interpret the same thing with clear and simple words to those who used to listen to my music. I played the vina until my heart turned into the same instrument. Then I offered this instrument to the Divine Musician, the only Musician existing. Since then I have become His flute, and when He chooses He plays His music. People give me credit for this music, which in reality is not due to me, but to the Musician who plays on His own instrument.

—HAZRAT INAYAT KHAN

Hazrat Inayat Khan, founder of the Sufi Order in the West, was born in India in 1882. A master of classical Indian music by the age of twenty, he relinquished a brilliant career to devote himself to the spiritual path. In 1910, acting upon the guidance of his teacher, he became one of the first teachers of the Sufi tradition in the West. For a decade and a half he travelled throughout Europe and the United States, giving lectures and guiding an ever-growing group of seekers. In 1926, he returned to India, where he died the following year.

A catalogue of books relating to Sufism and other spiritual traditions may be obtained from the publisher by writing to:
Omega Publications, Inc.
RD 1 Box 1030E
New Lebanon, NY 12125